RADICAL
HOMEMAKERS

Also available from Shannon Hayes

The Farmer and the Grill

The Grassfed Gourmet

Available at WWW.GRASSFEDCOOKING.COM

Forthcoming from Shannon Hayes:

*Long Way on a Little: An Earth Lovers'
Companion for Enjoying Meat, Pinching
Pennies and Living Deliciously*

RADICAL
HOMEMAKERS

Reclaiming Domesticity From a Consumer Culture

SHANNON HAYES

Left to Write Press
RICHMONDVILLE, NEW YORK

Book cover and interior design and production: Jill Shaffer
Proofreading and indexing: Steve Hoare

LEFT TO WRITE PRESS

270 Rossman Valley road
Richmondville, NY 12149
www.radicalhomemakers.com
518.827.7595

Left to Write Press is distributed by
Chelsea Green Publishing Company

QUANTITY SALES: Special discounts are available on quantity
purchases for groups and individuals. Please visit www.
radicalhomemakers.com for details, or call Left to Write Press
directly.

U.S. TRADE BOOKSTORES and WHOLESALERS:
Please contact Chelsea Green Publishing, 85 North Main
Street, Suite 120, White River Jct., Vermont 05001.
Orders: 800.639.4099; offices: 802.295.6300.

About Left to Write Press:

Left to Write Press is an initiative of Shannon Hayes and
Bob Hooper, who wanted to publish books completely on their
own terms, so they could earn a decent return on Shannon's
writing without selling their souls. We are now on our second
book, and we've managed to stick to our guns to keep it
written, published, edited and designed locally and regionally.
And we even managed to do it on recycled paper. Left to Write
Press expresses our agenda for an ecologically sound, socially
just world, where everyone is well-fed and happy. Now stop
reading this small print, and start enjoying our book!

DEDICATION

To C.M., as promised.

In memory of Arthur Frederick Horr and Evelyn Horr, who kept their family well on 300 jars of canned fruit each year from the backyard . . . and who taught me that buttercups truly are the best-flavored squash.

In memory of Auguste Magdalena "Hilde" Hayes, who showed me what kind of power can come from a kitchen.

In memory of Dr. Thomas A. Lyson, who, despite my low GRE scores and perfunctory rejections from various selection committees, felt I deserved a shot at a graduate-level education. Thank you for opening the door for me.

In memory of Ruth and Sanford, whose quiet hidden lives have transformed so many others.

CONTENTS

ACKNOWLEDGMENTS

I always wonder if anybody actually reads this section . . . but at least it gives me an opportunity to get a few things off my chest. I have a lot of people to thank for bringing this book to fruition. Let's hope I don't forget anyone . . .

First, thanks to Arthur "Butch" Wilson and Deb Trumbull from Cornell University's Department of Education. I used every trick you taught me to get through this book. I hope that doesn't embarrass you. Deb, you gave me the tools to answer my questions, and Butch, you gave me the confidence and power to keep it pragmatic.

Next, thanks are owed to the crew at the Middleburgh Library. You greeted my family warmly each time I staggered in with blazed computer eyes from doing the research and writing. You didn't yell at me when my kids rearranged the children's section, nor did you shush Ula when she paraded around the library dancing and singing "It's a Hard-Knock Life!" for everyone to hear, incriminating her mother in more ways than I care to explain . . . especially since it was on a day when we forgot her undies . . . You never asked any questions about all the weird titles I had you hunt down for me, and you never publicly chastised me for a late return. Can a library get any better than that?

And for all those needs that couldn't be met by the Library, there was Catnap Books in Cobleskill. You thoughtfully kept an answering machine running so that, when I decided I urgently needed a book at 4 am, I could just call down and leave you a message. Roberta and Jim patiently hunted down any titles I was having a hard time locating, and helped to keep my research budget under control. Your business is a gift to our community.

Thanks to Jane, David, Cress and Rocky, who always opened their door to me whenever I tottered down the road in need of a break from my writing. Depending on the time of day, there was either coffee or a cocktail to revive me . . . Now that's good neighboring!!

I am deeply grateful to Mary Jo Forbord, Registered Dietician and Executive Director for the Sustainable Farming Association of Minnesota, who first laid out those critical questions to me when she asked me to speak at the national American Dietetic Association conference. As the introduction will show, it was answering Mary Jo's questions that led to this book. Thanks also to the members of the Hunger and Environmental Nutrition practice group for all your support and encouragement with this project.

A super-huge I-Owe-You is due to the hundreds of men and women who never even met me, but who sent e-mails telling me about their lives, pushing me to keep going with the Radical Home-maker research. It can be very hard to get up in the predawn hours in the dark of winter to finish a book. A note of encouragement from a fellow Radical Homemaker goes a long way toward fueling the fire. Special thanks in particular are due to Denis and Alicia Stoltzfus, who opened their home and hearts to me in honest conversation as I sought to gain deeper insights into all the different ways Radical Homemaking could manifest itself.

A very deep and special thanks are owed to the twenty individu-als and families across the country who welcomed me into their lives, opened themselves up to me on tape, and allowed me to explore the workings of their minds. You fed my mind, gave my family and I food and soft pillows as we traveled, and filled us with hope and inspira-tion. Some of you have now become very dear friends. I wish I could name each of you, since you are the stars of this book, but I don't want to infringe on your privacy. You know who you are, and I am indebted to you. Special thanks go out to Dennis Olmstead and Julie Gleason who, when they learned of our traveling research project, insisted that we use their home as a resting place.

Another round of thanks are owed to the Radical Homemakers who've been great friends, book reviewers, and emotional support over the years. Holly Hickman happened to call me on the first day I thought of the book and pushed me to keep going with the idea. Dr. Kristen Case kept me talking about the research process, which kept me from feeling lost and overwhelmed. Nancy Kelly gave me free massage therapy and energy sessions to help me decompress and stay focused. All of you gave me faces to be accountable to as I wrote the book, reviewed my work, and filled me with confidence.

Thanks are also owed to my meat customers at The Round Barn Farmers' Market, whose generous patronage supported the printing and production costs of this book; to Linda McFall, who lent her professional editorial expertise *and* bought chickens; to those of you who helped critique cover images, tracked my progress, and challenged my ideas. You make every Saturday feel like a celebration of life.

Thank you to Fran McManus, who has steadily fed my mind and ideas from our first meeting over lunch six years ago. Fran organized the first public reading of *Radical Homemakers*, did a helluva job promoting it, and single-handedly told me how to fix the introduction — before she even *read* it. I honestly believe true editors are born and not made, and Fran has that gift. Thanks are also due to the folks who helped produce this book and take it to the world. Melissa Goldberg, my committed publicist (and another fellow RH); Kelly Beers, who tirelessly transcribed all those interviews; Steve Hoare, for the proofreading; Jill Shaffer Hammond for the cover and book design; and Charlotte Russell, the powerful beauty who so generously allowed us to photograph her (multiple times over) for the cover image. Thanks are also due to Dr. David Korten, whose profound thinking has so heavily influenced my work, and whose generous support when I finally worked up the courage to contact him was magnificent.

My name is on the cover of the book. I wrote the words. But the life that brings them about is a result of my family. My mom and dad, Adele and Jim Hayes, have made room for me on the family farm, enabling me to earn the money and grow the food I need to support my book habit and feed my family, while simultaneously making sure I have the flexibility to balance family, farm and writing. Dad was especially helpful in fleshing out ideas for the book; Mom was great at telling me to shut up when she'd heard me prattle on enough about it. She also suggested that I join her book club and engage in pleasure reading to spend some time outside my head. She's a smart lady, my mom.

Thanks are owed to my daughters, Saoirse and Ula, who quietly crept into my office each morning to give me kisses and hugs while I worked, who (admittedly with some coercion) eventually left me to get things done, then welcomed me back into the rest of the house with cheers and hugs when I finished writing each day. You traveled across country with the spirits of true adventurers, made friends wherever you went, and didn't really break all that much stuff during our home-stay visits. I'm very proud to be your mom.

Thanks, most especially, are owed to Bob. Words just aren't going to cover what this guy does. He keeps the girls quiet every morning while I work. He brings breakfast to my desk and keeps my coffee cup full so that I don't have to be interrupted. He sits with me for hours, reviewing ideas, challenging concepts, helping me to interpret research. He listens to the radio, tracks news stories and reads magazines, finding bits of information that contribute to my research. He sells books at every lecture, does all my PowerPoints for me, chooses and irons my clothes, packs my suitcase, washes my dishes, does the laundry, edits every one of my books and articles and claims to love my cooking. He cherishes me, makes me laugh, and fills my life with friendship, joy, humor, and unconditional love.

TOMATO-CANNING FEMINISTS

"For national and social disasters,
for moral and financial evils, the cure begins
in the Household."

—*Julia M. Wright*, The Complete Home, *1879*

"I don't know why I'm doing this." The deep heat of summer has found her way north to a pocked parking lot outside a peeling six-unit apartment building on the outer fringe of Durham, New Hampshire. Bob puts the car in park, but doesn't turn off the engine. Sensing my discouragement, he turns and stares at me head-on.

"Do you have enough data? We could skip out on this one." Skipping out sounds positively delicious. We're five hours from home. Five hours from our girls, who are staying with my parents at the farm. We could leave now, grab lunch on the road, and be home for bedtime stories. I let out an exhausted sigh and pull Susan Colter's paperwork out of my folder.

In the course of eighteen months, I'd received well over two hundred letters from women and men who were pursuing homemaking as a vocation for saving family, community, and the planet. After finding a time when I could break away from my family's farm, I chose which families I would visit in New England, carefully plotted each address on a map, then painstakingly scheduled each homemaker at a convenient time, with minimal back-tracking. When Susan's e-mail came in, I promptly put her name on the "must interview" stack. She was fresh out of a prestigious college, significantly younger than

1

anyone else who had written to me, and was already pursuing home-making and farming. I felt her young age would enable her to provide unique insights. Susan was my last stop on a carefully orchestrated research trip.

A few weeks prior, she had written a letter conveying her eager-ness for our dialogue. Two days before we were to meet, however, she e-mailed me to express apprehensions about doing the interview. She was reconsidering her life direction and wasn't sure if she fit the "radical homemaker" description any longer. At that time, I decided to hold to my original schedule and follow through with her. Besides, this young woman, more than any other respondent, seemed, from the nature of her correspondence, to want to talk with me. In my mind, this had become an interview I wouldn't need — done more for Susan's benefit than for my own. Now, road-weary, hot, hungry and homesick, Bob's idea to skip out seems logical. Logic doesn't prevail.

"I have to do this." In this style of qualitative research, dissonance and serendipity contribute as much to discovery as meticulous litera-ture reviews. I grab my recording gear, step out of the car, and head for the sloped landing tacked to the apartment on the back side of the building. Bob goes looking for an iced coffee. I approach the rot-ting steps, wondering if they will bear my weight. Susan greets me at the door. I enter her apartment, which she shares with her boyfriend and two other young women. I am immediately engulfed in a steam sauna from tomatoes canning in a boiling water bath.

"Both the farms where we work had bumper tomato crops," she explains. "We're trying not to let them go to waste." Her boy-friend sweats over a half-sized stove in a tiny kitchen that was clearly designed by a slumlord who thought "home cooking" meant boiling water for instant oatmeal. A copy of *The Ball Blue Book of Preserving* lies open on the kitchen table, covered with jar lids and spatters of tomato juice.

Susan shows me to a sofa in a makeshift living room. We sit down. Before I turn on my recorder, she hits me with my own words.

"I don't know why I'm doing this." But now we are both committed to our process. There is nothing to do but run the tape.

"I grew up in a fairly wealthy suburban household," she begins. Her parents both had demanding professional careers. But there was a trade-off for the upscale lifestyle.

> We sacrificed home. . . . My parents had to work so much, and we were eating a lot of take-out and convenience food, and it felt like that sense of building family around food got lost in the lack of time.

Susan explains that neither of her parents liked to cook, and they hired someone else to do the housekeeping. She reflects:

> . . . there was never a sense that they were particularly invested in having a home. . . . It was sort of "let's do as little as we can just to get by and make sure we're fed, and the house isn't an absolute disaster." The sense that I got was that that [home-making] was something to be avoided.

Susan's parents had high expectations of their two children, and she dutifully fulfilled them. She was a good student, she played sports, music, and pursued other extra-curricular activities. She earned admittance into a highly competitive, expensive private university. In her senior year of college, however, she spent a term in South Africa, and witnessed widespread hunger and poverty. Upon returning home, her university-centered career trajectory seemed meaningless. "The high pressure," she says, "became unattractive to me." She "wanted to slow things down," so she spent the next summer working on an organic vegetable farm. "Over the course of just a few months . . . my lifestyle really changed. . . . I was more focused on people and on needs." She tuned in to issues regarding sustainability and social justice. When she returned to school in the fall to finish her bachelor degree, Susan felt lost. "[I felt] this tremendous disconnect from it, as though we were going to class, and we were doing this sort of robotic classwork that felt irrelevant." She managed to complete the term, then returned home to an even more sobering situation. Her mother, now divorced from her father, was dying of cancer.

Ironically, as she assumed the role of her mother's caregiver and watched what remained of her family fall away, Susan began to experience what it meant to have a home:

> I got to take more of an active role as caretaker which . . .
> allowed me to sort of do it *my* way. And one of the ways I did
> it was by cooking for her. She couldn't do it herself, and really
> that was a way that I could be in the house and physically be
> near her and also give something to her which felt really pow-
> erful. . . . [Having a home] was something that seemed to just
> sort of evolve as she was dying, and it felt so good to have it.
> It felt so good to have my family in our home, in our physical
> home, and to all eat together and to talk together and spend
> time together, which we had never done a whole lot of.

That alone was great data to make the case for homemaking as a vocation. I could have turned off the recorder and joined Bob for an iced coffee. But I remembered that last e-mail Susan had sent me, where she was considering stepping back onto the formal career track. Why did she think she had to do this? "So you've identified that you want this," I say to her, "you want to have a family, to be with them full-time . . . and you don't think you can have it? You must feel —"

"Torn on a fairly daily basis," Susan finishes my sentence.

> The people my age I do know, who become interested in an
> alternative lifestyle, if you want to call it that, or who have
> come out of college . . . if they're interested in farming or arts,
> things that just don't enter into the traditional workplace . . .
> [they] come out bewildered by how to do it, or is it right to do
> it? Is it responsible to do that? — To not be building up a sav-

ings account, whatever, for whatever may come next? There's a sense of constant planning, and I'm totally guilty of that, of always planning for needing more, whether it be money, or space in a home, or that next degree. . . . there's always this pull to go and to keep forging ahead on that . . . societal scale.

I want to turn off my recorder. I want to whisk Susan out to the car and take her to meet some of her New England neighbors I'd just visited, to show her the many ways they have found to build a viable life in the world as a homemaker. Money becomes a marginal chit when a family can cultivate self-reliance and community interdependence. But she's not finished with me. She tells me about a conversation she had recently with a fellow woman farm worker:

It just sort of bubbled out of both of us. . . . [We] got into this conversation about farming and feminism and relationships and home . . . about feeling very conflicted about making money or not making enough money. We were really drawn to the idea of working with a partner, but did that somehow mean that we had failed at living up to the feminist ideal of going ahead and having this independent identity? That sense of independence, do we have to cast it aside in order to live on a humbler scale, or can you still . . . have your own identity within a family unit, or a tight community unit, and still have your own successes, however you define them? [Can you] have both of those? Is that possible? And if we forego the success image, are we then rejecting feminist ideals, are we just going back to the homemaker role that we were taught to think was primitive . . . a symbol of oppression for women?

I want to assure her of so many things. Whatever life path we choose, building an identity is important. Contributing to society in a meaningful way, challenging ourselves, and being true to our core are ideals present in all feminist theory. Working alone or with a partner to create a nurturing home is not antithetical to progress. Indeed, in a time of climate crisis, peak oil, and worldwide economic and social unrest, it may be the only thing that saves us. It is possible to be a feminist *and* to can tomatoes. These are the things I want to say to her. But I can't. Knee-deep in a quagmire of interview data, social science research, histories of domesticity and ancient cookbooks, on this particular August day I myself am still trying to figure out just what it means to be not just a homemaker, but a Radical Homemaker. How might I advocate for a meaningful and sustainable domestic life without inadvertently condoning the further subjugation of women?

The steam, the stewing tomatoes, this bright young woman who seriously questions her future, and the topic of my research, all suddenly feel too dangerous. It would be so easy to get this wrong, to steer her wrong. I blunder through the remainder of the interview, offer some limp-wristed tips for tomato-canning success, then hustle out the door to find my husband, to get back home to the unquestioning love and acceptance of my own kids, in my own home.

"How'd it go?" Bob looks refreshed, caffeinated, and ready to travel.

"I don't know." For what feels like the hundredth time this year, I question whether I even have the right to be probing these issues. "But if I can answer her questions, then we've got a book."

RADICAL HOMEMAKING – POLITICS, ECOLOGY AND DOMESTIC ARTS

I never intended to write this book. My mother's generation fought for the right to go to work, to achieve personal fulfillment through professional accomplishments. I charged through high school and college at full throttle, ravenously ambitious, eager to start my own career as soon as possible. At age sixteen, I attended high school during the day and I took college courses at night. My first college paper was about the psychological benefits of enrolling children and babies in day care. Full-time. I completed college before I was of legal drinking age, spent a year working overseas, another year administering a housing rehabilitation program for flood victims, then enrolled in Cornell University and had a Ph.D. by the time I was twenty-seven. I was ready to conquer the world in a big way.

My ambition was probably fueled by the fact that my primary and secondary schooling took place in a town on the rural-suburban fringe, in Cobleskill, New York, the only town in our county with not one, but *two* exits along the newly built interstate. It seemed Cobleskill students were cultivated to gaze longingly at those highway on-ramps, to dream of the day they would lead us away from an otherwise backward rural county. The trouble was, in my heart, I never wanted to leave home. My family's farm was just barely inside the district lines. We didn't actually live in Cobleskill, but in the next town over, with *no* interstate to be seen. West Fulton was far above the valley floor, at the northern edge of the Appalachian mountain chain, and the Appalachian agrarian culture was still very much alive throughout my childhood. During the week I worked to get straight A's in town. On the weekends and summers, I worked in the hills on a neighboring farm, where the inhabitants lived very well on only a few thousand dollars per year.

Ruth, the farm matron, kept chickens and a garden. She put up her vegetables for winter, sewed her clothes, and made pies and jams from berries picked on the field edges. Sanford, her octogenarian boarder, took care of the beef herd that supplied their winter meat, and kept the house, outbuildings, tractor and car in good repair. I loved every minute I spent with them, repairing fences, shoveling manure, cutting their grass, stacking firewood, raking leaves, and most especially, collecting my wages, which came in the form of mid-day feasts. I loved being on my family farm as well. I took great joy in spending time with my folks, spent endless days roaming the hills, and countless summer nights sleeping out under the stars.

Nevertheless, I faithfully adhered to my career track. But in an effort to find a path back to my own community, I studied subjects that I thought would help me get a job there, that would make me an asset to the local agricultural college or county government — rural sociology, sustainable agriculture, community and rural development, adult and extension education. So committed was I to finding a way home that Bob (my soon-to-be husband) and I took out a mortgage and bought a small cabin on fifteen acres even deeper into the hills, just seven miles from the family farm. Two weeks later he was fired from work. I never even got a job interview. The writing seemed to be on the wall. Sell the house, find jobs someplace else, leave town.

Bob and I were heartbroken. Our dream had been to help my family on the farm, to enjoy Ruth's and Sanford's friendship until the end of their days, to start a family in the place where I grew up, surrounded by a supportive community. Instead, we faced the same future that seemed inevitable for so many American couples — leave home to find work, fracture the extended family into nuclear units, and hope for ample salaries that would pay for the day care and assistance that loving relatives and neighbors could have offered at home.

My education had prepared me to accept this inevitability. But Ruth, Sanford and my family had, rather unwittingly, prepared me to reject it. Unlike so many people my age (I'm thirty-five), basic homemaking and self-reliance skills were part of my childhood foundational knowledge. My community and family practiced subsistence farming, food preservation, barter and frugal living as a matter of course. I had been taught in school to plan for a six-figure income in a dual-earning family. But I learned growing up that there was an arsenal of resources available that could offer a happy alternative lifestyle. Bob and I did the math. We could move away, take on dual careers, get a new house, own two cars to get to work. By the time we subtracted out what we'd pay for commuting, a new house, professional wardrobes, taxes, and buying rather than growing our food, we were only $10,000 ahead in annual income than where we would be if we stayed home and put our hearts and minds to work on our grassy hillsides. That was before we had figured in the costs for day care. Thus, Bob and I officially joined my parents on the family farm, I wrote cookbooks about sustainable food, we started a family, and we became homemakers.

The trick that Ruth and Sanford had taught us was simple. Mainstream American culture views the household as a unit of consumption. By this conventional standard, the household consumes food, clothing, household technologies, repair and debt services, electricity, entertainment, health-care services, and environmental resources. In order to be a "successful" unit of consumption, the household must have money. Ruth's and Sanford's household was not a unit of consumption. By growing their own food, living within their means, providing much of their own health care, and relying on community, family and barter for meeting their remaining needs, their household was essentially a unit of *production* (just not by the standards of a market economy). Thus, their *income* wasn't critical to their *well-being*. In fact, over the course of her life, Ruth even amassed considerable financial savings.

This was the model that Bob and I, together with my parents, adopted for our own lifestyle. Admittedly, there are some modern twists and indulgences on Ruth and Sanford's ways. We are not the sort of folks who would willingly don sackcloth. The month of May will find me out in the fields with my father during lambing season, while Bob watches the girls and Mom prepares the gardens. By the end of the month, our farmers' market season is in full swing, and Bob and I are selling Sap Bush Hollow meats every Saturday. Our daughters come to the market to meet their friends, or stay at the farm with Grammie and Pop Pop. During the week, the kids join me as I help move fence, milk the family cow, and do chores. On chicken processing days, Bob heads down to the farm, and the girls and I stay home to go for hikes, visit the neighbors, or explore the woods in search of fairies. The entire family labors throughout the season, tending livestock, cutting meat, making sausages, keeping records and weeding gardens, but there is ample time for us to take turns with vacations, canoe trips, afternoon swims and naps, and evening cocktails. As late summer rolls around, like Ruth, I pull out my canning gear and work 'round the clock to put up peaches, pears, plums, green beans, beets, tomato sauce and even some homemade stews. A giant crock fills first with sour dill pickles, then myriad fermenting mixtures of summer vegetables, then finally, at the season's end, with cabbages for a winter's supply of sauerkraut. Before mid-October, we team with friends to press cider; Mom pulls mountains of bright orange, yellow and deep green squashes out of the garden, which we stow away in our coldest rooms; I render pork and beef fat for lard and tallow for soaps and cooking; a fellow farmer swaps us a supply of storage onions and potatoes in exchange for meat; and the farmers' market closes for the season. We harvest the turkeys for Thanksgiving, and then begin our winter's rest . . . and play. Where Ruth and Sanford lived most of their lives in the confines of Schoharie County, during the winter months we take a different path. Our incomes and ecological concerns don't allow for cheeky weekends in Paris, but they do, every few years, allow for some pretty extraordinary extended travels. . . . Those trips have included renting a home for three months in rural France (where cheeky weekends in Paris *were* doable), a winter in Argentina researching a book, or extended trips across the country by train. The years that don't find us boarding planes or trains during our resting months are still full of fun. We take the girls to area museums or on short mini-vacations for home-school study to learn about the pilgrims, our colonial history, witch trials, Native Americans, or to hear some live music. We do science experiments at our kitchen table, read long novels aloud at night, play music and sing by the fire, enjoy cider and popcorn while playing games (or fighting over toys), or pile up on the couch to watch a movie. Sunny wintery days find us out for walks, hiking through the woods on snowshoes, or sledding down the road.

My family has always understood that the key to success as farmers wasn't necessarily how much money we made, but how much money we didn't have to spend. What's good for farming is also good for homemaking. There are, admittedly, some things we do without. We limit restaurant visits, take advantage of local thrift stores, wear our clothes until they are threadbare, have only one car in our family, and we forego health insurance, both from inadequate finances and a conscientious objection to corporate health care (this will be discussed in further detail later in the book). We pay cash, make use of sliding scales and barter for the health-care services we require. We celebrate birthdays and holidays with verve, but Bob and I do not exchange gifts (although we do find or make a few things for our daughters). We make very heavy use of our library, and commit to keeping our car off the road at least one day each week during the growing season and two to four days a week during the winter. Because we produce so much of our own food, grocery shopping only needs to happen every other month. Using such tricks and accepting a few limitations, Bob, the girls and I have lived very, very well on less than $45,000 per year.

Along this path, naturally, I became a local-food advocate. After writing two cookbooks about working with sustainably raised meats, I found myself taking on the role of a spokesperson for the integration of ecologically sound, humane animal production into a sustainable diet. (I felt like the dairy princess for the grass-fed meat movement.) As a result, in 2007, I was invited to speak at the national conference of the American Dietetic Association. My charge was to explain to several hundred dieticians what *exactly* this grass-fed meat movement was, why the darn thing wouldn't go away, and to justify why

Americans should be willing to spend money on food that was so much more expensive than what could be found in the grocery store.

As I tooled away on my presentation, the final requirement was the most troubling. I could come up with lots and lots of reasons *why* we should be willing to pay more for our food. Social justice. Ecological benefits. Stronger local economies. Superior nutrition. Animal welfare. Saving farmland. Reversing global warming. Reducing our reliance on fossil fuels. But I realized then, that *why* was never going to matter if Americans couldn't figure out *how* to afford it. Up until then, the grass-fed movement had been pegged as a niche farming vocation that appealed to the wealthy folks who were in search of higher-quality foods. It was not regarded as an option for the rest of America.

But truth be told, when I crunched the numbers, a farmers' market meal made of a roasted local pasture-raised chicken, baked potatoes and steamed broccoli cost less than four meals at Burger King, even when two of the meals came off the kiddie menu. The Burger King meal had negligible nutritional value and was damaging to our health and planet. The farmers' market menu cost less, healed the earth, helped the local economy, was a source of bountiful nutrients for a family of four, and would leave ample leftovers for both a chicken salad and a rich chicken stock, which could then be the base for a wonderful soup. But when push came to shove, I knew that Burger King would win out. The reason? Many people don't even know how to roast a chicken, let alone make a chicken salad from the leftovers or use the carcass to make a stock. Mainstream Americans have lost the simple domestic skills that would enable them to live an ecologically sensible life with a modest or low income.

Ordinarily a calm public speaker, my hands shook when I stood in September of 2007 before an audience of 600 professional registered dieticians, many of whom were women. I had a painful message to deliver, one that I considered leaving out every time I rehearsed my speech. Eating local, organic, sustainably raised, nutrient-dense food was possible for every American, not just for wealthy gourmets or self-reliant organic farmers. But to do it, *we needed to bring back the homemaker*. As I made this claim, my toes curled in the tips of my shoes. The room was completely still. And then, before I could continue on, the crowd burst into spontaneous applause. I learned in conversations afterward that I had called attention to the elephant in the room, a simple truth that was felt by so many dieticians who were trying to help families reclaim good nutrition and a balanced life.

As I looked more closely at the role homemaking could play in revitalizing our local food system, I saw that the position was a linch-pin for more than just making use of garden produce and chicken carcasses. Individuals who had taken this path in life were building a great bridge from our existing **extractive economy** — where cor-porate wealth was regarded as the foundation of economic health, where mining our earth's resources and exploiting our international neighbors was accepted as simply the cost of doing business — to a **life-serving economy**, where the goal is, in the words of David Korten, to generate a living for all, rather than a killing for a few[1], where our resources are sustained, our waters are kept clean, our air pure, and families can lead meaningful and joyful lives.

More than simply soccer moms, Radical Homemakers are men and women who have chosen to make family, community, social jus-tice and the health of the planet the governing principles of their lives. They reject any form of labor or the expenditure of any resource that does not honor these tenets. For about five thousand years, our culture has been hostage to a form of organization by domination that fails to honor our living systems, where "he who holds the gold makes the rules." By contrast, Radical Homemakers use life skills and relationships as a replacement for gold, on the premise that he or she who doesn't *need* the gold can *change* the rules. The greater our domestic skills, be they to plant a garden, grow tomatoes on an apartment balcony, mend a shirt, repair an appliance, provide for our own entertainment, cook and preserve a local harvest or care for our children and loved ones, the less dependent we are on the gold.

These thoughts led me to wonder if salvation from our global woes — the rampant social injustices, climate change, peak oil — was going to be dependent upon the women, upon questioning all the hard-fought battles of both the first and second waves of feminism that have swept this country. Women, after all, have been the home-makers since the beginning of time. Or so I thought.

Upon further investigation, I learned that the household did not become the "woman's sphere" until the industrial revolution. A search for the origin of the word *housewife* traces it back to the thirteenth century as the feudal period was coming to an end in Europe and the first signs of a middle class were popping up. Historian Ruth Schwartz Cowan explains that housewives were wedded to *husbands*, whose name came from *hus*, an old spelling of *house*, and *bonded*.[2] *Husbands* were bonded to houses, rather than to lords. Housewives and husbands were free people who owned their own homes and lived off their land. While there was a division of labor among the sexes in these early households, there was also an equal distribution of domestic work. Once the industrial revolution happened, however, things changed. Men left the household to work for wages, which were then used to purchase the goods and services that they no lon-ger were home to provide. Indeed, the men were the first to lose their domestic skills as their successive generations forgot how to butcher the family hog, how to sew leather, how to chop firewood.

As the industrial revolution forged on and crossed the ocean to America, men and women eventually stopped working together to provide for their household sustenance. They developed their sepa-rate spheres — man in the factory, woman in the home. The more a man worked outside the home, the more the household would have to buy in order to have the needs met. Soon the factories were able to fabricate products to supplant the housewives' duties as well. As sub-sequent chapters in this book reveal, her primary function ultimately became chauffeur and consumer. The household was no longer a unit of production. It was a unit of consumption.

The effect on the American housewife was devastating. In 1963, Betty Friedan published *The Feminine Mystique*, documenting for the first time "the problem that has no name," *housewife's syndrome*, where American girls grew up fantasizing about finding their hus-bands, buying their dream homes and dream appliances, popping out babies, and living happily ever after.[3] In truth, pointed out Friedan, happily-ever-after never came. Countless women suffered from depression and nervous breakdowns as they faced the endless meaningless tasks of shopping and driving children hither and yon. They never had opportunities to fulfill their highest potential, to challenge themselves, to feel as though they were truly contributing to society beyond wielding the credit card to keep the consumer culture humming. Friedan's book sent women to work in droves. And corporate America seized upon a golden opportunity to secure a cheaper workforce and offer countless products to use up their paychecks.

Before long, the second family income was no longer an option. In the minds of many, it was a necessity. Homemaking, like eating organic foods, seemed a luxury to be enjoyed only by those wives whose husbands garnered substantial earnings, enabling them to drive their children to school every day rather than putting them on the bus, enroll them in endless enrichment activities, oversee their educational careers, and prepare them for entry into elite colleges, and to win a leg-up in a competitive workforce. At the other extreme, homemaking was seen as a realm of the ultra-religious, where women accepted the role of Biblical "help meets" to their husbands. They cooked, cleaned, toiled, served and remained silent and powerless. Bob and I fell into neither category. And I suspected there were more like us.

I was looking for a different type of homemaker — someone who wasn't ruled by our consumer culture, who embodied a strong ecological ethic, who held genuine power in the household, who was living a full, creative, challenging and socially contributory life. For lack of a better word, I wanted to find folks who were more . . . *radical*. I began writing and speaking more on the subject, and in November of 2007 I posted a call on my Web site, seeking such homemakers:

> If you have learned to live on less in order to take the time to
> nourish your family and the planet through home cooking,
> engaged citizenship, responsible consumption and creative
> living, whether you are male, female, or two people sharing the

role, with or without children, full or part-time, please drop me
a line and tell me your story.

With the help of a full page story that appeared in *The New York Times* and a few other magazines, blogs and newspapers, my inbox filled up with over two hundred letters. Unable to fully document the lives of all these people, I selected twenty homemakers to interview, seeking a balance of young and old, rural, urban and suburban, single and married, male and female, with children and without. I wanted to know who these people were, how they chose their life paths, how they were faring in our American economy. I wanted to see their domestic lives with my own eyes, to gauge the balance of power in their relationships, to gain insights about their impact on their local communities. I wanted to know if they were able to thwart the chronic depression that Betty Friedan wrote about, and if so, how they did it. I wanted to understand their tactics for both surviving and thriving. I packed up my family whenever we could squeeze away from the farm, and we eventually worked our way across the country, from Maine to Los Angeles.

As I got to know each of these families, I learned that most Radical Homemakers do not have conventional jobs. They simply refuse to work to make the rich richer. They do have some form of income that comes into their lives. But they were not the privileged set by any means. Most of the families that I interviewed were living with a sense of abundance at about 200 percent of the Federal Poverty Level. That's a little over $40,000 for a family of four, about 37 percent below the national median family income and 45 percent below the median income for married couple families.[4] Some lived on considerably less, few had appreciably more. Not surprisingly, those with the lowest incomes had mastered the most domestic skills and had developed the most innovative approaches to living.

I learned that Radical Homemaking is a domestic choice made by all the adults in a household. It is true that a man may work outside at a job that honors the four tenets of ecological sustainability, social justice, family and community, while the woman stays home. But the reverse may also be true. Sometimes neither partner works outside the home. As we'll see later on, this is in no way a throwback to the 1950s household. Nor can it be confused with some form of ultra-conservative religious sect. Radical Homemakers draw on historical traditions to craft a more ecologically viable existence, but their life's work is to create a new, pleasurable, sustainable and socially just society, different than any we have known in the last 5,000 years. While they learn from history, they do not seek to recreate it in all forms. Women are not second-class citizens. The governing tenet of social justice precludes treating any member of the family as subservient.

Some of the Radical Homemakers I came to know professed a strong spiritual faith. Others did not. If there was one unifying belief among them, it was to question all the assumptions in our consumer culture that have us convinced that a family cannot survive without a dual income. They were fluent at the mental exercise of rethinking the "givens" of our society and coming to the following conclusions: nobody (who matters) cares what (or if) you drive; housing does not have to cost more than a single moderate income can afford (and can even cost less); it is okay to accept help from family and friends, to let go of the perceived ideal of independence and strive instead for interdependence; health can be achieved without making monthly payments to an insurance company; child care is not a fixed cost; education can be acquired for free — it does not have to be bought; and retirement is possible, regardless of income.

As for domestic skills, the range of talents held by these households was as varied as the day is long. Many kept gardens, but not all. Some gardened on city rooftops, some on country acres, some in suburban yards. Some were wizards at car and appliance repairs. Others could sew. Some could build and fix houses; some kept livestock. Others crafted furniture, played music or wrote. All could cook. (Really well, as my waistline will attest.) None of them could do *everything*. No one was completely self-sufficient, an independent island separate from the rest of the world. Thus the universal skills that they all possessed were far more complex than simply knowing how to can green beans or build a root cellar. In order to make it as homemakers, these people had to be wizards at nurturing relationships and working with family and community. They needed an intimate understanding of the life-serving economy, where a paycheck is not always exchanged for all services rendered. They needed to be their own teachers — to pursue their educations throughout life, forever learning new ways to do more, create more, give more.

In addition, the happiest among them were successful at setting realistic expectations for themselves. They did not live in impeccably clean houses on manicured estates. They saw their homes as living systems and accepted the flux, flow, dirt and chaos that are a natural part of that. They were masters at redefining pleasure not as something that should be bought in the consumer marketplace, but as something that could be created, no matter how much or how little money they had in their pockets. And above all, they were fearless. They did not let themselves be bullied by the conventional ideals regarding money, status, or material possessions. These families did not see their homes as a refuge from the world. Rather, each home was the center for social change, the starting point from which a better life would ripple out for everyone.

Home is where the great change will begin. It is not where it ends. Once we feel sufficiently proficient with our domestic skills, few of us will be content to simply practice them to the end of our days. Many of us will strive for more, to bring more beauty to the world, to bring about greater social change, to make life better for our neighbors, to contribute our creative powers to the building of a new, brighter, sustainable and happier future. That is precisely the great work we should all be tackling. If we start by focusing our energies on our domestic lives, we will do more than reduce our ecological impact and help create a living for all. We will craft a safe, nurturing place from which this great creative work can happen.

A note on how this book is organized: This volume is divided into two sections. Part One is more in-depth and theoretical. It looks at the history of domesticity and feminism, and provides an in-depth critique of our current cultural and economic systems. My aim is to demonstrate how Radical Homemaking can function in rebuilding a life-serving, socially just and ecologically sustainable economy while honoring the values of feminism. In Part Two, the Radical Homemakers themselves speak out. Rather than listing each family I interviewed and rattling off the pertinent lessons they offered, I have organized Part Two as a discussion of the overarching themes and lessons I gleaned from their interviews and letters in aggregate. My intent is to give a clear picture of the many ways this lifestyle can work, to explore the homemakers' most common decision-making processes and their tactics for thriving. Essentially, Part One is the theory and Part Two is the practice. My hope is that the two parts, in balance, create for readers an opportunity to evaluate this way of life and to see how it fits into a picture of great social change. Naturally, each of the people who participated in the study is a worthy subject on their own. And since their lives reflect different segments of our American culture, I assume that their personal stories will also be of interest. Thus, the appendix includes in-depth stories of all the different people who participated in this research, arranged alphabetically.

AUTHOR'S NOTE: *All of the quotes and anecdotes are taken directly from interviews and letters with twenty different Radical Homemaking families. In order to honor their privacy, their names, along with a few details about their lives, have been changed. The only exceptions are three individuals — Erik Knutzen, Kelly Coyne and Nance Klehm — all of whom write and speak on subjects that tie in very strongly with the Radical Homemaking movement.*

Part One
WHY

CHAPTER ONE

A WOMAN'S PLACE

"[W]oman's work within the home
[is] not directly useful to society, produces nothing.
[The housewife] is subordinate, secondary, parasitic."
— Simone de Beauvoir, *The Second Sex* (1949)

"So in a way, you could say I'm just another
unprepared youngster in this, but . . . I know I'm not
going to starve. . . . I can be more self sufficient.
And what's more liberating than being self-sufficient?"
— Stormy McGovern, Radical Homemaker

"We are not wiser, we are not better,
we are not stronger than our predecessors,
but we have their accumulated knowledge
and wisdom to build upon."
— William Coperthwaite[1]

In running the homemaking banner up the flagpole, I understand that I may garner two different salutes — one with a full hand lifted respectfully at eyebrow level, and a second where only a single finger is raised. For generations now, the homemaker banner has come to represent two primary struggles. In the first, the homemaker is viewed as a subservient loser in the battle of the sexes, where a man has presumably gained power over a woman if she stays home. In the second struggle, woman faces off against woman; the struggle for autonomy, self-fulfillment and economic independence is pitted against society's need for nurturers.

The trouble with both positions is that they are framed by a model for organizing human affairs based on domination. David Korten calls this the "Empire" model, and it has presided over human history for the last five thousand years. In it, he explains, society maintains "a system of dominator power and elite competition. Racism, sexism and classism are endemic features of Empire."[2] Within this model, a woman's struggle for autonomy and self-fulfillment is satisfied if she participates in the market economy in a way that gains her prestige and economic power. In other words, she only gains respect if she's got a good job. If she opts to forego the job, a woman is valued as a nurturer only if there is a dollar figure attributed to her services, demonstrating how she, too, empowers the economic machine both by enabling her husband to spend more time at work and by helping children to grow up with a greater capacity to compete in the global marketplace. Interestingly, we tend to think of the conflict between self-fulfillment and the need to nurture as a female issue, leaving men no honorable option but to participate in the race for prestige and power, almost entirely ignoring their own need to nurture.

It is natural that men today assume that their life path will be defined by the struggle for power, as history by and large only tells us such stories. We rarely learn about the glories of great egalitarian and peaceful cultures; our stories center on how one culture or hero has "won a victory" over another. And in most instances, the central characters in these tales were almost exclusively men. Even our prevalent religious traditions have taught us that the gender of the almighty and powerful God is male.

ANCIENT LESSONS

We didn't always live this way. Human civilization was not always defined by the quest for power and the worship of the powerful. In fact, for a large part of human history (about 10,000 years), egalitarian cultures were the norm. While there may have been a division of labor between the sexes, *difference* did not imply superiority or inferiority. That is because, according to feminist scholar Riane Eisler, men and women worked together in these early cultures as partners.[3]

Evidence from several Neolithic societies and the Catal Huyuk (one of civilization's first towns, 6500 BC–5000 BC) indicates that worship centered around the ability to create, rather than to destroy. A common religious image from this period depicts a birthing woman. Eisler tells us that all of the cultures that had significant technological breakthroughs had one common feature — they worshipped a goddess. An important distinction she points out, however, is that while these cultures were matrilineal (meaning they traced family history through the mother), they were not *matriarchical* or *patriarchical*. They did not rank one half of humanity over the other. Rather, Eisler says, they organized their society on a partnership model, or what Korten today calls "Earth Community."[4] By such an orientation, human partnerships lay the foundation for creative cooperation, in which the aim of society is to grow the potential of the whole, rather than to expand the power of a few.

Under this model, Eisler points out, these early societies had phenomenal accomplishments, including breakthroughs in agricultural production, livestock domestication, housing improvements, and the invention of weaving and sewing. The arts flourished. According to conventional archaeology, social organization and the earliest technologies among humans were a result of men working together to hunt and kill. Alternative evolutionary models advanced by Nancy Tanner, Jane Lancaster, Lila Leibowitz and Adrienne Zihlman suggest that initial evolution and social progress were brought about by relationships between mothers and children.[5] These scientists argued that our erect posture was a result of freeing hands not for hunting, but to advance from foraging (eating as one moves) to gathering and carrying food so that it could be stored and shared. The first handmade artifacts were not weapons, but vessels for carrying food and offspring, and tools used by women to soften foods for their babies. Interestingly, in Catal Huyuk and other neolithic societies, archaeologists have also found sculptures of elderly men, sometimes sitting in poses similar to Rodin's *The Thinker*. According to Eisler, this suggests all elders, both male and female, had important and respected roles in these societies.

Thus, for thousands of years, human history was defined by creative achievements and cooperative relationships until, as Eisler explains, nomadic tribes invaded these agricultural settlements. The nomadic tribes had a different social system, where male gods of war were worshipped, violence was more prevalent, and authoritarian social structure was normal. "The way they characteristically acquired material wealth," says Eisler, "was not by developing technologies of production, but through ever more effective technologies of destruction."[6] Rather than worshipping the power to create, these cultures worshipped the power to conquer, and therefore dominate.

The cultural shift from a partnership to a dominator (or Empire) society was not completely owing to these conquests. However, this was the point where the ability to dominate gained strength over the ability to cooperate. Eisler is quick to point out that the root of the problem was not *men* as a sex; rather, the change came about through the adoption of a social system that revered the power to take life more than the power to give it. Anyone, male or female, who did not conform to this ideal was marginalized, as was their contribution to society.

DARWIN'S AWARD

Flashing forward to the late 1800s, we meet the premier contributor to our initial understanding of evolutionary biology, Charles Darwin. There is hardly a scholar alive who will question the importance of his work, and it is fascinating to consider its inadvertent impact on American domestic culture and the role women played in it. While admittedly there are many who would disagree, historian Glenna Matthews argues quite convincingly that Darwin's interpretation of women's roles in evolution contributed greatly to modern prevailing views that the role of nurturing and creation is secondary to physical dominance.[7] Matthews asserts that Darwin held a highly reductionist view of women, suggested that their reproductive capacities were their only contribution to human evolution, and explicitly stated that women were biologically inferior to men. Investigating the history of domesticity, Matthews argues that Darwin's theory of sexual selection, or perhaps more accurately, the public's interpretation of his work, played a major role in our emerging cultural disdain for matters of the home. Claiming that the genesis for human evolution was in the male struggle for mates, Matthews suggests Darwin appointed male activity as the front line for its progress. To oversimplify a bit, the guys had to keep coming up with new tricks to win over the girls. Thus, the guys kept evolving, while the girls just stood around and picked the best mate to breed with. Each new generation of humans became more evolved as a result of these male advancements. On the other hand, it could also be argued that woman's power to select her mate and determine the most desirable traits for future generations indicates that evolutionary advancement was directed by the girls (my personal vote was that it was probably a team effort, since it takes two to tango).

Either way, since his writings were a clear departure from the serpent and the apple story, Darwin's work stimulated the secularization of our society and changed the way we talked about the home. Until that point, the merits of a home were often described using the transcendent (and value-laden) language of religion, such as "loving" and "nurturing." Once society became more secular, transcendent values seemed old-fashioned and unscientific.[8] Functioning from the premise that human societies only advance through domination, Darwin, or more likely the interpreters of his work, attached a scientific validity to the notion that matters of the home were trivial and marginal to progress and relegated to "the weaker sex."

Domination, either by males or females, is a relatively newfangled notion for the organization of human societies. As David Korten points out, it "is no more than a five-thousand-year blip in the four-to-five-million-year arc of human learning about ourselves and our possibilities."[9] Nevertheless, it plays a central role as we attempt to understand our views of home and domesticity, and how they have changed in the last fifty years. More importantly, shedding the dominator model and embracing a cooperative ideal will be central to clearing the path for the truly egalitarian homemaking that can serve as our foundation for radical cultural change and ecological restoration.

THE MONEY-MAKING POTENTIAL OF A HOUSEWIFE:
"WHAT DOES IT PROFIT A MAN?"

The diminishment of homemaking's greater value and its consignment to women became firmly ensconced throughout the 19th century. In the years following World War II, the vision of the American Housewife primly dressed on the steps of her suburban home as she kissed her husband good-bye, shuttled her children off to school in the station wagon, then returned home to iron her sheets and wax her floor was so powerful, it inspired the iconic Suzy Homemaker Doll and toy appliance series. Americans had a renewed picture of happiness, and it was the job of the housewife to embody it, until Betty Friedan shattered the image with her 1963 classic, *The Feminine Mystique*.[10] Friedan pinpointed the "mystique of feminine fulfillment" as the core of Post-War American culture. Girls were raised to believe the greatest challenge in their lives would be to win their husbands, and the rest of life would be a happily-ever-after of new ovens and dishwashers, and the perpetual birthing of children as a way to ensure eternal youth. "The feminine mystique," explained Friedan, "says that the highest value and the only commitment for women is the fulfillment of their own femininity."[11]

The trouble lay beneath the surface of the dream, referred to by doctors as "housewife's syndrome." According to Friedan, most women suffered the condition in silence, thinking they were alone in their experience of emptiness, depression, anxiety and desperation. "It was a strange stirring," she writes, "a sense of dissatisfaction, a yearning that women suffered . . . As she made the beds, shopped for groceries, matched slipcover material, ate peanut butter sandwiches with her children, chauffeured Cub Scouts and Brownies, lay beside her husband at night — she was afraid to ask even of herself the silent question — 'Is this all?'"[12]

By and large, the prevailing thought was that there could be no problem with American housewives, as they enjoyed more material

wealth than any other women in the world. The problem could not be
identified in terms of poverty or sickness. In fact, Friedan noted, "it
may not even be felt by women preoccupied with desperate problems
of hunger, poverty or illness. And women who think it will be solved
by more money, a bigger house, a second car, moving to a better
suburb, often discover it gets worse."[13] The middle-class American
housewife's life had become, essentially, meaningless. The industrial
revolution and subsequent rise of America's consumer culture had
demoted homemaking from a craft tradition to the mindless occupations of primping the house, shopping and chauffeuring.

Magazines and television bombarded American women with a
public image about who she was supposed to be, and she lost the "private image to tell her who she is, or can be, or wants to be."[14] Friedan
reviewed magazines from 1939 through the early 1960s and found
they depicted a changing image of the American woman. In 1939 the
magazines featured stories about plucky, fearless women with both
professions and adoring men, but ultimately with some goal or vision
entirely their own; but by the 1960s they had degenerated to the
point where they were "crammed full of food, clothing, cosmetics,
furniture and the physical bodies of young women, but where [was]
the world of thought and ideas, the life of the mind and spirit?"[15] The
true role of the American housewife, Friedan explains:

> . . . is to buy more things for the house. In all the talk of femi-
> ninity and woman's role, one forgets that the real business of
> America is business. . . . Somehow, somewhere, someone must
> have figured out that the women will buy more things if they
> are kept in the underused, nameless-yearning, energy-to-get-
> rid-of state of being housewives.[16]

Indeed, she was quite right. Continuing her investigation, Friedan
met with a motivational researcher, "a man who is paid approximately
a million dollars a year [in the 1960s] for his professional services in
manipulating the emotions of American women to serve the needs
of business."[17] "Properly manipulated ('if you are not afraid of that

word,' he said), American housewives can be given a sense of identity, purpose, creativity, the self-realization, even the sexual joy they
lack — by the buying of things."[18] The researcher allowed Friedan
to peruse his studies, and indeed, she found that most of the unfulfilled emotional needs confronting American housewives were seized
upon by advertisers as marketing opportunities.

For example, through in-depth surveys, the researcher discovered
housewives' frustrated need for privacy, which was translated into an
opportunity to sell families a second car. "Alone in the car," the study
suggests, "one may get the breathing spell one needs so badly and
may come to consider the car as one's castle, or the instrument of
one's re-conquered privacy."[19] He uncovered the need to do creative
work, and linked it to an opportunity to sell cake mix:

> Every effort must be made to sell X Mix, as a base upon which
> the woman's creative effort is used. The appeal should empha-
> size the fact that X Mix aids the woman in expressing her
> creativity because it takes the drudgery away. At the same time,
> stress should be laid upon the cooking manipulations, the fun
> that goes with them, permitting you to feel that X Mix baking
> is real baking.[20]

In another report, the motivational researcher capitalizes on the
housewives' need to experience personal authority:

> Justify her menial task by building up her role as the protector
> of her family — the killer of millions of microbes and germs.
> . . . Emphasize her kingpin role in the family. . . . help her to
> be an expert rather than a menial worker . . . make housework
> a matter of knowledge and skill, rather than a matter of brawn
> and dull, unremitting effort.[21]

The means for doing this, he suggested, was by introducing new
products, because housewives "look forward to new products which
not only decrease their daily work load, but actually engage their

emotional and intellectual interest in the world of scientific development outside the home."[22] The need for a sense of achievement was met through offering sales and bargains. The "need to learn and to advance in life" would be filled by the department store. "We symbolize our social position by the objects with which we surround ourselves," one of the reports explained. "A woman whose husband was making $6,000 a few years ago and is making $10,000 now needs to learn a whole new set of symbols. Department stores are her best teachers of this subject."[23]

The most frightening conclusion of the researcher's analysis was this glaring truth: "The store will sell her more if it will understand that the real need she is trying to fill by shopping is not anything she can buy there."[24] Friedan's pointed analysis of the situation was that housewives were being manipulated by corporate America, sold an image of happiness, and then were unable to fulfill their greater potential as human beings.

It was no small wonder that Betty Friedan's book sparked the revolution that sent American women into the workforce in droves, seeking opportunities to challenge themselves, fulfill their creative potential, and have a meaningful impact on society. However, in a grim foreshadowing of the outcome of this shift, Frieden remarks, "I wonder if the challenge and the opportunities for the American economy and for business itself might not in the long run lie in letting women grow up, instead of blanketing them with the youth-serum that keeps them mindless and thing-hungry."[25] American businesses' efforts to keep women mindless in the home eventually melted away. Instead, it seized an even greater opportunity, whereby a cheaper labor force could be recruited and even more products could be sold to fill the empty spaces that were now left at home.

In fairness, not all careers are soul-sucking ventures (if they were, I wouldn't be investing so much time in writing this book). The balancing act with a good career is to achieve personal fulfillment, to contribute to society, but also to honor the four tenets of ecological sustainability, social justice, family and community. The argument I lay out here is levied against the vast majority of American occupations that fail to achieve these terms. It is *not* directed at those true life-serving vocations that make the world better for everyone.

2 EARNERS = 2 INCOMES = DOUBLE THE BUYING POWER

It is not hyperbole to say that we live in a society where corporations are fundamentally directing, if not ruling, our economy. They have become the ultimate dominators in an Empire where the masses have been lured into believing that corporate survival is essential to the well-being of the common folks. However, for-profit corporations are not structured to benefit the welfare of society; they are structured to make money. "Under the prevailing interpretation of corporate law," policy analysts Lee Drutman and Charlie Cray explain, "corporations have one primary duty: to make money for shareholders . . . In pursuit of this one goal, they will freely cast aside concerns about the societies and ecological systems in which they operate."[26] And when women left the home and entered the workforce, the corporations' charge was not to figure out how to accommodate women's needs to make money or to hand them opportunities for creative expression and personal fulfillment. Their intent, their *duty*, was to find a way to profit from the maneuver.

If the household was to be empty all day, then an assortment of products could be marketed on grounds that they would minimize domestic duties upon returning home, or fill the void left by family members' absence from each other. As women joined men in the workforce, opportunities to spend the paychecks were plentiful, including professional clothing, labor-saving home appliances, entertainment, exercise equipment, luxury vacations and, most significantly, processed foods.

By the 1950s, our nation's food system was rapidly industrializing. Cheap oil made it possible for fresh foods to be available year-round, and factories made it possible to produce canned foods far cheaper and faster than a housewife could do with her surplus garden produce. Once both men and women were working, and no one was home to bag lunches or fix dinner, then an enormous market opened wide. Processed convenience foods flooded the grocery stores, office buildings, gas stations, office supply stores, restaurants, street corners, rest stops and schools. Our dietary habits changed dramatically. In one telling example, U.S. per capita production of high fructose corn syrup, the essential ingredient in most processed and convenience foods, and a major contributor to obesity, was about 0.03 pounds per person per year in 1967. By 1977, that figure had jumped to 9.6 pounds per person per year; by 1987 it was 47.7; by 1997 it was 60.4 pounds per person per year.[27] From 1960–1962, 44.8 percent of the U.S. population was overweight or obese. By the late eighties we crossed the halfway mark, and by 2001 over 66 percent of our population was overweight or obese.[28]

The disruption of having husband and wife gone from the home all day created opportunities to commodify the needs of the vacant household. Alise Jansons, who parented and managed a brain injury program prior to joining the ranks of the Radical Homemakers, describes her family's descent into the dual-income home life:

> The laundry would rot. I would forget about it in the washing machine. And you lie in bed and these weird lists go through your head, like "Oh my gosh! This is what I have to do [and] . . . I have to do this . . . and this . . . and this . . . and this." You're processing work stuff. You have to do take-out food and you can't be thrifty and you don't have the time to recycle or do anything that's better [for the environment] . . . Everything is about time saving, time saving. . . . When you come to that working mom thing, sure you can do it, but you're cutting a lot of corners and the corners that you're cutting, I think, are the important corners for our society and our environment. . . . The time-saving things that you do, there's a price that goes along with that.

That price, she feels, was paid not only in earnings spent, but in her family's quality of life.

THE GOLDEN HANDCUFFS

When Rosie the Riveter and then her daughters of the late sixties and seventies joined the workforce, they entered a world that had been defined as a man's sphere since the dawn of the industrial revolution, when husbands first left their positions as co-stewards of the home to take on work for wages. Since that time, the wage-earning world has revolved around the cycle of a man's life. Thus, the period of time wherein a man establishes his value in the workforce and begins his significant career accomplishments is the same time when women are in their childbearing years.[29] As simple biological reality, women who hope to raise children are handicapped in the workday world from the moment they enter it. Julie Hewitt, a Radical Homemaker who left a corporate career, had her own interpretation of the quest for professional advancement: "You broke the glass ceiling or whatever it was . . . [but] that was something sold; that was a bill of goods." Pamela Stone, a sociologist who investigates work-family issues, published a study in 2007 showing how high-achieving, educated women are forced out of the workplace.

The women in Stone's study had enjoyed tremendous success in their professional lives, but at a considerable price. "Prestige, hefty remuneration, a modicum of job security, and generous benefits were offset by long hours, extensive travel, and unrelenting 24/7 demands."[30] Time demands and family conflict were an element of their lives to be taken for granted as working mothers attempted to fulfill the requisite sixty-hour work weeks and round-the-clock requirements for accountability. It was this pressure, played out in a dramatic unfolding of events, that led Julie Hewitt to step off her corporate path and begin her life as a Radical Homemaker.

Julie's first pregnancy ended prematurely with an emergency cesarian-section where she learned she'd given birth to a baby girl with Down syndrome. "I went back to work kind of . . . numb," she says. "I got six months off . . . and then David [her husband] got three, but when he was taking his paternity leave, I went back to work and really hadn't absorbed the full reality of dealing with a kid with special needs."

At the time, Julie didn't question her obligation to her employer or her commitment to her corporate career:

> I thought I would be able to go out and do something fabu-
> lous and not really have to deal with her day-to-day needs. I
> thought I could hire a nanny or something, which really wasn't
> realistic at all, nor was it really anything I wanted. But you
> get caught up in the mindset of "well, this is what everybody
> does." All these power women at [X-Corporation], they all
> go off and have a baby and six months later, they're back and
> they've got nannies. . . . It's the mindset, it's the culture . . . you
> don't even think about it; you're on autopilot.

Still, Julie says, the adjustment was extremely hard. During the first nine months of her daughter's life, she says, "I was just kind of not fully in my body." After her six-month maternity leave ended, Julie had to return to work, even though her daughter required open heart surgery. "I couldn't get any more time off," she says. "My boss said 'no.' She [my daughter] was in the hospital having open heart surgery, David was on paternity leave. I would drive from [X-Corporation] to the hospital every day after work. . . . it was just nuts."

Had it not been for her daughter's condition, Julie may have kept going with her stressful work-family routine, owing to the company's salary vesting schedule:

> They call it the "golden handcuffs," because you have to stay
> there for four and a half years to get all of your options back. I
> was only there for three years when I had [my daughter] . . . I
> was like, "I just can't [continue]; she needs early intervention;
> she's sick all the time." . . .

Julie and David ultimately decided to accept the penalty of fore-going the vesting schedule for the sake of their family. The women in Pamela Stone's research were forced to make similar sacrifices, which they couched as a "feminist choice," when in truth there was no choice at all. Stone acknowledges the hardships women face in their careers, stating that, "it is the workplace, stuck in an anachronistic time warp that ignores the reality of the lives of high-achieving women."[31] She regards the exit of highly talented women as the canary in the mine, "a frontline indication that something is seriously amiss in too many workplaces."

Just as corporate America has externalized the costs of the environmental damage it causes to the poorer nations left to cope with them, so too does it externalize its labor costs through its unfair treatment of female employees. The workplace has treated more than just the high-achievers unfairly. The National Women's Law Center reports that, even in today's "politically correct" climate advocating for income parity, women still make less money than men for the same work. Women working full-time year-round make $0.78 for every $1.00 earned by their male counterparts; working mothers earn only $0.73, and single mothers earn only $0.60 for every $1.00 earned by a man.[32] In one study, women's annual earnings decrease by 30 percent as a result of a period out of the workforce for two or three years (an average amount of time career-women would take off to start a family).[33] A Cornell University study found that mothers are penalized on the job market — they are 44 percent less likely to be hired than non-mothers with equivalent qualifications.[34] After women take a leave to begin a family, they discover that reentry into the professional world is "exceedingly difficult," says economist Sylvia Ann Hewlett, founder and president of the Center for Work-Life Policy. The Cornell study concluded that, "Unfortunately, only 74% of off-ramped women who want to rejoin the ranks of the employed manage to do so."[35]

And herein lies a moment of truth. When a person opts to pursue the radical homemaking life described in this book, to forego conventional employment to build a sustainable home life, the odds are that he or she will not be able to reverse their decision. The handwriting is on the wall: if you leave the workplace, in most instances, they will not want you back. The good news is that the odds are even greater that, once one steps out of this dysfunctional relationship, she or he won't *want* to go back.

WHAT (WHO) IS "THE ECONOMY" FOR?

Research shows us time and time again what most of us already know — the workplace, particularly corporate America, treats most women poorly. Many are overworked, time-starved, and face unrelenting accountability. At the same time, employees live in fear that they will lose their jobs. If we had a boyfriend or spouse who treated us this badly, most of us with healthy self-esteem would peg him as an abuser and dump him. Yet our culture compels us to behave like codependents in a dysfunctional relationship with the corporate economy.

Social scientists and work-family advocates diligently fight to improve the system — to increase remuneration, to garner more satisfactory leave time, to demonstrate to employers women's talent and value. Their efforts go toward making tiny upgrades in a relationship that, for too many people, simply doesn't work. To follow the abusive relationship analogy, it would be like a therapist working with a wife-beater to at least stop smacking her around on Sundays. We overlook the greater damage these workplace relationships cause in our lives for the sake of economic survival — both for our households and for our national economy. But in these efforts to continue and make minor improvements in this injurious relationship, we fail to ask the essential questions: What is our economy for?; Isn't it supposed to serve *everyone?*; Are our families truly served by an economy where employees are overworked, where families do not have time to eat meals together, an economy that relentlessly gnaws at our dwindling ecological resources? In David Korten's words, a true, living economy "should be about making a living for everyone, rather than making a killing for a few lucky winners."[36]

HIGHER EDUCATION

Discussing attrition of working women from high-achieving careers, sociologist Pamela Stone expresses concern for the "brain drain of sophisticated talent and expertise that workforce projections show we can scarcely afford to lose."[37] Further, she worries about women's future entitlements to higher education if they are not able to endure these abusive workplace relationships: "What does it say to the prestigious schools where they have been educated and trained? What message does it send to the top-drawer firms that hire them?"[38] By turning our backs on the extractive economy, will we forfeit our entitlement to a good education?

This, to me, seems highly unlikely. If a school determines a student a worthy educational investment *only* if she or he is a notable participant in the global market economy — an economy prone to stimulate worldwide social injustice, ecological havoc and domestic unrest, that feeds into an empire of domination whereby only a few can garner the resources rightfully owned by all — then its accreditation should be revoked and academicians should be ashamed to serve them. Universities should not be facilities merely for employee training with the aim of generating a qualified labor pool for corporations and top-drawer firms. The purpose of higher education should be to prepare students to perpetually teach themselves, cultivate their interests, talents and skills, and ultimately use them to serve their communities in a meaningful way. At this point in human history, it is incumbent upon educational institutions to consider how their services are preparing our students to restructure our society along the partnership model, so that we may be a true Earth Community where we recreate our civilization to live harmoniously on the planet, allow plenty for all, and recover our ecological health.

This is the new paradigm embraced by the Radical Homemakers. In the old paradigm, women chose the gilded cage or the glass ceiling. If they chose the gilded cage and stayed home, they became slaves to the marketplace image of the happy (shopping) homemaker. If they opted for the glass ceiling, they entered the workforce, where they became enslaved to their employers and hoped that they could fulfill their family dreams without getting tossed out like a used Kleenex. In the paradigm of the Earth Community, Radical Homemakers have chosen to stop investing their life energy in any employment that does not honor the four tenets of family, community, social justice and ecological balance. Instead, they invest themselves in the support of family, community, and environmental stewardship so that those things, in return, will pay them lifelong dividends. In Wendell Berry's words, "the only preventive and the only remedy is for the people to choose one another and their place, over the rewards offered them by outside investors."[39]

VALUE WITHOUT DOLLARS

As women's place in the workforce has become the norm in the last fifty years, the American household has changed to accommodate the shift. Agriculture rapidly industrialized and generated highly processed foods that supplanted most home cooking; skills were replaced with products, thrift with income, and time with convenience. As the home became increasingly devoid of enterprise and creativity, few could blame women for fleeing the hearth. However, during the same fifty years, our health, happiness and well-being have also dramatically declined. The abandonment of the kitchen, the loss of personal finance skills despite rising household incomes, the relentless increase in busy-ness and the compulsion to replace emptiness and loneliness with consumer products have put us on course for an ecological, social and cultural train wreck.

Perhaps saddest of all is that Americans seem to have surrendered their entrepreneurial spirit to the god of employment. Success, in our country, is now defined by money earned, by promotions, by continued servitude to an employer (or by eventually pressing others into service). Our gauge of success and personal worth has become so reliant on external validation that women and men now find it difficult to believe that a life centered around the home can satisfy their needs for personal fulfillment and genuine achievement.

Alise Jansons, who left her job managing a brain injury program explains: "[At] a high-end job . . . you get a lot of praise . . . you always have some supervisor saying 'Good job!' and 'Great!' and

'Here's your performance review!' Well, you don't get that at home."
Rebecca James, who resigned from a position teaching emotionally
disabled children, describes the same phenomenon:

> At school you had this compartmentalized list of things that
> you had to get done, and you knew they were done because
> they weren't on your desk anymore, or because they involved
> paper. . . . [There were] outside tracks of progress and linear
> tasks, and they stayed somewhat linear. . . . You get interrupted,
> but the tasks are still ordered and linear. And everything here
> [at home] is a crash course for me all the time . . . You really
> have to trust yourself, and you have to be self-sustaining in
> terms of feeling that you've accomplished something.

In many respects, our society still values mothers who opt to stay
home with their children, and Radical Homemaker parents are able
to feel confident they are making a "social contribution." But those
who have opted to forego having children often find it difficult defining (and defending) the accomplishments and achievements of their
home-centered lives. Penelope and John Sloan are a young couple in
Vermont who have secured modest financial independence, but often
feel awkward when articulating their life choices within conventional
parameters. "'So, what do you do?' That's a really strange question to
us," says Penelope:

> It's a question that we don't have a really good answer for,
> because what *do* we do? We get to live our lives however
> we want, is what we do. In a sense, according to the rules of
> society, we're retired because we're not out there working in a
> career, earning a paycheck. . . . so it's a strange kind of thing
> and I think that's where the [discomfort] comes in, because
> how do you explain to people in a nice little sound-bite that
> you chose this different path?

In Julie Hewitt's mind, the labels, resumé builders, and linear to-do lists that once defined success have simply become unimportant. "They're so temporary. I mean, you're on your deathbed; [are you] going to say 'Well, thank God I got the golden clock at my 40th retirement party?'. . . It's just meaningless."

Still, the value of rebuilding the home, the foundational unit in our society, offers seemingly few opportunities to garner the traditional trappings of success. This disparity in valuation of work can exacerbate power struggles in those couples where one person is employed and the other works at home. In efforts to ameliorate this, some social scientists have attempted to assign dollar values to domestic work. In truth, however, since domestic work does not actually bring in dollars (unless it is done for a third party), such imaginary figures really only place a heightened value on paycheck work. As Jonathan Rowe has observed, the mentality that underlies our economy "assumes that the only activities that have reality and value are those in which money changes hands." If money does not change hands, then the actions "dwell in a kind of netherworld where they await the beckoning of the market to attain actuality and life."[40]

Sylvia Tanner is a Radical Homemaker in Maine who once worked as an environmental analyst before she rebuilt a derelict cabin to make a solar-powered home where she raised her son. She frames the argument this way:

> So, if I go out to an office, let's say I work as a scientist for
> the state and I earn the money to pay for someone to install
> a floor for me, and I earn the money to pay to buy organic
> tomato sauce and salsa and whatever, that's considered real and
> respectable. But if I just do it myself, somehow or other that's
> not as respected.

Kelly Robideau, a Radical Homemaker living north of San Francisco also asks, "Why is it that people assume that the paid work is inherently more valuable?" For her, even seemingly trivial endeavors at home have an in impact her community:

Because for my family, having me home, making jam, [which
my husband] can take to his friends at work for Christmas
gifts . . . and we know that we're supporting the woman who's
got the last strawberry patch [in the region] . . . on so many
levels it's valuable to me, and I think that . . . there's that
assumption that if it's not paid work, then it's not worth doing.
. . . [But] there still needs to be the food made, there still needs
to be somebody taking care of the community.

Nevertheless, Friedan and many feminist scholars before and
after her have maintained that equality, security and human dignity
are impossible to achieve without earning one's own money. Without economic independence, they argue, a woman cannot marry for
love, she cannot escape an intolerable relationship, and she cannot
pursue an independent existence if she prefers to remain single. The
feminist concerns that women are enabled to have self-determination and independence are, of course, entirely valid. However, when
they are framed *only* in the context of participation and prevalence in
the market economy, they are trapped by the confines of the Empire
paradigm where personal economic power is the only security. This
position is untenable if domestic partners, in order to feel safe from
each other, must place harsh demands on their own family in order
to extract from the economy (and, hence, the environment) twice
the salaries, twice the commuter cars, double professional wardrobes,
meals away from home, etc.

Furthermore, though Friedan asserts that a domestic partner can
be intolerable and repressive, so too can be a job. A domestic partner
can be domineering and abusive — so too can be an employer. A
domestic partner can terminate a relationship, leaving one with no
means for support — so too can a corporation. Radical Homemakers, in their move toward a new paradigm of partnership and Earth
Community, are not the brand of feminists seeking security through
economic independence. In most cases, they view "economic independence" as an imaginary condition; if a wife, say, is reliant upon her

husband's paycheck, he, in turn, is dependent upon the vicissitudes, or even the whims, of his employer. They are both vulnerable if their life skills are limited to whatever they are able to do for a paycheck. They are more stable if the paycheck is only a small percentage of the livelihood, and life skills, increased self-reliance, community and family networks supply the rest.

Naturally, the Radical Homemakers who came forward to tell their stories verbalized no need to escape their marriages; undoubtedly, if they felt trapped or unhappy, they would not have been interested in talking with me. But as I spent time with happily married Radical Homemakers, egalitarianism was a resounding theme in their discussions of their domestic lives. In these households, men and woman share both authority and responsibility. As we will see, these homemakers have evolved a more sophisticated view of what constitutes an economy, and they have surrendered a false sense of independence to embrace genuine *inter*dependence. In place of conventional employment, these men and women build security through frugal living, domestic skills and reduced material needs. They have opted to trust and actively nurture their personal partnerships and to cultivate a web of family and community that supports them.

WHO IS DOING THE DIRTY WORK?

Theologian Thomas Berry noted that Western civilization has appropriated human reality and value to life *outside* the home.[41] Thus, it is only natural that many feminists, working in the context of a power struggle between the sexes, suggest that the only way to achieve equality is for women to *exit* the home. The trouble, however, is that everyone still needs a home. If both partners work outside the household to maintain perceived value in our society, then someone else must do the domestic work. The power struggle that may be alleviated when both husband and wife become working professionals is merely transferred to someone lower on the social ladder. Kelly Robideau offers a tragicomic example in her own community:

I have a neighbor across the street, both parents work at home, and they have a full-time nanny. She's a wonderful nanny . . . but I feel sorry for the baby, because I feel like he's not getting his parents. . . . Actually, this [nanny] is from Mexico and she has children that she's not taking care of because she's here taking care of somebody else's child. . . . And the mother (who employs this nanny), her job is placing nannies. So she has a nanny, and the nanny takes care of her child because she's busy placing nannies [for celebrities]. . . . So to me, there's something fundamentally wrong about that. This mother, who has two teenage children in Mexico, is here taking care of another family's child, and you know, economically that's what she needs to do, but it's unjust. . . . It's unfair on every level. It's unfair to the little boy across the street, and it's unfair to his nanny's children in Mexico, and I don't know where it ends.

The issue of transferring domestic labor to lower socio-economic classes was not lost on early feminists. Historian Glenna Matthews points out that nineteenth-century advocates for women's rights also struggled with this issue.[42] She writes that some adopted an openly elitist position: "a letter to the *Woman's Journal* in 1870 contended that only those who have no vision beyond the kitchen should be doing the housework. Bright women should aspire and drudges should keep the home fires burning."[43] Echoes of this view often reverberate in today's modern school system, where domestic skills are directed toward those students who do not appear to be "on a college track" (apparently college-bound students will not need to know about maintaining a household or personal budget!) Socialist forefathers Engels and Lenin also wrestled with questions of domestic duties and concluded that the only way for women to achieve true equality was through full involvement in industrial production. Neither Engels nor Lenin viewed domestic work as meaningful in its own right, so they, too, decided that it could be relegated to low-status women, and they offered the cozy-sounding proposition that this be accomplished by socializing child care and food preparation.[44]

"Only the material feminists," author Dolores Hayden asserts, "argued that women must assert control over the important work of reproduction which they were already performing, and reorganize it to obtain economic justice for themselves."[45] These late-nineteenth-century feminists made demands for both remuneration and honor for their work. Uniquely, Hayden says, "they were not prepared to let men argue that a woman's equality would ultimately rest on her ability to undertake 'man's work' in a factory or an office."[46] Nor, however, were they prepared to assert that men should pick up their fair share of the housework.[47]

Radical Homemaking is a movement seeking social justice on all levels. As Glenna Matthews reminds us, "if such work is despised, it will be performed by someone whose sex, class, or race — perhaps all three — consign her to an inferior status. If such work is despised, we will be much more likely to allow corporate America to manipulate the nature of homes and of housework."[48] For there to be true social egalitarianism, then the work of keeping a home must be valued for its contribution to the welfare of all. However, homemaking must also allow room for the self-actualization and creative fulfillment that was missing from the lives of so many housewives of the last half century, who suffered under the tyranny of "the feminine mystique."

SOMETHING MORE

There is more to our lives than a partner, children and a clean house. What Betty Friedan identified in her work was that, by merely attending to these three elements (and the consumerism that each came to entail), women were failing to self-actualize. Their lives might be amply busy, but still feel empty and devoid of meaningful and challenging work. As Kelly Robideau, the Radical Homemaker living outside San Francisco, observed, "If taking your child to get professional photographs . . . or organizing playgroups . . . is the biggest thing on your agenda, it's no wonder that that's unfulfilling."

Friedan argued that the root of both feminism and women's frustration lay in the emptiness of the housewife's role, because "the major work and decisions of society were taking place outside the home."[49] However, at this point in history, the work to heal our ecological wounds, bring a balance of power into our economy and ensure social equity starts with our choices about what to eat, what to buy (or, more importantly, what not to buy), what to create, and how to use our time and money. Indeed, the major work of society needs to happen *inside* our homes, putting the homemaker at the vanguard of social change.

Nevertheless, Friedan raised a critical point: "*The only way for a woman, as for a man, to find herself, to know herself as a person, is by creative work of her own. There is no other way.*"[50] What Friedan understood, but what many of us ultimately forgot, is that simply landing a job does *not* guarantee self-actualization. At the same time, the homemaker who simply learns to cook dinner, keep a garden and patch blue jeans will probably not find deep fulfillment, either. Those who do not seriously challenge themselves with a genuine life plan, with the intent of taking a constructive role in society, will share the same dangers as the housewives who suffered under the mystique of feminine fulfillment; they face what Friedan called a "nonexistent future."[51]

Wondering if my interviewees were in danger of contracting "housewife's syndrome," I looked for signs of it in my interviews. I asked questions about experiences with depression, sense of meaning, and personal fulfillment. Admittedly, I am *not* trained as a psychologist. But after conducting all the interviews for this book, I could see a pattern. The Radical Homemakers seemed to be on a three-stage path:

RENOUNCING: In this first stage, the Radical Homemaker is increasingly aware of the illusory happiness of a consumer society. They recognize and question the pressures and compulsion to purchase goods and services that they begin to feel they could provide for themselves "if only . . ." This stage is marked by growing introspection, doubting the ultimate worth of their careers, identifying their true sources of contentment, and seeking better alignment of their personal values with their life's trajectory.

RECLAIMING: In the second stage, the "reclaiming" period, Radical Homemakers were recovering the many skills that enabled them to build a life without a conventional income. This "phase" can take a few years or a lifetime, and homemakers will perpetually return to it as they build ever more skills. Initially, this is an exciting and tremendously fulfilling period, as people regain their self-reliance. Interestingly, if the homemakers dwelled only in this realm for too long, they began to manifest some symptoms of Friedan's housewife's syndrome — malaise, feeling lost, aimless, or occasionally depressed, or wondering "what's this all for?"

REBUILDING: Those homemakers who seemed most satisfied and committed to their life choices over the long haul had entered a "rebuilding phase." In this period, they took on genuine creative challenges, tended toward engagement with their communities, and made significant contributions toward rebuilding a new society that reflected their vision of a better world either through artwork, writing, farming, fine craftwork, social reform, activism, teaching, or a small business.

Entering the rebuilding phase did not preclude a return to the other phases. The myriad stages of life are forever presenting new challenges that require everyone to occasionally retreat from the public sphere to regain skills and life balance, and to critically evaluate the societal givens that they may have to consider at that time. For instance, along the homemaking path, this retreat might happen in order to: evaluate whether the conventional prenatal care system is consistent with a family's values; learn new parenting skills; examine the education system and explore the best methods for helping our children to learn; figure out how to cope meaningfully with a limiting health condition. Once a homemaker has gone through all three phases initially, the rest of his or her life becomes a balancing act of honoring each of them.

The choice of these individuals to become homemakers is not an act of submission or family servitude. It is an act of social transformation. Homemakers who entered the rebuilding phase did not then abandon the home to pursue a new passion. Rather, they fulfilled a dream of homemaking articulated by some of the earliest feminists. Susan B. Anthony visioned that "when society is rightly organized, the wife and mother will have time, wish and will to grow intellectually, and will know the limits of her sphere, the extent of her duties, are prescribed only by the measure of her ability."[52] Antoinette Brown Blackwell pictured a world where women moved from "bound to rebound," between the home and the world, with energies for both.[53] She was one of the few who argued that this would only be possible if men returned to their rightful place as full participants in domestic life.

It is time we come to think of our homes as living systems. Like a sour-dough starter, the home's survival requires constant attention. A true home is inhabited by souls who live, breathe, eat, think, create, play, get sick, heal and get dirty. It will wither in an antiseptic condition. A true home pulses with nonhuman life — vegetable patches, yeast, backyard hens, blueberry bushes, culturing yogurt, fermenting wine and sauerkraut, brewing beer, milk goats, cats, dogs, houseplants, kids' science projects, pet snakes and strawberry patches. A living system cannot respect the hours on a time clock and requires the involvement of all the inhabitants in order to thrive. When we can see our home as a living system, when men and women both play a role in its care, even if one of them goes out to a job for part of the day, we have taken the first steps to restore the important partnerships our Neanderthal ancestors innately understood. We will have moved toward creating a true Earth Community.

CHAPTER TWO
HOME ECONOMICS

"A thatched roof once covered free man;
under marble and gold dwells slavery."

Roman philosopher Seneca (3 BC–65 AD)[1]

Betty Friedan passed away in 2006 after a long life during which she witnessed fully the second wave of feminism that *The Feminine Mystique* sparked in the United States. In the final edition of her book (1997), however, she warned in her foreword that there was a bigger battle than sexual politics looming on our horizons:

> . . . the sexual politics that helped us break through the feminine mystique is not relevant or adequate, is even diversionary, in confronting the serious and growing economic imbalance, the mounting income inequality of wealth, now threatening both women and men.[2]

Friedan pointed out that we have been living in a culture of greed that has been distracting Americans from a growing sense of anxiety and insecurity. She cautioned that it was easier to absorb ourselves with rage between "women and men, black and white, young and old . . . than to openly confront the excessive power of corporate greed."[3] We have bigger battles to fight.

As I have already emphasized, it is not my intention with this book to draw men and women away from the valuable outside-the-home work of seeking justice, healing our sick, serving our communities, educating our citizens, or any other vocation, *as long as it genuinely honors* the four tenets of family, community, planet and social justice. Too many Americans, however, are finding themselves working as wage slaves in employment that fails to honor this quartet. We must realize that we can be empowered and find opportunity when we live opposite to the corporate-centered world. In order to revive our culture and create a vibrant society that does not depend on a consumer-driven and ecologically rapacious economy, more of us need to look homeward to create a life-nurturing alternative. Gandhi taught us that "to believe in something, and not to live it, is dishonest." Thoreau warned that failing to honor our conscience was a form of self-inflicted violence: "Is there not a sort of bloodshed when the conscience is wounded? Through this wound a man's real manhood and immortality flow out, and he bleeds to an everlasting death."[4]

Doubtless, the suggestion of creating a life-nurturing alternative to our existing consumer society still has countless key-punching economists puckering their mouths, rolling their eyes, and trying to persuade their sons and daughters that such an effort is fruitless. These folks go home at night and, sometime between heaving take-out on the table and finding the TV remote, they offer parental guidance, urging their daughters to grow up to continue the fight for fair treatment in the workforce, and their sons to practice their necktie knots so that they will be able to comfortably don their daily noose in adulthood.

It has been programmed into the conscience of many Americans that *any* alternative to the status quo will have a detrimental effect on the economy. Thus, as social critic John DeGraaf has observed, for any movement to succeed, whether it be for environmental protection, worker rights, or food security, advocates must first prove "that their suggestion will not adversely affect economic growth or the Dow Jones Industrial Average."[5] In short, advocates for social change are under obligation to prove that they will do no harm to corporate America, because corporate America has become inextricably linked with mainstream culture. It dominates over our political system, foreign policies, food system, environmental policies and practices, music and entertainment, even our educational system.

Since corporations claim no legal accountability other than to make money for their shareholders, we are living in, and largely governed by, an extractive economy that is divorced from our life systems.

Curtailing any social movement by offering deference to an extortionate economy is no longer acceptable. "It's long past time for a new framing offensive," argues DeGraaf, "one that turns the obligatory question on its head and shifts the burden of proof to those who resist change. Imagine bumper stickers, posters, internet messages, a thousand inquiries visible everywhere, asking a different question: What's the economy for?"[6] Our national (now global) economic principles have served only a handful of powerful elites. In the process, it has wrought havoc on our culture, our planet, and on the lives of most who serve it. By rebuilding our home lives according to values of social justice, ecological sustainability, and family and community security, we begin the process of dismantling the extractive economy and creating in its place a life-serving economy that enables us to meet our needs while thriving in harmony with our earth and spirits.

THE EXTRACTIVE ECONOMY: HOW DID WE DEVELOP IT, WHO SERVES IT, AND WHO BENEFITS?

Americans did not always embrace the corporation as a central axis of our culture. These legal structures first reared their heads in this country when Europeans settled along the East Coast, a process that was overseen by a series of British colonial companies chartered by the crown in order to explore, extract wealth and develop markets in the New World.[7] This arrangement eventually proved unacceptable to the colonists who, at the Boston Tea Party, finally rebelled against the Tea Act of 1773, which was imposed to benefit the financially troubled East India Company, in which the king and members of parliament were personally invested[8] (apparently, history repeats itself with the idea of government bail-outs). Homemakers, notably — the women of the colonies — had determined that they could operate their homes using local resources, and the colonies began a boycott of British goods. Thus empowered, rebels were able to respond to the Tea Act by dumping 90,000 pounds of East India Company tea into Boston Harbor, provoking the revolution that was not just about political independence from the crown, but about economic independence from British corporations.[9] The good news here is that we already have a history of confronting corporate control. The bad news is that after overthrowing corporations, we eventually succumbed to them once more.

Corporations regained their foothold in this country as quasi-governmental institutions created through acts of government for the expressed purpose of creating national infrastructure, such as canals or turnpikes. Originally, they were limited in size and were entitled to only limited rights specified within their charters. But slowly, states began loosening their control over the corporate form. Corporations were able to grow bigger, and their legal status eventually devolved from what policy analysts Lee Drutman and Charlie Cray describe as "creatures of the state," "mere business organizations," to "independent entities . . . 'persons' with constitutional rights."[10] The legal devolution proceeded to the point where today, explain Drutman and Cray, "they have very little accountability to the public, and the ability of the people to use public institutions, such as governments, to control corporations is largely circumscribed."[11] This weakness of our public institutions has resulted in corporations committing countless social, economic and ecological crimes. "If these corporations were ordinary persons," Drutman and Cray argue, "they would probably be locked up and put away for life for what they had done. In some states, they would even be executed."[12]

The prevailing belief is that the sole legal and ethical obligation of corporations is to generate financial returns for the shareholders. David Korten points out that nowhere is this spelled out in any legal legislation; nonetheless, it has become deeply embedded in our legal culture and case law. "It is a pure case of judge-made-law based on the arguments of corporate-interest lawyers," he explains.[13] The publicly traded limited-liability corporation is now presumed to be prohibited from exercising the same moral responsibilities legally expected of any sane adult in our country. Based on the atrocious violations of civility they have committed, Korten argues that most corporations, if they were actual human beings, would be diagnosed as sociopathic. In fact, to demonstrate this, anti-tobacco activists successfully filed paperwork in March of 2003 to create a new tobacco company in the state of Virginia. In the articles of incorporation, the *stated purpose* of "Licensed to Kill, Inc.," was "the manufacture and marketing of tobacco products in a way that each year kills over 400,000 Americans and 4.5 million other persons worldwide."[14] No questions were asked, no legal challenges were raised. After paying the appropriate fees, Licensed to Kill, Inc., was licensed to conduct business.

What has changed within our cultural psyche to condone or even be complicit in a social system that permits a corporation like Licensed to Kill to operate legally? Worse still, what kind of indoctrination have we succumbed to that would lead us to conclude that the profitability of a corporation such as Licensed to Kill (or Union-Carbide or Altria . . .) is linked to our personal well-being? Korten argues that this is simply a fallout from the Empire/dominating model for organizing human affairs. According to the conventional wisdom of this model, human beings are believed, at their core, to be "an inherently unruly and self-centered species prone to violence and lawlessness." With such a low image of ourselves, we accept the notion that we need a ruling class "and the competition of an unregulated market to impose order."[15] Thus, we are inclined to engage in commerce not because we have "needs," but in order to keep our corporations, our rulers, upon their thrones. In 1854, Thoreau observed this exact phenomenon during the industrial revolution:

> I cannot believe that our factory system is the best mode by
> which men may get clothing. . . . as far as I have heard or
> observed, the principal object is, not that mankind may be well
> and honestly clad, but, unquestionably, that the corporations
> may be enriched."[16]

This perverse kowtowing to corporate well-being continues into this millennium. Many Americans can recall recent history when, following the attacks on September 11, President G. W. Bush advised us to be patriotic by going shopping: "Get on board; do your business around the country . . . get down to Disney World in Florida [where his brother was governor]; take your families and enjoy life the way we want it to be enjoyed." In the same speech, he even explained that "One of the great goals of this Nation's war [on terror] is to restore public confidence in the airline industry."[17] The message was clear — our survival is supposed to be dependent on corporate survival.

We have come to believe that the viability of the corporate world is integral to our social and individual progress. Corporations provide jobs that pay us money to buy food, houses, cars, new clothes and radios and televisions and movies and vacations . . . and this has come to be how we define *progress*. However, as eco-theologian Thomas Berry pointed out, "this sense of progress is being used as an excuse for imposing awesome destruction on the planet for the purpose of monetary profit, even when the consequences involve new types of human psychic and physical misery."[18] We have confused "more money" with a "better life." Living with this pathology, we find ourselves sicker, our life systems becoming perilously destitute. Yet, simultaneously, our society seems willing to sacrifice ever more in order to achieve this misconstrued "progress."

The first sacrifice we make to this extractive economy is our time. Writer and social critic Jonathan Rowe wryly observed that we attribute little or no value to our time, unless it is used in a process whereby money changes hands.[19] It matters not *what* the time was used for, so long as the trade resulted in the generation of dollars. "It could go to thinking up new ways to seduce children into drinking more cola, or plotting ways to subvert clean air laws," notes Rowe. "So long as the time has flowed into the market and increased the churn of money there, it has been used beneficially where the economic mind is concerned." Once we have sacrificed our time to the extractive economy, there is even more money to be made, because we now must use our hard-earned cash in order to purchase substitutes for the time we've traded. We buy take-out and fast food when we don't have time to cook dinner. We buy prescription drugs when we no longer have time to take care of our health and get ample rest. We buy luxury goods for our loved ones as a substitute for spending time together. We throw out our shoes when the soles wear thin, toss our electronics into landfills when they stop working properly, because it takes too much time to repair them.[20] In the long run, we wind up cash-poor and time-destitute, while corporate America accumulates our wealth.

Yet another sacrifice made at the altar of the extractive economy is the vitality of our local communities. Whether rural or urban, prior to World War II our communities and their economies were, in many ways, inseparable. Our neighbors were not simply the people who lived next door. They were our partners in commerce, our local service providers, our local educators. Now, as Wendell Berry has observed, in most communities and neighborhoods, the residents are merely neighbors with no economic relationship to each other.[21] Instead, they are participants in the broader extractive economy, which has siphoned off the communities' resources. Agricultural land, once used for local food production, is commandeered for a global industrialized food system, housing subdivisions, strip malls of absentee-owned franchises, and highways to accelerate delocalization of the community. In the wake of extractive economics, water supplies are polluted, mountainsides are mined and, typically, local autonomy is overrun by corporate influence. With local economies fractured and marginalized, people are left with few options but to garner a living by working for and purchasing from the extractive economy. Even our schools appear to be directed to serve the extractive economy as well; instead of helping children to be self-learners, entrepreneurial and inventive, the priority is to make them "competitive in the global marketplace" and "good at following directions," or in other words, to become diligent servants in corporate commerce and the extractive economy.

With the American community compelled to always look outside itself for its basic needs, it becomes merely a shared address on a map. It is no longer a site for the intertwining of people's lives for mutual sustenance. As an example, look no farther than Benton-ville, Arkansas, birthplace of Wal-Mart, the company that enjoyed approximately $45 million in sales every *hour* in 2008.[22] In 2007, Bill McKibben reported that, despite the $90 billion fortune shared by the three heirs, the city of Bentonville runs at a deficit and is unable to afford a needed sewage treatment plant.[23] It is ironic that, after overthrowing imperial/corporate rule in the 1700s, Americans have not only re-accepted it, but have come to think that it is imperative for the well-being of our nation.

Our gravitation toward corporate welfare is due largely to our national faith in the Gross Domestic Product, a dollar figure that measures the total market value of all the goods and services we produce in a given period. The problem, explained Yale economists William Nordhaus and James Tobin in the 1970s, is that the GDP, while it gauges the nation's market production, does not provide a true measure of our well-being.[24] For all its complicated adjustments of variables, GDP simply quantifies market outputs, but it has no qualitative reference to their actual productive value. If it is made and sold, it is a positive number. But when the GDP places equal value on the sale of new clothes, cars and Happy Meals as it does on anti-depressants, palliative health care, and divorce lawyers (and it does), then it only measures the vigor of the nation's market, not the vitality of the nation's people.

The Genuine Progress Indicator (GPI) is an alternative measure of national well-being vetted by social and economic scientists. In addition to counting consumer spending, the GPI attributes value to housework and volunteer efforts, and balances it out against other factors for well-being, such as income inequality, crime, environmen-tal degradation, and loss of time. With annual total market value of all goods between $13 and $14 trillion, the United States has the highest GDP in the world. It has gone up by approximately $12 tril-lion since the mid-1970s.[25] However, the GPI of the United States has remained stagnant since the 1970s.[26] As of 2001, only 20 percent of the population owned 84 percent of the wealth. That leaves 80 percent of Americans to share 16 percent of the remaining assets.[27] Of the one hundred largest economies in the world, fifty-one are corporations and forty-nine are nations.[28] CEOs now typically earn 475 times as much as the average worker.[29]

Is it possible that, if more Americans sidestep the conventional workforce and make their homes the central focus of their lives, the economy will suffer? If we are talking about the extractive economy that serves America's elites and protects its corporations, then the answer is yes. And rightfully so. Our economy should not be dedicated to the enrichment of corporations. The true definition of the word *economy*, taken from Greek *oikonomia* — from *oikonomos*, household manager — refers to "the management of household or private affairs and especially expenses."[30] Reflecting on this, we see that the economy should be serving the people — families, in their homes — not the reverse.

Money is simply a tool. We use money as a proxy for our time and labor — our life energy — to acquire things that we cannot (or care not to) procure or produce with our own hands. Beyond that, it has limited actual utility: you can't eat it; if you bury it in the ground, it will not produce a crop to sustain a family; it would make a lousy roof and a poor blanket. To base our understanding of economy simply on money overlooks all other methods of exchange that can empower communities. Equating an economy only with money assumes there are no other means by which we can provide food for our bellies, a roof over our heads and clothing on our backs. Further, when we assume that money is the only means by which we can accomplish these things, then our economy serves only those people who possess it. It does not value the regenerative work that must be done in order to provide the resources that every soul, human and nonhuman, needs to live.

When women and men choose to center their lives on their homes, creating strong family units and living in a way that honors our natural resources and local communities, they are doing more than dismantling the extractive economy and taking power away from the corporate plutocrats. They are laying the foundation to

re-democratize our society and heal our planet. They are rebuilding
the life-serving economy.

TOWARD A LIFE-SERVING ECONOMY

The extractive economy is terminal. Contrary to media propaganda,
we cannot tweak a few policies here and there and create never-end-
ing growth. Resources will be depleted, living systems will crumble,
spirits will break. By contrast, a life-serving economy will endure
because it serves everyone and is based upon renewing the health of
the land and water, the vitality of the forests and pastures. It regards
all life forms as mutually supportive, equally important contributors.
Cooperation, sharing and nurturing are as essential to an authentic
life-serving economy as money and muscles. The wealth it is built
upon is real and regenerative, rooted in healthy citizens and natural
resources. Unlike the extractive economy, it is not built upon resource
depletion or deferred costs.

In 1987, at the United Nations Environment and Development
Conference, delegates proposed that an international agreement on
sustainable living principles be written as a governing guide for individuals, businesses, organizations and nations. This idea snowballed
into a worldwide grassroots effort that, in 2000, gave birth to The
Earth Charter. The document outlines four interdependent principles for a sustainable way of life, which serve as the governing forces
of a life-serving economy:

1. Respect and care for the community of life
2. Ecological integrity
3. Social and economic justice
4. Democracy, nonviolence and peace[31]

In order to build a life-serving economy on these principles, we
must accept that the basic foundation of our wealth is sunshine and
water, not fossil fuels or other nonrenewable resources. We must
embrace the principles of social justice and non-exploitation, and

agree that our exchange of dollars must not come at the expense of someone else, whether they are local or on the other side of the planet.

Once we have accepted these principles, the life-serving economy allows what many of our spiritual traditions have taught — that each of us has a calling or right livelihood that enables us to serve the common good, and in finding this calling, we will be most happy. Few, if any, spiritual teachings call us to seek the accumulation of money, stuff, power, or other purely selfish interests. Further, in a life-serving economy, we individually accept responsibility for creating our own joys and pleasures. We do not rely upon corporate America to sell us these things. We take personal and collective responsibility for supplying many of our needs. In taking these steps, we discover that true economic assets, unlike money, are intangible. Wendell Berry defines some of these assets as: culture-borne knowledge, attitudes and skills; family and community coherence; family and community labor; cultural or religious principles such as respect for gifts (natural or divine), humility, fidelity, charity, and neighborliness.[32]

By cultivating these assets, Radical Homemakers simultaneously build a life-serving economy while reducing their reliance on the extractive economy. They are building a bridge from the old to the new. Husbands and wives in healthy marriages opt to trust their relationships and invest their efforts into their mutual home, rather than devising ways to be economically protected and independent from each other. Multigenerational families may discover that complete financial independence from one another is costly, or perhaps that shared homes, property or resources reduce the costs of housing, elder care, child care or even food and maintenance costs. Young families find that humility enables them to accept help from willing parents without stigma, or vice versa, reducing their duplicative demands on an extractive economy. The seasoned homemaker takes joy in teaching gardening and food preservation, or sharing any other myriad skills with her neighbors, both building her community's capacity to provide for itself and stimulating her own intellect. A family avoids buying a new car by virtue of a son's mechanical gifts. A rural hamlet creates its own Christmas traditions through a community exchange of songs, poems, stories and potluck suppers.

In the life-serving economy, the political spectrum fades away, particularly as Americans discover that the majority of us share many of the same values. The Center for the New American Dream reports that 96 percent of Americans believe we need to take personal action to conserve energy and protect the environment. Eighty-six percent feel the phrase "more is better" no longer characterizes the American dream; rather, they crave "more of what matters."[33] The majority of Americans feel that as a society, we are too focused on working and earning money and not focused enough on family and community.[34] Americans worry about our materialistic culture and fear it has negative consequences for our society, environment and world.[35] A large majority of Americans claim a willingness to take personal actions to reduce their consumption and materialism.[36] The Democratic and Republican parties no longer define the political battles in our country. As this poll data clearly indicates, the vast majority of us want to do away with our extractive economy and replace it with one that honors our need for time and togetherness, restores our ecological systems, and provides for everyone, regardless of politics, race, income, education, or spiritual beliefs.

Eco-theologian Thomas Berry referred to the challenge we all now face as the "great work" whereby humans, nonhumans and the whole of the Earth community must support one another. Radical Homemakers play a critical role in meeting this challenge. We do this by raising our children to understand their place in healing this world, reclaiming the skills our local communities require for sustainable self-reliance, and changing our economy from one that is extractive to one that is life-serving. The choice to become a homemaker can no longer be dismissed as a retreat from the "real" world. It is a full, head-on engagement with the major tasks our society is confronting. And as we will see in the next chapter, this will not be the first time that homemakers have changed history.

CHAPTER THREE

FROM SELF-RELIANCE TO COMMODIFICATION

"We started leaving the home to go to work
in order to support the home. We have been doing
this for so long that we have forgotten the purpose
for which we sold ourselves in the first place."

— William Coperthwaite[1]

Columnist Ellen Goodman once remarked that "Normal is getting dressed in clothes that you buy for work, driving through traffic in a car that you are still paying for, in order to get to the job that you need so you can pay for the clothes, car and the house that you leave empty all day in order to afford to live in it."[2] Life in America was not always like running on a hamster wheel. There was a time when the home was not just a place to sleep at night, nor a gilded cage for a marginalized stay-at-home woman. In fact, there was a time in our nation's history when homemakers wielded great power for reforming our society. As we embark on a new quest for social justice, for living harmoniously on this planet, and for uncovering deeper meaning in our lives, we must understand how our homes morphed from productive social units to isolated consumption units, and the impact this deterioration has had on our culture. With this understanding, the path to recovery will come to light.

PRE-INDUSTRIAL HOMES
Housework, we have come to presume, is women's work. However, if we trace the history of the household back to its origins in thirteenth-

century Europe, we uncover a different reality. "Housewife" was a term that did not enter into our language until the feudal period was coming to an end and the world saw the first signs of a middle class emerge. "Housewives" were women who were married to husbands; *husband* comes from *hus,* the older spelling of house, and *bonded,* as in one who is bonded to a house, rather than to someone else.[3] Because they owned or rented their house, these couples had a unique title in the emerging social structure; they were neither members of the aristocracy, nor peasantry. They stewarded the land around their home to gain their sustenance and made their own decisions about how to manage their livestock and other domestic resources. The couples' economic security was a result of their combined efforts to produce for their household.[4] Historian Ruth Schwartz Cowan notes that while there was a clear division of labor in these thirteenth-century homes, there was not necessarily a clear line drawn between a man's sphere and a woman's sphere. Men made cider and mead; women made beer, ale and wine. While the women made and mended clothing made from cloth, the men produced anything made of leather. Both had tasks to fill "the interstices of their days"[5] — women sewed and spun, men chopped wood and fashioned tools and utensils. Both performed jobs that required strength and stamina — men hauled wood; women washed clothes. Both men and women would milk livestock, draw water, weave, and peel apples and potatoes. Much of their work was a team effort. Men would grow flax; women would break it and spin it into linen.[6] Women nursed and cared for the children; men made the cradles, and mowed the hay and sheared fleece to fill the mattress ticking. In contrast to modern times, the household was the source and locus for sustenance and survival. It was not a separate entity to be supported through outside means.

These early households were, by and large, self-sufficient, but they did require a limited market economy to supply those materials and objects that they could not produce for themselves. Families would exchange whatever surplus product they had produced in order to acquire the additional articles they needed.[7] The success of the household relied on the presence of both sexes. Domestic duties were too great to be accomplished by one person. Further, the culturally imbued division of labor meant that generations of men had learned the male jobs, and generations of women had learned the female jobs. Without division of labor, no one person, regardless of strength and stamina, could master all of the requisite skills to accomplish all of the tasks to be done.[8]

This pattern of life found its way across the ocean, where the colonial American home became the foundation for production in the New World. Since most colonists did not reside in cities, they had to produce much of what they needed. They raised their food, cured their bacons and hams, made their own soap, wove fabric and sewed their own clothing.[9] This lifestyle continued even after the industrial revolution, when pioneers set out across the frontier. Husbands and wives would usually have some help at different times — local youth who worked as servants or day laborers before they married and acquired their own land — but prior to the widespread adoption of slavery in the late 1600s, most help in these households came from children, other relatives, and neighbors. While European villages may have had specialized artisans — "butchers, bakers and candlestick makers" — such market infrastructure was not yet established in colonial America. With the exception of certain materials, such as lead, glass, or paper, or specialized tasks that required the attention and tools of a skilled craftsman (or "smithy"), colonists produced virtually all of their fundamental necessities within their households.[10]

The success of the home, and the concomitant survival of colonial society, rested on the laborious efforts of *both* husband and wife. Despite the teamwork, the underlying form for organizing society was still based on the hierarchical dominator model, and thus women did not share the same status as men. According to historian Glenna Matthews, women from the colonial period would describe their work with phrases such as "my narrow sphere," "my humble duties," or "my little domestick affairs." "In other words," writes Matthews, "a home was seen as serving the purely private ends of providing for the needs of those who lived in it, and the housewife had no reason to think of herself as vitally linked with the world outside the home."[11] All of that was about to change.

THE CULT OF DOMESTICITY

During the 1760s and 1770s, relations between the colonies and the British Empire were becoming contentious and unraveled, particularly in light of a series of tariffs imposed on imported goods. Matthews points out that, suddenly, seemingly petty concerns — the type of cloth used to make a suit or the foods served at the table — acquired a significant political relevance. In order to have the tariffs repealed, colonists engaged in a series of boycotts. "The boycotts would not have worked," says Matthews, "without the cooperation of women acting within their own households." The result of their participation, she says, was that women gained "a new self-respect and a rationale for entering into political discussions."[12]

Patriotism was not defined merely by willingness to wield a musket or throw tea into Boston Harbor. A Declaration of Independence also took place in the early American household with the refusal to use British imports and, quite interestingly, in the cultivation and celebration of a regional cuisine. Prior to the Revolution, the common guide to running a household, Gervase Markham's *The English Huswife: Containing the Inward and Outward Vertues which ought to be in a Compleate Woman*, printed in the British Empire, was commonly sold throughout colonial America.[13] The book contained a lengthy section on cookery, information on seasonal planting, advice on dairying and brewing, several recipes for medicinal remedies for "griefes in stomacke," and cures for consumption and even the plague. Colonial women soon found, however, that the book did not serve them well as they learned to use the resources of their new native land. Colonial cooking was vastly different from cooking in the British Isles, but the changes went unacknowledged until Amelia Simmons printed, at her own expense, the first edition of *American Cookery* in 1796, which came to be recognized as the first truly American cookbook. In it, Simmons documented the culinary changes that would forever separate the American housewife from her continental ancestors. She acknowledged the importance of locally derived ingredients such as Indian corn, and recorded the first recipes for "Indian Pudding," "Johny Cake or Hoe Cake," and "Indian Slapjacks." She wrote recipes for "Pompkin" Puddings, "Crookneck, or Winter Squash Pudding," Jerusalem artichoke, as well as for the medicinal remedy Spruce Beer. She wrote that roasted turkey should be accompanied by the uniquely American cranberry sauce, and that bacon could be smoked with America's plentiful corn cobs.[14]

As citizens of the new republic discovered that the affairs of the household were integral to their freedom from colonial rule, the home became the center of the culture for a period of time that historians now refer to as "the cult of domesticity."[15] Women assumed the status as society's moral authorities, novels appeared that celebrated the role of the housewife, and more cookbooks appeared on the market, offering a greater variety of advice and cuisine. The home was seen as the vanguard for producing patriotic and virtuous citizens, and women, raising their children, wielded responsibility for the civic education of our population. Benjamin Rush, who represented Philadelphia's signature to the Declaration of Independence, wrote that women "should not only be instructed in the usual branches of female education, but they should also be taught the principles of liberty and government; and the obligations of patriotism should be inculcated upon them."[16] With an entire nation in agreement with these ideals, by 1860 the literacy rates of men and women were equivalent, and girls had as much access to education as boys.

Women's influence within society grew stronger, and family size became smaller. When Alexis de Tocqueville wrote *Democracy in America*, he noted that, even relegated to the domestic sphere, the influence of American women upon their culture was vast.[17] The importance of the family was greatly underscored during this time as well. Abolitionist, reformer and Unitarian clergyman Samuel May argued that, while children were young, "the family . . . ought never to be neglected for the service of the state, by the father any more than the mother" but once grown, both sexes should endeavor to contribute to the "common weal."[18] The preponderance of such thinking laid the groundwork for housewives' participation in the political shaping of our nation. The resonant political role of women was evident in the fight to end slavery, when abolitionist housewife Harriet Beecher Stowe became, in the words of Abraham Lincoln, "the little woman who made this big war" through her 1852 novel, *Uncle Tom's Cabin*.

Following the Civil War, the Cult of Domesticity was fueled by one of America's most influential thinkers, Ralph Waldo Emerson. Writing at the start of the nation's industrial revolution, Emerson promoted the home as the moral foundation for a truly democratic society. "But the reform that applies itself to the household must not be partial," he wrote. "It must correct the whole system of our social living. It must come with plain living and high thinking; it must break up caste, and put domestic service on another foundation."[19] Pointing to the growing aspirations brought on by the industrial revolution, he wrote, "Give us wealth, and the home shall exist. But that is a very imperfect and inglorious solution of the problem, and therefore no solution. Few have wealth, but all must have a home."[20] Despite his efforts to uphold the political power of the domestic unit, Emerson was already losing ground. The industrial revolution was well underway in Europe before it spread to the New World, and the effect it had on the status of the household on both sides of the ocean was profound.

THE DOCTRINE OF SEPARATE SPHERES

When the industrial revolution found its way to post-colonial America, society changed quickly to meet its demands. Merchants, shopkeepers and peddlers had to insist on cash payments, rather than on in-kind trade. Farmers, too, suddenly found themselves in need of cash to acquire new farm equipment to increase their yields beyond simple surplus. The industrial revolution brought changes to the family hearth as well. The wood-burning fireplace was replaced by the wood-burning cookstove, which was then replaced by the coal-burning stove. The coal-burning stove reduced the man's labor to find and split firewood, but it required that he sell his product or take a job outside the home in order to have the cash to afford the fuel.[21] Once he no longer had to cut, haul and split firewood, it was no longer imperative for his son to learn these skills. Factories took many more of the man's domestic tasks. They produced boots and shoes, removing the requirement for him to tool leather; they produced pottery and tin ware, removing his need to carve, whittle or otherwise craft utensils.[22] The development of the meat-packing industry removed the family's need to raise and slaughter their own animals. One by one, men's domestic duties were taken over by the factories. Within a short period of time, their skills for raising and butchering a hog, making cider, repairing ironware, making shoes, cups or bowls for their families, or for wielding an axe became unnecessary. What a man needed to know was how to make salable product or keep a job to pay cash for his family's necessities. Thus, these were the new lessons he taught his son.

The industrial revolution may have freed men from their household labors in order to work in the factories, but most people still needed a home, and homes still needed to be maintained. Though boys no longer learned the crafts their fathers practiced, girls continued to learn to cook, sew and maintain the household. Girls also may have gone to work in factories in their late childhood or early adulthood, often to earn wages so that a male in the family could pursue an education to enter a profession (now that wages were a necessity). But with men's labors now permanently committed to the workplace, it was presumed that girls would eventually leave their jobs, marry, and return to the home and raise a family. Thus, while our culture quickly came to assume that separate spheres for men and women are an age-old tradition, it was only in the early 1800s that the idea became entrenched.

The industrial economy altered nearly every aspect of home life. The rearing and education of children was reoriented with the assumption that they would become employees, rather than owners of their own homesteads or enterprises. To hold a good job was the aspirational force behind their childhood training. The family's eating patterns changed as well; traditionally, dinner was served midday, enabling the cook the benefit of working during daylight hours, and supper was a light repast, taken just prior to sundown, before the family would head off to bed.[23] But once men were gone to factories all day and children were off to school, this pattern changed, and dinner became the principal meal,[24] pushing the daily labor of housewives later into the evening. Most importantly, families came to think of "work" and "home" as separate places, with "work" most typically being the realm of the man, and "home" the domain of the woman.[25] Before long, "work" also came to mean the "real world," where one's labors had value, leaving the home a site for thankless toil.

More families were living in cities, and factories made it possible for them to purchase things that they once had to make, such as cloth or soap. At first sight, it may seem as if the housewife's labors, like the husband's, were relieved by the industrial revolution, but this was not necessarily the case. The ability to purchase manufactured cloth alleviated the need to weave, but it resulted in more labor. Cotton required frequent laundering, which required that families needed more changes of clothes, so the labor of weaving was supplanted with more sewing and more washing. The availability of gas lights alleviated the task of candle-making, but the globes required daily cleaning to remove the soot. Myriad devices were invented during the first one hundred years of the industrial revolution with the intention of easing household burdens, but in truth, says Schwartz Cowan, they did nothing to spare the housewife labor; they simply reorganized her work processes.

Doubtless, many significant improvements in quality of life resulted from modernization. Toward the end of the 1800s, the family diet was likely more varied, the typical house had more heat in the winter and more space to accommodate the family, personal and household hygiene improved, and clothes were cleaner. However, with husbands now gone off to work, families having relocated closer to the factories but farther from the support of relatives, and with her children spending more time in school, the housewife was left increasingly isolated at home with a mountain of work. Writing "A Domestic Problem" in 1875, Abby Morton Diaz outlined the typical labors for a woman in her position:

Setting tables, clearing them off, keeping lamps or gas-fixtures
in order, polish stoves, knives, silverware, tinware, faucets,
knobs, &c.; washing and wiping dishes; taking care of food left
at meals; sweeping including the grand Friday sweep, the limited daily sweep, and the oft-recurring dust-pan sweep; cleaning paint; washing looking-glasses, windows, window-curtains;
canning and preserving fruit; making sauces and jellies, and
catchups and pickles; making and baking bread, cake, pies,
puddings; cooking meals and vegetables; keeping in nice order
beds, bedding, and bedchambers; arranging furniture, dusting
and 'picking up'; setting forth, at their due times and in due
order, the three meals; washing the clothes, ironing, including doing up shirts and other 'starched things'; taking care of
the baby, night and day; washing and dressing children, and
regulating their behavior, and making or getting made, their
clothing, and seeing that the same is in good repair, in good
taste, spotless from dirt, and suited both to the weather and
the occasion; doing for herself what her own personal needs
require; arranging flowers; entertaining company; nursing the
sick; 'letting down' and 'letting out' to suit the growing ones;
patching, darning, knitting, crocheting, braiding, quilting, —
but let us remember the warning of the old saying ['If you
count the stars, you'll drop down dead'], and forebear in time.[26]

Beyond a doubt, there was a new "domestic problem" in our country. The work level was tremendous without the aid of husbands, children, extended family or domestic servants. However, as is the case
in our culture, problems are only problems for a short time before
enterprising individuals identify them as marketing opportunities.

THE FRAGMENTED HOUSEHOLD

Once the industrial revolution had fully swept the country, the Cult
of Domesticity withered away. With most of the occupants of the
household gone for most of the day, the family home was no longer considered the heartbeat of the culture, nor a wellspring for

transcendent values. Increasingly, it was regarded as a mire of drudgery. Initially, the remedy, at least in the middle class, was to find "good
help," meaning reliable, competent, inexpensive, obedient domestic
servants. In just a short period of time, the labor that husbands,
children, extended family and community once contributed to the
household had become an element that needed to be purchased.

Soon the industrial values of maximum efficiency were called
upon to rescue the housewife from her burdens. Even before many
homes had been electrified, there was a push in the marketplace to
create labor-saving appliances. There were ample money-making
opportunities in relieving the housewife of her duties. The food-pro-
cessing industry got its foothold in the economic boom following
the Civil War, taking advantage of the railways, urban expansion, and
national advertising opportunities.[27] By the late 1800s, commercial
canneries had sprung up. The competition among them led to a series
of mergers that ultimately resulted in the birth of the multinational
corporation Del Monte, whose copywriters were soon able to con-
vince housewives that factory-canned goods were superior to what
they could produce at home.[28] In 1925, Clarence Birdseye patented
his technique for freezing food, and by 1934, thirty-nine million
pounds of frozen food were processed annually and sold to owners
of new freezers.[29]

Even the core of the home — nurturing and caring for the family's health and well-being — was sellable. Advertisements for patent
medicines filled the pages of women's magazines (themselves, a new
phenomenon), and cookbooks soon stopped offering housewives
recipes for preparing their own remedies.[30] Nursing became a profession, and the sick were moved out of family homes and into hospitals,
which benefited from a middle class willing to pay for care. By 1900
the job of preparing the dead for burial, once an important, (if lach-
rymose) family rite of passage, had left the home and was taken on
by morticians.[31]

As a whole, the nation eagerly embraced the shift toward industrial technologies. All household work was viewed as drudgery that
ideally could be supplanted by the marketplace. By the end of the

First World War, most housewives had the job of managing machinery instead of people. The craft traditions once so integral to the home — food and beverage production and preservation, healing, shoemaking, weaving, sewing, soap making, toy making, education and furniture making, to name but a few — were no longer the domain of the household. With each of these developments, the American home lost its grip on production and slipped more and more into the realm of consumption. The tools and techniques of housekeeping became increasingly reliant upon manufacturers and service professionals. The industrialization of food production made families simply consumers of food, rather than producers. Housewives were no longer health-care providers; they and their families were health-care consumers.

All of this was aided by the booming advertising industry, which came of age in the 1920s. During this time, marketers pioneered new techniques for luring buyers. One associate editor of *Advertising and Selling* hit on a national selling phenomenon when he remarked, "I want advertising copy to arouse me, to create in me a desire to possess the thing that's advertised, even if I don't need it."[32] And in that moment, American corporations found a new goal. Opportunity was no longer limited to simply easing the housewife's domestic duties; it could be found in convincing her to buy what she *didn't* need. Then, in 1927, E.R.A. Seligman introduced the concept of installment buying, putting the final touches on our newly created culture of consumption.[33]

As forms of household production were out-sourced to a corporate America, increasing efficiency had become something of a religion, as well as the ultimate justification for exploiting the Earth's resources for material gain. In the process, the American home was left empty, cared for by a woman whose labors had been de-skilled to the point where her obligation to society was to function as a consumer, buying those services and goods for her family that she and her husband, just two or three generations prior, would have worked together to provide. She no longer needed to make strawberry jam, home remedies, or sew her children's garments. Her home-based duties were to clean, fix the evening meal, and tend the children when they were home. However, her days were not idle. Even though corporate America was producing most of the goods and services her family needed, the American housewife was still responsible for procuring them. And for that, she now needed the greatest tool that would lead to the fragmentation and disconnection of her home, family and community — the automobile.

MARRIAGE TO THE AUTOMOBILE

One would expect that the proliferation of household conveniences that defined the marketplace of the mid-20th century would have liberated the long-suffering housewife from her grinding chores. However, upon examining domestic time and labor studies from the period, historian Glenna Matthews explains that the time spent on housework declined very little, if at all.[34] This was largely owing to the widespread adoption of the automobile, which became to the 20th-century housewife what the cast-iron stove had been to her counterpart in 1850 — the means by which she did the majority of her work.[35] The union of a housewife with her car perpetuates even to this day. When conducting her research with stay-at-home moms, Pamela Stone shares a comment from one mother, who uses her car as a vehicle for parenting, as well as driving:

> "They tell you it when you're driving them to piano lessons,
> and from the back of the car comes this little voice, 'Mom,
> what do you think about this?' In some ways I think it's easier
> for them to talk to the back of your head." Meg continued that
> these back-of-the-head conversations provided unparalleled
> opportunities for "a lot of moral guidance and developmental
> guidance that I'm doing for my children on the fly."[36]

Perhaps there is some solace that modern mothers are attempting to parent behind the wheel, since the average American adult today spends twice as much time driving than the average American parent spends interacting with his or her children[37]; however, since such parenting styles contribute to our culpable distinction as the world's number one consumer of oil, it seems a dubious method to parlay moral education. Nonetheless, the spread of suburban communities following World War II makes it difficult to imagine raising a family without logging thousands of miles in an automobile.

The socially isolating effect of suburban development may not be simply an unfortunate afterthought. The idea of the suburb was actively promoted by corporations before the war. Factories were perpetually facing labor unrest, and the corporations believed they would face fewer strikes if workers no longer lived in close quarters in the cities.[38] Thus, corporations encouraged home ownership in the suburbs as a way of "fostering a stable and conservative political habit," which was confirmed at Herbert Hoover's 1931 National Conference on Home Building and Ownership, intended to support home ownership for men "of sound character and industrious habits."[39] For those men who had shed their ancestral skills for home stewardship, who had learned to be well-behaved factory employees, who had subsequently raised their families away from relatives, the prize that now awaited them was a single-family dwelling, isolated from their factory cohorts and far from the communities they had built up in their city neighborhoods.

With the aid of a car, each worker would drive to the workplace; with the aid of a second car, each wife could shuttle her children to school and other activities, and then outfit each of these homes with food, clothing, furniture, dishes, silverware, and adornments. The housewife's job title might as well have been changed to *chauffeur*. Perhaps the moniker would have stuck, had there not been further opportunities to exploit her role as a homemaker.

FROM HOME ECONOMICS TO CONSUMER SCIENCES

When *The Feminine Mystique* was released in 1963, it launched the second wave of feminism, sending women into the workforce in droves. However, women had been in the workplace long before that, though not in the same numbers. Some held jobs to supplement their husband's income; others worked as secretaries while they were single, perhaps hoping to find a husband in a young executive; and some had heartfelt career ambitions. Among the latter women were a group of academic scientists who were cornered by male dominance in the university. On September 19, 1899, ten women and one man (Melvil Dewey, creator of the Dewey Decimal System) convened a meeting in Lake Placid, New York, where they defined a new discipline that would become, for many years, the only field in academia where a female scientist might become a full professor, department chair, or dean — home economics.[40]

The pioneering home economists believed they were finally making room for women in the American university system, but in truth, they were actually pigeon-holing them. Home economics would become the only academic discipline where women could find work as scholars. Another even larger glitch in the system, argues historian Glenna Matthews, was the subsequent need for home economists to shroud themselves in robes of authority, thus separating the knowledge *they*, as *experts*, could offer, from that conventional wisdom held by the lowly housewife. To achieve this, the housewife, a fixture in American culture, was now demoted to the level of lowly amateur, compared to the professional, salaried, "expert" home economists. However noble their intentions, "Those who attended the Lake Placid conference nonetheless set a process in motion by which the devaluation of the female craft tradition . . .was greatly accelerated," writes Matthews. "This was because, in order to establish their own profession as worthy, they perforce needed to denigrate the quality of housewifely competence."[41] In order for the home economist to rise up, the housewife needed to fall down in the eyes of the American public.

Matthews writes that, for the most part, the field of home economics was misconceived; it was simply not possible to "help" housewives by "systematically disparaging [their] life experiences and judgement."[42] Nevertheless, the discipline did have some positive effects. The average life expectancy of a woman went from forty-five in 1900 to seventy-eight in 1985, an achievement for which the sanitation experts deserve a considerable amount of credit.[43] The experts also played an important role in World War I, when households were asked to alter their diets to enable food distribution to the soldiers. Through the U.S. Department of Agriculture, home economists published a series of popular pamphlets to help housewives make the necessary amendments to their family's diets, such as "Do you know corn meal?," "Save Sugar," or "A whole Dinner in One Dish." Despite good intentions, their efforts also contributed to the growing culture of consumption, as well as the growing disdain for housewives as an empty-headed lot. One of the most notable figures for contributing to both of these downfalls was writer and home-economist-turned-marketing-expert Christine Frederick.

Frederick's career started in the pages of *Ladies Home Journal*, when she began applying the principles of scientific management to housekeeping for the benefit of American housewives. She was a great believer in the power of advertising as a way to educate women about the technological breakthroughs in modern housekeeping, and this belief ultimately led her into the industry. In 1929 she wrote a book called *Selling Mrs. Consumer*, wherein she abandoned the idea of communicating with housewives about new housekeeping, and instead communicated directly with advertisers about how best to market to women. "'Consumptionism' is the name given to the new doctrine; and it is admitted today to be the greatest idea that America has to give to the world," wrote Frederick, "the idea that workmen and the masses be looked upon not simply as workers or producers, but as consumers. Pay them more, sell them more, prosper more is the equation."[44]

In order for "consumptionism" to be successfully launched in American culture, Frederick argued that the marketers must get through the female gatekeepers: "Every article of family use, even those beginning with exclusively male interest, like automobiles and radio, have slowly come into a woman's purchasing fold. . . . Since but a mere small fraction of income goes for family purposes, it is of course inevitable that woman should dominate family expenditure."[45]

What marketers needed to understand, however, was that
Mrs. Average Consumer was, according to Mrs. Frederick, rather
dim-witted:

> Mrs. Average Consumer has a vocabulary of only about 1,200
> words, but adding that though her stock of words may be
> small, she has rapid turnover! . . . Mrs. Average Consumer's
> education consists approximately of a sixth grade school edu-
> cation. 95 or 96% of Mrs. Consumers know only what the
> grade schools taught them, and many have forgotten much
> of that! Mrs. Average Consumer does not know more, intel-
> lectually, than the present 14 year old adolescent, if as much.
> She would not know how to define the word "philanthropy"
> or "courage," or describe the difference between "poverty" and
> "misery" (although she may be feeling it) or between "charac-
> ter" and "reputation" or "laziness" and "idleness," or between
> the words "revolution" and "evolution." She has a "memory
> span" for only seven digits.[46]

Her low estimation of the American housewife, combined with
her "expertise" on how to appeal to her, created a noteworthy career
for Christine Frederick, but cemented the American housewife as
unintelligent and easily manipulated, regardless of her stage in life:

> There are undoubtedly four distinct age periods for women
> consumers, and I classify these as follows:
>
> 16–22: Narcissistic and Self-Gratification Period: In this
> period general family goods is more or less uninteresting. . . .
> Personal adornment, pleasure, vanity, excitement, style — these
> are the predominating appeals.
>
> 22–28: Romantic Home Building Period: This covers the
> period when young couples are thinking about or actually set-
> ting up new homes, and is a most important consumer period,

for it marks the creation of the new generation of homes, often with distinctly individual ideas of change from the old generation. The new and radical are the most powerful appeals in this period.

28–38: Alert Home-making, Cooking and Housekeeping Period: This represents the apex of the modern consumer attitude; the period when women are most approachable and suggestible, alert and open-minded. They are still ratable, in America as young women, and they are still energetic, youthfully and fashionably dressed. Furthermore the appeals of logic, economy, health, sanitation, hygiene, labor saving and efficiency have their maximum opportunity in this period, while fashion, personal appearance, pleasure and up-to-dateness are also still appeals of great power.

38 onward: Parenthood and Relaxing Period: In this period luxury attains a higher place in consumption because of the gradual accumulations of wealth and earning power, and appeals to luxury and comfort, travel, new housebuilding, health, etc., bear fruit. In sheer volume, this is the maximum period of consumption, but conservatism, habit and preference begin to rule out consumption of certain goods on which younger women will take a chance.[47]

Matthews argues that Christine Frederick's transmogrification from pioneering home economist to advertising woman is evidence of just how easy it was for corporate America to "buy" home economists as their spokeswomen. While the home economists were not necessarily greedy or weak-willed, the compulsion of the era to perpetually "modernize" made it difficult to draw the line between a legitimate transfer of new knowledge and the advancement of marketing interests. Regardless of intents, there was a definite synergy between the field of home economics and corporate America, and the advancement of both depended upon further reducing the role of the housewife, undoing the craft traditions that had informed her work for centuries, and convincing her that the "experts" knew better. So came forward writings that suggested that: "women, isolated in the home, were isolated, too, from human progress"[48]; "Even the intelligent housekeeper still talks about 'luck with her sponge cake!' Luck! There is no such word in science, and to make a sponge cake is a scientific process!"[49]; "Happily the days are passing when the feeling prevails that 'anyone can keep house.' We have been a long time in learning that housekeeping is a profession for which intelligent preparation is demanded."[50] Thus reduced to a clueless ninny, the American housewife and her family fell victim to the most dangerous of team efforts between home economists and corporate America — the destruction of the American palate and the rise of the industrialized food system.

A TASTELESS FOOD CULTURE

From the proceedings of the Lake Placid conference in 1899, one of the most salient themes to emerge was the need to overrule the palate of American housewives and their families. What the family thought tasted good should not take precedence over what the pioneering home economists felt to be good nutrition. "A favorite device," writes Matthews, "was to imply that there was something suspiciously sensual — and not at all scientific — about a too-enthusiastic enjoyment of food."[51] "The 'breaking of bread,'" wrote one home economist, "is a universal sacrament and it is given to men primarily for the strengthening of their bodies, not for the gratification of their palates."[52] Another home economist suggested that selecting food because of flavor would lead people away from the "higher life," and another suggested that the less memorable our food was, the better: "It is a great waste of time to spend several hours preparing an elaborate dish which will be eaten in fifteen minutes, and after that time will not make the partaker any happier. The test of good food is to have no reminder of it after eating."[53] Home economist-turned-marketing-expert Christine Frederick discussed this supposed fortunate transition when she wrote *Selling Mrs. Consumer*:

I have traced dramatically the caveman dragging the dead buck to the cave, where he turned over its preparation to the cavewoman. And she, bending low, with constant basting and turning and watching of the fire, gave it undivided attention for hours. This is cooking. In contrast, I have called attention to the young farm girl of today in a western state who raised a prize pig as part of our splendid agricultural extension work. This girl gave her "Buster" just precisely so much cornmeal to eat, just so much buttermilk, just so much shorts; carefully measured amounts and kinds of foods at proper intervals — foods that were selected for definite nutritive value. Her prize pig received "rations," or a "balanced meal," and became a prize pig because he was fed, and not merely cooked for! "Feeding," and not "cooking" has long been the slogan of the stock raiser desirous of producing a prize pig or any other animal. But it is only very recently that the housewife has learned to feed her family, and stop just cooking for it. Feeding implies a knowledge of nutritive values, while cooking implies nothing more than an appeal to taste.[54]

And thus, with the birth of a new discipline for teaching Americans how to manage their households, came the dangerous lesson that they should not trust their own taste buds. Once our sense of taste had been dismissed as unscientific, we were easy targets for an industrialized food system intent on destroying our local food culture and replacing it with factory-farmed livestock, produce, and highly processed food products. Culinary historians John and Karen Hess equate the rise of America's industrialized food system with the "rape of the palate," and argue that, since modern Americans are now "weaned on junk foods and soda pop," our sense of taste has been numbed.[55] With a lost sense of taste, we are no longer aware of what we are eating. The average American ingests approximately fourteen pounds of chemicals per year in the form of food additives (such as colorings, artificial flavorings, preservatives and emulsifiers), pesticides, herbicides, antibiotics, hormones and heavy metals.[56] Write the Hesses:

> . . . now they 'whiten' their instant coffee with a synthetic
> powder or a superpasteurized fluid that needs no refrigeration,
> and they apply an aerosol chemical to their desserts in place of
> whipped cream. As for cheeses, there is really only one, though
> it comes in as many flavors as Jell-O. It is a compound of milk
> solids and lots of water and chemicals, synthetically flavored,
> and it is sold, often pre-sliced, in airless packages.[57]

The industrial food system's intensive use of inexpensive petroleum to produce food in the cheapest way possible has resulted in bizarre transportation patterns. Seventy-five percent of the apples sold in New York City are brought in from the West Coast or overseas, despite the fact that upstate New York produces ten times as many apples as the city residents will consume.[58] In order to ship apples (and countless other fruit and vegetables) long distances, industrial growers cultivated varieties that would transport better and sacrificed the flavor inherent in the older, locally-marketed varieties. When, in the 1970s, the public was on the verge of abandoning the now lousy-tasting apples, rather than returning to the older and more flavorful varieties, the apple industry partnered with Kraft foods to promote the Waldorf salad, a mixture of Delicious apples and Miracle Whip.[59] Owing to this industrialized global food production system, over the last 100 years, 75 percent of plant genetic diversity has been lost and 30 percent of livestock breeds are at risk of extinction.[60] Seventy-five percent of the world's food comes from twelve plants and only five animal species,[61] making our global food supply highly vulnerable to disease and famine. In the process of losing our sense of taste and myriad food varieties, we've allowed the extractive economy to take virtually complete control of our food supply. Where homemakers once grew and processed a considerable amount of their food in their own backyards, a few powerful multinational corporations have now stepped in. Six companies control 98 percent of the world's seed sales,[62] four companies slaughter 81 percent of American beef,[63] and four companies control 70 percent of American milk sales.[64]

With our palates destroyed and our homemakers now divorced from the food production process, Americans know nothing about their food. Three generations of us have managed to walk this earth without understanding the fundamentals of food production — when to plant seeds, when certain foods are locally in season, how to put up garden produce, what cows, pigs, sheep and chickens eat, how they are slaughtered and processed, or the labor that food production entails. When we are unaware of these things, we are also blithely unaware of the industrialized food system's destruction of our land and resources, of its abuses of human labor, of its propensity to poison our land, water and bodies with toxic chemicals, of its rapid consumption of our dwindling petroleum resources.

We are not simply unaware of how our food is produced. We have such little understanding about it, that we are willing accomplices in horrendous, environmentally destructive food waste. According to Timothy Jones, a University of Arizona anthropologist, 40 percent of the food grown in the United States is lost or thrown away.[65] Upon studying household waste streams, Jones discovered that 14 percent of our trash was perfectly good food, unspoiled and in its original packaging. Since very few people have enough time to keep their own gardens and/or the inclination to compost, all but 2 percent of this wasted food ends up in landfills, where it produces methane, a major source of greenhouse gases.[66] Our inability to produce and process our own food also results in Americans spending one of every eleven food dollars on packaging.[67]

Interestingly, once homemakers were persuaded that their palates were not to be trusted and they should offer their faith to the gods of industrialized food production instead, we got fat. One of the most pervasive ingredients in processed foods is high-fructose corn syrup. In 1967, U.S. per capita production of HFCS was 0.03 pounds per year. By 2006, that number had increased to 58.2 pounds per year.[68] Now, 66 percent of adult Americans are currently overweight or obese.[69] Americans gained an average of ten pounds just during the 1990s, enough to boost airline fuel costs by $275 million per year.[70] Worse still, our children have fallen victim to our reliance upon industrialized food. They are included in our fat statistics, and today's children are now the first generation expected to have a shorter life expectancy than their parents. Unfamiliar with the taste of a truly home-cooked meal, these kids are the direct targets of $10 billion per year in advertising from food companies.[71] With homemakers' surrender of their taste buds also came the surrender of family meals. Only 28 percent of American families dine together every day,[72] despite studies showing how family meals predicted healthy adjustment and school performance for children.[73] How strange and sad — that so many parents invest small fortunes in tutors and extra-curricular activities in order to enrich their children's education, when what most kids really need is time around the kitchen table with parents and a home-cooked meal.

Since colonial times, American women have come to enjoy justly deserved freedoms and rights that their ancestors never experienced. Certain technologies have spared drudgery, and improvements in sanitation practices improved our overall health. At the same time, however, the role of the home has moved from being the central form of economic production and survival, to a separate sphere that is considered ancillary to our culture. Men and women, both vital to the original household economy, have since forgotten the craft traditions tied to keeping a home. Thus, by the time men were fully ensconced in the workforce and the children were gone to school, the women were left, isolated, at home. They were still charged with procuring food and necessities to ensure the comfort and survival of their families, but now they did it as chauffeurs and shoppers. A job that once connected them to the seasons, to their communities, to their creativity and ingenuity is now reduced to the role of consumer. It was no small wonder that Betty Friedan found so many women suffering from "housewife's syndrome" during the 1960s, or that many conventional homemakers, solely consumers and babysitters, continue to suffer that malaise today.

We have lost the innate knowledge and traditional crafts essential to countless functions for our daily survival, with the end result being a disconnection from our communities and our natural world. So complete is this detachment that we are unaware of the ecological and social damage created by mass production for our daily needs. Screened from the production process, we buy chicken breasts without considering the workers in poultry factories who must breathe toxic fumes, or the loss of topsoil from irresponsible grain production. We purchase our detergents and cleaners without considering the ingredients that might be poisoning our families and our water supply. We buy inexpensive clothing, never considering who must produce the fiber, weave the cloth and sew the garments for paltry wages, or what country must have its rivers polluted with dyes. No matter where we live, we expect fresh tomatoes in December and iceberg lettuce in January, regardless of the fact that it took more calories to grow and ship them than they deliver when we eat them.

This is not to say that every homemaker must start weaving cloth and hand-washing their family's clothes; with few exceptions, most of us will always rely on the broader industrial system for something. But for each daily need that we re-learn to provide within our homes and communities, we strengthen our independence from an extractive and parasitic economy. As we realize the impact of each choice we make, we discover ways to simplify our demands and rebuild our domestic culture.

When we regain connection with all that sustains us, we regain creative spirit. We rediscover the joy that comes with using our hands and our minds in union to nourish, nurture and delight in our families; we tap the source of true creative satisfaction, the ecstasy that accompanies a home that lives in harmony with the earth's systems, and the certitude of a life guided by principles of social justice and nonexploitation.

CHAPTER FOUR

HOME WRECKERS

> "While many Americans are
> reluctant to criticize our way of life,
> it is clear that Happy Meals
> are not quite doing the trick."
>
> — Psychologist Bruce Levine,
> *Surviving America's Depression Epidemic*[1]

Since the industrial revolution, our culture has inculcated into our men that the smartest and noblest among them will behave in school, study their lessons diligently, demonstrate a strong work ethic, and become an ideal employee someday, earning a decent salary to provide for their families. Since the mid-1960s, seeking equality and professional opportunities for self-fulfillment, women have followed the same prescribed path. So deeply embedded is this ethos that it is difficult to imagine a life in which one eschews the quest for validation of our self worth from teachers, principals and employers, and instead seeks prosperity in a satisfying and creative home life.

No doubt, it appears the life of diligent employment pays off in the United States, as most Americans seem able to spend lots of money on mass-produced consumer goods. Between 2000 and 2007, the amount of furniture we purchased, measured in pounds, more than doubled.[2] Between 1991 and 2007 the amount of clothing Americans purchased doubled.[3] As the world's number one consumer of oil, we have a car for every 1.3 people[4]; and our affluence generates four and a half pounds of trash per day, per person.[5] From the looks of things, it would seem that Americans have been enjoying a great big happy-go-lucky spending spree, harvesting the rewards of their hard work and dedication, particularly since, in the last fifty years, our gross domestic product (GDP) has tripled.

But there is abundant evidence to the contrary. Despite our enormous GDP, psychologists Ed Diener and Martin Seligman have shown that, since World War I, there has been a dramatic split between income and life satisfaction.[6] Economic data, particularly the GDP, has long had a starring role in our national political agenda. That is because we have traditionally assumed that there is a positive relationship between happiness and purchasing power: having more money will increase our well-being. To the contrary, Diener and Seligman have found that, despite our economic boom, there was no rise in Americans' life satisfaction. In fact, they discovered that beyond a moderate level of income (about $10,000 per person per year), there was virtually no correlation between increased income and well-being. Furthermore, rather than becoming happier, over recent decades Americans have become more miserable, with higher rates of distrust, depression, and anxiety. In 1998, while president of the American Psychological Association, Martin Seligman addressed the National Press Club about America's depression epidemic:

> We discovered two astonishing things about the rate of depression across the century. The first was there is now between ten and twenty times as much of it as there was fifty years ago. And the second is that it has become a young person's problem. When I first started working in depression thirty years ago . . . the average age of which the first onset of depression occurred was 29 . . . essentially middle-aged housewives' disorder. Now the average age is between fourteen and fifteen.[7]

In 2000 it was estimated that annually, 750,000 Americans attempted suicide, more than 2,000 people per day. In 1999 suicide was the eighth leading cause of death in our country, and the third leading cause of death among teenagers.[8] Psychologist Bruce Levine reports that today, it is estimated that 20–25 percent of Americans use psychiatric drugs and 10–15 percent abuse alcohol and illegal psychotropic drugs. Seven to twelve percent engage in compulsive gambling and, he adds, "Millions more compulsively view television, video games, and pornography; play the stock market; overeat; shop for things they don't need, and flee their helplessness and hopelessness in countless other ways. Increasingly the U.S. economy is based on diversions and anesthetizations."[9] Evidence of this economic fact can be seen in the $12 billion self-storage industry (larger than the U.S. music industry),[10] where we house our unused stuff, or the fact that new homes today have three times the closet space of a typical 1950s home.[11] Richard Layard, a British economist who has studied happiness, says that mental illness in the United States accounts for a quarter of the total of all diseases in entirety.[12]

Physical illnesses and ailments also plague Americans. Dr. Stephen Bezruchka, physician and professor at the University of Washington School of Public Health, upon examining our national health indicators such as infant mortality and life expectancy, concluded, "In the early 1950s, the U.S. was one of the healthiest countries in the world, but by 1960, it had sunk to the 13th healthiest. . . . Since then we have continued to fall, so that we are now 25th, behind almost all other rich countries and a few poor ones, as well."[13]

In 2005, editors of *The Economist* magazine proposed an alternative gauge to the Gross National Product for evaluating our nation's economic health, one which accounted for indicators such as divorce rates, community life, well-being and political freedom. It found that the United States ranked thirteenth, behind even Spain, where the citizens earned only 60 percent as much money.[14] Psychologist Michael Yapko observes that when other societies achieve America's standard of living, their rates of depression increase.[15] He found that in those societies where depression is less prevalent, there is less emphasis on technology and consumerism and greater emphasis on family and community. Richard Layard reports that outside our current cultural practices — in most other countries and at most times in history — as people have become wealthier, they have opted to work less, forfeit their potential surplus income and, instead, "spend" it on a fuller private life. This is consistent with scores of studies indicating that material wealth does not create happiness. "We keep looking outside ourselves for satisfactions that can only come from within," explains psychologist Richard Ryan. But in humans, true happiness comes from achieving intrinsic goals, like self-satisfaction or giving and receiving love, as opposed to extrinsic goals, such as monetary wealth, fame and status. "We've documented that unhappiness and insecurity often initiate the quest for wealth," says Ryan.[16] There seems to be a perpetual loop where unhappiness and insecurity feed the quest for wealth, which, because it distracts us from achieving intrinsic goals, furthers our unhappiness and insecurity.

Apparently, dedicating our lives to garnering increasing material wealth from the marketplace has not brought the enduring rewards we expected. As a nation we suffer from a depression epidemic that affects even our children; the average American child in the 1980s reported greater anxiety than the average child receiving psychiatric treatment in the 1950s.[17] Our physical health as a nation is poor; the American Heart Association estimates that 80,000,000 people in the United States have one or more forms of cardiovascular disease, and the Centers for Disease Control calculate that clinical obesity more than doubled from 1974–2004 to a rate of 32.9 percent in adults, and increased from 5 percent to 16.7 percent in children. For every two marriages in this country, there is a divorce before eight years.

Whether or not these damning statistics can be attributed to the work-a-day world or American affluence, the perceived risks of reducing the family income seem less threatening when we consider that our psychic health, nutrition, and relationship stability could all improve when we redirect our energy toward our homes and the people with whom we share them. The conventional lives many of us lead right now are, in the words of Thoreau, "lives of quiet desperation."[18] Many families and personal lives are falling part, owing to three major home wreckers — the compulsion to overwork, the reckless pursuit of affluence, and the credo of individualism.

THE COMPULSION TO OVERWORK

In 1884, writer, architect, artist and socialist William Morris presented a lecture in Leicester, England, where he proclaimed:

> . . .the waste of making useless things grieves the workman
> doubly. As part of the public he is forced into buying them,
> and . . . as one of the producers he is forced into making them.
> . . . he is compelled to labour joylessly at making the poison
> which the truck system compels him to buy. . . . I beg you to
> think of the enormous mass of men who are occupied with
> this miserable trumpery, from the engineers who have had
> to make the machines for making them, down to the hapless
> clerks who sit day-long year after year in the horrible dens
> wherein the wholesale exchange of them is transacted, and the
> shopmen, who not daring to call their souls their own, retail
> them amidst numberless insults which they must not resent, to
> the idle public which doesn't want them but buys them to be
> bored by them and sick to death of them.[19]

Indeed, the woes of work have plagued Western society since the industrial revolution imposed the time clock upon us. Despite labor regulations, the number of hours we toil today is more than the medieval peasants endured during the feudal period.[20] From 1973 to 2000, the average American worker added 199 extra hours onto their annual work schedule, the equivalent of nearly five extra workweeks per year.[21] According to sociologist Juliet Schor, the famously squeezed middle class shouldered an even greater labor burden between 1979 and 2000, and increased their work hours by 660 per year — a total of nearly twelve weeks. Americans now work more hours than any other industrialized country, including famously industrious Japan.

These hours have done nothing to further our productive efficiency as a nation. John DeGraaf writes that in 1970, Western Europeans were producing 65 percent as much as Americans per hour, but by 2000 their productivity was up to 95 percent. Unlike us, however, Europeans dropped their number of working hours to about 80 percent of U.S. hours, opting for "time affluence" over monetary wealth.[22] Their consumption of goods did not increase during that time, so instead of opting to buy more stuff, they chose to safeguard more time away from the workplace. This is one of the reasons, Bill McKibben argues, why Europeans may enjoy a significantly lower divorce rate.[23]

Overwork is accepted, even *valued*, in American culture. Even with the United States at the vanguard of the technological revolution that brought us such marvels as computers, the Internet, and wireless communications, our overall work hours did not decrease as expected. Rather, work demands actually increased. Says Juliet Schor, "the labor requirements of technology have very little to do with how many jobs an economy generates or how long people work at those jobs."[24] As in the industrial revolution, the introduction of labor-saving technologies resulted in the further accumulation of wealth for the company owners, and greater labor burdens for the workers. Schor explains that with the hi-tech revolution came structural changes in the labor market that made it difficult for employees to avoid increasing work hours. There were fewer full-time union jobs available as part-time, contingent and temporary work became more commonplace. "Finding a full-time job with good security, benefits, and promotional possibilities had gotten harder and harder over time," writes Schor. "Landing one of those plums meant that long hours came with it."

Offering those same "plums" with benefits come at a high cost to employers as well, furthering the incentive to overwork existing employees for overtime pay, rather than taking on the additional costs (health insurance, payroll costs, retirement, etc.) of new employees.[25] The pressure to labor excessively is also fuelled by the downsizing trend, says Joe Robinson, author of *Work to Live*. Many Americans now engage in "defensive overworking," attempting to protect themselves from future layoffs by working through their vacations. Expedia.com commissioned a study on this phenomenon and found that Americans gave 175 million days of paid vacation back to their employers in 2002. "It was a $20 billion gift to business," writes Robinson.[26]

Mandatory off-the-clock work is also becoming a common phenomenon in the workplace. This can happen in subtle ways, such as when employees devotedly carry their Blackberries, cell phones and laptops along on vacation to tend to business matters during their time away. It can also happen through not-so-subtle, patently illegal routes, such as when supervisors require employees to punch out, then return to work. A 2004 report in *The New York Times* about the increase in off-the-clock work stated that it was happening because middle managers faced greater pressure to lower labor costs, and their bonuses could be tied to such cost-cutting measures.[27] Eileen Appelbaum, director of the Center for Women and Work at Rutgers University, explained that employees willingly comply with these illicit mandates in order to protect their jobs.

Despite all these intrusions upon our personal lives, most Americans are willing to look the other way. Our culture has placed a high value on the willingness to clock hours for an employer, and to protest is almost shameful. Jonathan Rowe has observed that "a sanctity has grown up around the assault on time. It is as though temporal exhaustion, and the self-exhaustion it involves, is a devotional act, almost a form of communion."[28] He adds that "the kind of pride a medieval monk might have felt, or been tempted to feel, at his endurance in prayer, people today feel at their capacity to multi-task, to cram more in." Rowe's analogy to devotional acts is not mere coincidence. In fact, clock time gained a foothold in Benedictine monasteries, long before factory owners seized upon the idea, he says. When St. Benedict declared a war on idleness, the monasteries revived the Roman hour and began organizing their day around it. Within a few hundred years, the spiritual aversion to idleness eventually evolved into the Americans' beloved "Protestant work ethic" where, says Rowe, "fitness for the Kingdom was seen in the ability to acquire this world's goods." Thus it seems that two great habits that contribute to the destruction of our lives and the pollution of our planet, namely overwork and over-consumption, have entered our psyche via our spiritual beliefs.

This misguided honor-bound duty to work long hours can cause impaired judgement and excessive fatigue, can result in injuries within and outside the workplace, can generate irritability at work and home, and contributes to disrupted personal, family and community life. In one study, hyper-busy American couples reported finding only twelve minutes per day to speak with each other.[29] Further, when employers compel workers to accept unwanted work, they also deny access to the unemployed and under-employed who seek it, says Barbara Brandt — "the millions of Americans in the contingent workforce who are struggling to subsist on insecure, low-paid temporary or part-time work, and the millions of people who are seeking work, but remain jobless."[30]

The dearth of time at home even reaches our companion animals. According to Camilla Fox, National Campaign Director of the Animal Protection Institute, pet sitting has become one of the fastest-growing sectors of the pet service industry, offering dog walking, feeding, full-time day care, playgroups, leash walks and snuggle time. "Mechanized gadgets for pets are also taking the place of time-stressed humans," writes Fox. "The billion-dollar pet supply industry has produced an array of toys (some costing as much as $500) that don't require the presence of humans at all."[31] These services and products are meagre substitutes for the human-animal bond. Thirty to forty percent of animals brought to veterinary clinics are obese, a condition linked to poor diet, lack of exercise and anxiety-based overeating. Twenty–forty percent of pets, mostly dogs, suffer from separation anxiety from their caretakers, which has become the number-one behavior problem in dogs.

The surprising irony is that all of this overwork has not increased our collective bottom line one whit. Americans' personal savings rates dropped into the negative numbers in 2005, and have only just climbed to slightly over 3 percent by the end of 2008, compared to the 11–14 percent savings rate of Europeans at the end of 2006[32] (notably, these figures precede the economic collapse of 2009, in which most Americans' personal savings were further diminished, if not obliterated). Recalling the words of William Morris, the 19th-century writer quoted above, our labors have generated a thriving market for all the products bought and sold to assuage the maladies caused by our time lost to the workplace. The "growth economy" has emerged in such items as prescription drugs for stress-related disease, mobile entertainment and communications, fast food, mental health services, "human-free" pet toys, and services such as child care, tutoring, and house-cleaning — all the "valueless" work typically handled by the homemakers.

"But men labor under a mistake," wrote Thoreau. "The better part of the man is soon ploughed into the soil for compost. By a seeming fate, commonly called necessity, they are employed, as it says in an old book, laying up treasures which moths and rust will corrupt and thieves break through and steal. It is a fool's life, as they will find when they get to the end of it, if not before."[33] Hopefully, we will figure this out long before the end of our lives, if not for our personal sake, then for the sake of the planet. Our overworked drive toward affluence is rapidly degrading the Earth's ecological health as well as our own. When compared to the Europeans, with their reduced working hours, Americans fall far behind in the race toward sustainability. EU countries require half the energy consumption per person as does the U.S. Measured by the "ecological footprint," an index that estimates the amount of land and water necessary to support an individual way of life, the average American consumes twenty-four acres; the average European's footprint is twelve acres.[34]

Juliet Schor explained that, while our economy was booming a few years back, it reinforced a "work-and-spend" cycle, wherein consumer norms accelerated. Seeking a salve for the stress of overwork, people engaged in "an orgy of consumer upscaling."[35] In order to afford their "retail therapy," they needed to work more. In the end, the consumption of luxury goods increased dramatically, the aspiration to possess them spread widely throughout the culture, and real consumption expenditures per person doubled.

The ecological fallout of the work-and-spend cycle reaches beyond affectations of wealth. When we toil at a job all day, we eat "on the run"; then, too tired to cook when we are finally home, we rely on convenience and packaged foods to feed the family, rather than nutritious, sustainable, locally grown foods, which require that we spend at least *some* time in the kitchen. The ideas of keeping a small garden to supply some of our food or visiting our farmers' markets seem like preposterous impositions on our time. Recycling takes too much effort. Composting seems irrelevant. So that everybody in the household gets to work or school promptly, families typically have multiple cars and send multiple drivers often in the same direction simultaneously. Considering its concentric effects, overwork has a significant correlation with increased ecological footprint. "An American working twenty to forty hours a week requires about twenty-three acres of the earth to support him," writes Bill McKibben. "Someone working more than forty hours requires nearly twenty-eight acres."[36]

Psychology professors Tim Kasser and Kirk Warren Brown also have found strong associations between ecological impact, working hours, and income. Typically, it has been assumed that supporting a life-sustaining, ecologically friendly economy is an option available only to the affluent. However, Kasser and Brown found that the reverse is true — those with greater material wealth have a greater ecological impact, and those who work fewer hours seem better able to support the ecological health of the Earth.[37] Reminding us that "correlation does not necessarily imply causation," Kasser and Brown have nevertheless found "statistically significant associations between fewer work hours, on the one hand, and both happiness and ecological well-being, on the other."[38] It seems only logical that higher consumption would lead to greater ecological impact. Contrary to our customary response of spending money to solve societal problems, this is a case in which spending *less* money is a solution. And therein lies the power of the Radical Homemaker to create these changes: the more homemakers are able to do for themselves — whether it be cooking, preserving or growing food, mending clothing or purchasing it used, fixing cars and appliances to avoid replacing them, cleaning with vinegar and water rather than toxic chemicals, or making rather than buying gifts and toys — the less time they exchange for money, the fewer natural resources they require from the planet, and the less they rely upon (and the less they are complicit in) the global extractive economy.

Quoting an anonymous author from 1821, Karl Marx re-echoed: "Wealth is liberty — liberty to seek recreation, liberty to enjoy life, liberty to improve the mind: it is disposable time and nothing more."[39] Observing a third-world village in the Philippines, Jonathan Rowe saw precisely how this form of wealth functioned when he noticed that there was not a clock to be found and he experienced "a strange absence of time." "People rise early to beat the sun," noted Rowe. "They prepare meals, wash clothes, visit, rest. All this proceeds at its own pace."[40]

From personal experience on my family's farm, I have learned that simply removing my wristwatch can return some of this temporal wealth. With the watch gone, I stop worrying about how productive I am, whether the cow was milked efficiently, or the fence moved fast enough. Without worrying how much is done in a day, there seems ample time to grow the food, enjoy a long meal with my family, read to my children, take them swimming in the farm pond, and nap with them through the heat of the day before resuming the evening chores. No, my income does not amount to much. But I have time to be with my family, time to enjoy long, drawn-out lunches, time to nap. Temporal abundance buys far more daily pleasures than a paycheck can provide.

THE RECKLESS PURSUIT OF AFFLUENCE

Affluenza is a state defined by social critics as "a painful, contagious, socially transmitted condition of overload, debt, anxiety, and waste resulting from the dogged pursuit of more."[41] The "more" that is pursued takes many different forms, including more money, more status, more cars, bigger houses, more . . . stuff. If we are still (quite mistakenly) gauging the health of our society based solely on material productivity, then Americans' affluence prior to the current economic crisis may have seemed like a good thing. From 1950 to 2002, global economic output increased by over $40 trillion.[42] Even with the rapid spread of consumerism in Asia, Americans still lead the world in consumption. In 2007, China and India accounted for $1.6 billion of the world's consumer spending, compared to America's $9.5 trillion.[43] Two-thirds of our $14.2 trillion economy has been derived from consumer spending. But buying all that stuff consumes more than our dollars, it consumes time, too; the New Road Map foundation reports that a typical American now spends six hours a week shopping and only forty minutes playing with their kids. Naturally, all this consumption takes its toll on our ecological resources. It also drains Americans' pocketbooks, leaving many with personal savings in the negative numbers, while the folks at the helm of the consumer machine just keep getting wealthier. If such behavior is devastating for our personal pocketbooks, our family life and our earth community, what drives us to live like this?

Advertising. In 1923 a promoter speaking to a group of Philadelphia businessmen laid his finger on the brilliant psychology behind sales:

> Sell them their dreams . . . Sell them what they long for and
> hoped for and almost despaired of having. Sell them hats by
> splashing sunlight across them. Sell them dreams — dreams
> of country clubs and proms and visions of what might happen
> if only. After all, people don't buy things to have things. They
> buy hope — hope of what your merchandise will do for them.
> Sell them this hope and you won't have to worry about selling
> them goods.[44]

As described earlier, such marketing efforts stripped homemakers down to the role of mere consumers by promising American housewives lives of domestic bliss, but then left them with an unfulfilled and empty existence. While homemakers may have been the original targets of the forces of a consumer culture, they are by no means the last. Once women joined the workforce, corporate America had a

wide range of marketing options to pursue. And our citizens willingly accepted the sales pitch. The passive acceptance of commercials
is practically a national pastime. The average American home now
has more televisions than people, and at least one is turned on at any
given time over eight hours per day, during which time each typical
American watches it for more than four hours.[45] The result is a zeitgeist defined almost exclusively by the corporate interests behind the
advertising and even the programming. James Twitchell, author of
Branded Nation, notes that "much of our shared knowledge . . . comes
to us through a commercial process of storytelling and branding."[46]
We see images of happiness, and they are connected to things that
can be purchased. Family together-time is linked to fast-food restaurants. Meaningful friendships are linked to soft drinks. Fun is linked
to toys. Prestige is linked to automobiles. This practice convinces us
on some level that the objects we see in front of us will bring us the
happiness and fulfilment we crave. But the data on happiness cited
above (or, perhaps more accurately, the national misery data) indicates that the reverse is true.

Even when the commercials aren't running, our mass media still
pushes us to aspire for more than we currently have. It raises our
standards for comparison. Research has shown that happiness is
often a relative phenomenon. Thus, in determining happiness, one's
perceived status in comparison to others' is often more important
than actual amount of income.[47] Television programs or ads depict-
ing lives of prosperity inflate our ideas about what everyone else has,
and therefore what we should aspire to. Even if we don't turn on the
television, these marketed images about happiness and "the good life"
find us. The Internet is plastered with advertising and promotions
disguised as stories. Media conglomerate Clear Channel operates
900 radio stations across the country, deciding what messages most
Americans are listening to in their cars or on their radios at work. A
few years ago, its former CEO Lowry Mays unabashedly remarked,
"We're not in the business of providing news and information . . .
We're simply in the business of selling our customers products."[48] The
magazine industry brags that it is 66 percent more effective than tele-

vision at selling cars, and that it is the most influential source for convincing people to buy packaged goods, to generate word-of-mouth buzz, and for driving brand favorability.[49] Wherever we turn, it seems we are being fed a commercial message to strive for more money, more status, to demonstrate our accomplishments by consuming, and ultimately to contribute to the $9.5 trillion annual spending goal.

There is a paradox in Americans' queer eagerness to rely upon this market-and-spend system, and to measure our quality of life by what we can afford — especially when most of us worry that we will not be able to meet our basic needs for health care, child care, education, housing, or retirement. In order to allay these enduring fears, we have tended to identify increased income as the only solution. But often the objective of seeking ever-growing income ultimately exacerbates this insecurity, rather than resolves it. Beyond side effects of material affluence — time poverty, more dependence on products, greater ecological impact, etc. — the contentment it can deliver is elusive, even illusory. Consider the fundamental evidence in the happiness research — as our incomes have grown, we have become no happier.

Sociologist Juliet Schor points out that just as happiness is often relative, so too our personal sense of adequacy is often comparative — that we are likely to define our self-worth in terms of how we measure up to everyone else.[50] She argues this is particularly dangerous today; we no longer worry about "keeping up with the Joneses." Instead, we now compare ourselves to those glamorous people we see on televisions, in movies, in magazines, or in the music industry. Psychologist Oliver James explains that when our societies encourage perpetually rising expectations, and those expectations exceed our ability to meet them, "we feel either aggressively resentful or depressed."[51] Or, in the words of Gore Vidal, "it is not enough to succeed. Others must fail."

Perpetually rising desire for more income and luxury consumer goods clouds our ability to accurately predict what life events will make us truly happy or unhappy. The happiness we anticipate from "good" things — the lucrative job, the promotion, fame and wealth, the new car, the ideal waist size, the perfect hair — tends to be temporal, explains Richard Layard, because we quickly habituate to the new circumstance.[52] The excitement of the new acquisition may thrill us for a brief period, but after its "newness" fades to "normalness," we return to our prior state of contentment (or discontentment) and reach for the next promise of happiness. Psychologist Bruce Levine describes this as "the faith of fundamentalist consumerism," where one believes it is possible to find an object or a life event that, once acquired or experienced, "can predictably manipulate moods without any downsides."[53] At the same time we may overestimate the unhappiness that would ensue from losing an unfulfilling job, failing to earn a promotion, or having to forego a new car. "These mispredictions demonstrate that we probably count too much on conditions to make us happy," observe Deiner and Oishi, adding, "It would be a mistake to sacrifice close relationships or interesting work in order to pursue a job that was uninteresting but lucrative."[54]

Life gets away from us when we over-invest our energies into acquiring objects and achievements that provide only temporary satisfaction. We worry about our jobs rather than enjoy our lives. We work harder and accept burdensome debts in order to afford luxuries, forgetting that we've sacrificed the leisure time to enjoy them. Peter Whybrow, professor of neuroscience and human behaviour at UCLA, explains that the endless pursuit of more has sped up the pace of life worldwide. "Everybody could work all day and all night . . . the world is still going on while the rest of us are asleep. We've essentially taken the brakes off the business cycle." The result, he says, is that "We are pushing ourselves to our physiological limit." One cannot observe this driving pace of life without noticing the predictable outcomes of obesity, Type II diabetes, sleep deprivation, anxiety and depression.[55]

Back in 1970, Swedish economist Staffan Linder warned that our excessive consumption would catch up with us.[56] The ability to acquire stuff is not always a blessing, Linder felt, and he predicted that as the volume of our consumer goods grew, increasing requirements for their care and maintenance would rob us of our time better spent on human relationships. Even if they look as though they "have it all," many people who have (literally) bought into the materialistic values of the consumer culture are suffering. Kasser and Brown found that individuals with such a life orientation reported "lower personal happiness and life satisfaction; more anxiety, depression, and physical health symptoms; poorer quality interpersonal relationships; decreased contributions to one's community; and more damaging ecological behavior."[57]

Whether or not America's adults reorient their relationship to the consumer culture, corporate advertising has vigorously seized upon our youth, pushing them to be an enduring market force. American children, "tweens" and teens, are estimated to spend or influence spending of around $670 billion per year, making them a key target for advertising. Corporations spent $15 billion marketing to children in 2004,[58] teaching them what to want, what to eat, how to behave, and encouraging them to nag their parents. One recent study revealed that convenience and fast foods and sweets comprised 83 percent of foods advertised during television programs heavily viewed by children.[59] Corporate efforts to reach our kids are now easier than ever; a recent newspaper article reports that 68 percent of children now have their own television in their bedrooms.[60] Further, an international forum for consumer organizations, recognizing the use of the Internet, cell phones, and other media, expressed concerns about "the emergence of new 'stealth,' 'guerrilla' and 'viral' marketing techniques, such as . . . text messages and computer games targeted [at] children which encourage them to consume foods of low nutritional value." The group also acknowledged "the problem of 'pester power' in which marketers urge children to pressure their parents to purchase such foods."[61] Through broadcast media, communication technologies, within school facilities and even curricula, corporate America now finds it easier than ever to train a new generation to accept the dubious notion that the pursuit of "more" will make them happy.

Aside from being the target of these marketing predations, children are also subject to the malaise associated with economic wealth. A study of affluent suburban families found that the dogged pursuit of status and material wealth beyond a $120,000-per-year family income starts adversely affecting children. While affluent suburban children seemed to fare better than most prior to their teenage years, by the time they were in high school, wealthy kids reported greater use of cigarettes, alcohol and hard drugs than any other control group — including the inner-city kids. They also showed higher rates of depression and anxiety, especially girls, who were three times more likely than average teenage girls to exhibit clinically significant depression.[62] The researchers found that isolation from adults played a major part in the problem. The demands of parents' professional careers and kids' excessive extra-curricular activities ate away family time and fed into the kids' distress. Worse, the increasing pattern of family members to retreat to their respective bedrooms with a television, computer and mobile phone, isolated from family and community, plants the seed for the final home wrecker — individualism.

THE CREDO OF INDIVIDUALISM

In 1987, British Prime Minister Margaret Thatcher declared an end of society: "There is no such thing as 'society.' There are just individuals and their families."[63] Indeed, the architecture of today would suggest the same. In 2004, the International Builders Show in Las Vegas showcased the new "ultimate family home." What used to be a family room had been broken up into a media center and a "home management center." There was a personal playroom for each of the kids (separate from their bedrooms). The boy's playroom had a 42-inch plasma screen TV, and the girl's personal playroom was accessed through a secret mirrored door in her bedroom. Under the stairs, the family dog had its own room. The builder of the model unabashedly explained the idea behind the design: "We call this the ultimate home for families who don't want anything to do with one another."[64] After decades of selling home designs featuring open floor plans where family life could revolve around kitchens and gathering areas, the new millennium finds architects who have been asked to wall things up with private Internet alcoves, his-and-her offices, and increasing numbers of extra rooms for individual diversions. William Sherman, chair of the Department of Architecture at the University of Virginia, observed that all these parceled spaces increased the isolation of family members. "People don't even gather in the same spot to watch TV anymore," he noted.[65]

Family TV time is not the only group activity that has succumbed to the individualistic rage. As mentioned earlier, today only about 28 percent of families eat together each night; of those, only 25 percent report spending more than 31 minutes sharing the weeknight meal.[66] We have come to a point where the family home is merely a shared roof, and where family members succeed in almost completely avoiding each other. An evening may pass with Dad in the den watching a movie while Mom is upstairs watching cable TV; one kid may be playing video games in his room, while the other browses the Internet. Nobody has to fight, talk about their opinions or feelings, or help each other solve life's problems. Every family member can be passively entertained while they shut out each other and their surrounding world. Some surveys have reported that as many as 75 percent of Americans admit that they don't even know their next-door neighbors. "That's a novel condition for primates," who are instinctively social creatures, observes Bill McKibben.[67]

Going against these social instincts takes a powerful toll on human society. Sociologist Robert Putnam studied the ways communities work through their collective problems and described "social capital," or citizens' interconnections and ability to trust and support each other. Strong social capital, he argues, heightens people's awareness of how their fates are linked, and it encourages people to cultivate whatever personal traits are best for society. Putnam reports evidence that people whose communities are rich in social capital are better able to cope with trauma, fight off illness, avoid depression, and lead healthier, happier lives.[68] Not surprisingly, in recent years when Americans have been suffering from a depression epidemic, there has also been a dramatic decline in social capital. Putnam attributes this to: the time and money pressure faced particularly by two-career families; the isolation brought on by suburban sprawl and the commute where each person drives to work in his or her own car; the effect of passive and solitary diversions, such as television, that focus more on entertainment than information; and finally, most importantly, "the slow, steady, and ineluctable replacement of the long civic generation by their less involved children and grandchildren." In short, our fragmented society has forgotten how to be civically engaged. Our housing, work and entertainment patterns have encouraged an individualistic society, where life is built or destroyed through the money each person brings in or fails to bring in. We've lost the skills our grandparents once had for building a quality of life by engendering solid family relationships, commitment to our neighbors, service to our communities, and engagement in open dialogue about the collective good of our society.

Our mythic notion of the "rugged individualist" has changed somewhat from its classic American ideal. As always, we equate freedom with independence, but we've come to equate independence with *financial* independence, the ability to purchase what we need or want whenever we need or want it. But there is a flaw in this equation — if our freedom is tied to the ability to buy what we need, then we are not independent at all. We are reliant on an employer or business to provide us with money, and a company to produce things and sell them to us. If we reject the isolationist view of individualism and instead embrace *interdependence*, in a sense a communal self-reliance, then our personal freedom will be more genuine.

This, in fact, is one of the keystones to the empowerment of Radical Homemakers. Sylvia Tanner, who lives in a solar-powered cabin in New England, attributes much of her ability to live a self-determinant life to her relationships with her friends and community. She discovered that money was significantly less important when relationships were well-nurtured. Malnourished relationships, she observed, even with neighbors, can be costly:

> The nuclear family . . . I don't think it's been really healthy,
> actually, that you have mom and dad and the kids . . . isolated
> in this house, this big house . . . and they're all doing every-
> thing themselves . . . and they all have their own lawnmower
> and their own washing machine and their own dryer, and it's
> like, everybody is duplicating everything . . . [On my own road

here,] you can see two, you know, "mamma-mobiles," the huge
SUV and a Subaru wagon following each other out, often,
down the road, all the way to the next city. That's 20 miles [to
drop off their kids at the same school], then 20 miles back, and
then 20 miles to pick them up, and 20 miles back. So that's 80
miles a piece [each day].

Amanda Shaw, divorced from her husband and living in a trailer-
park home, has observed how such individualistic behavior deeply
burdens the single parents who are her neighbors:

She's a single mom and she's got to go out and work to pay
the bills. She can't stay home. . . . She's driving in at 7:00,
[she's] just getting home [when the kids do], [she's] got to
shower, no time to cook . . . [she's] tired, she just wants to
get to bed and [she's] got to start all over. . . . So [this] mom
has to go out, but yet there is a mother [nearby] that . . .
gets to stay home, a neighbor lady. . . . So let's have a little
'I'll-cook-for-you-and-then-you-can-help-me-do-this.'

Sylvia underscores that there is a deeper value to cultivating
interdependence with our family and community members, beyond
just saving dollars, time and ecological resources:

We used to have the need for each other, and the doing for
each other was really valuable. And it also enabled people of
all different levels of social status and income and intellect and
training and skills to be of use to other people. So even if you
weren't the sharpest knife in the drawer, and even if you didn't
have a lot of money . . . you were still able to toss hay bales
or you were still able to pound a nail, or you were still able to
carry lumber . . . or help split firewood.

By contrast, today the balance of power favors those individuals
who, for whatever reason, are able to acquire the largest paycheck.

Within our complex society, we have found that money is easier to trade than skills, services or caring. Thus, only those who have money are able to have their needs met or to have the dignity of feeling of some worth to society. Those without money remain powerless and disenfranchised, even though they possess skills and abilities to contribute to the welfare of our communities.

Individualism and the unknitting of community have led to a breakdown in our ability to work effectively with our community's resources. Kelly Coyne and her husband Erik Knutzen are Radical Homemakers living in Los Angeles. When they first set about learning how to garden in their urban backyard, the only information they could find about growing food came from books written by authors in temperate climates, where it is common knowledge, for example, that the gardener plants seeds in the spring. It took Kelly and Erik a lot of trial and error before they learned that L.A. gardeners need to plant in October. A simple connection with a gardening neighbor, or a simple cultural understanding that it is okay to knock on a door to ask for help, might have spared Kelly and Erik years of frustration.

When local relationships are intact, and the cultural norm is to make use of them, our individualistic behavior slips away, our connections expand and our life satisfaction increases. We learn that no man is an island, and that it is asinine to aspire to such a thing. Richard Layard found that people who stayed in the communities where they were raised, who stayed in contact with their family and childhood friends, enjoyed lives that were more stable and marriages that held together.[69] In fact, "the more individualistic the society," observes Bill McKibben, "the higher the divorce rate, which may explain why in those dynamic states of the Sun Belt, people divorce twice as much as the inhabitants of old-fashioned New England."[70]

Strongly interdependent local relationships generate stronger local economies that typically make more efficient use of resources and offer greater economic return to the community members. In fact, every dollar that is spent locally has three times the economic impact of one that is given to an absentee retailer whose headquarters are located far away from the community.[71] Thus, letting go of our overly individualistic habits of not knowing our neighbors, not talking to our family members, of entertaining ourselves in isolation can open us up to far greater things. Our family lives can be healthier, our local ecology will be restored, and our local economies can begin to recover.

But thwarting the home wreckers will take more than sitting down to a meal with the family or meeting the neighbors. It means letting go of our attachments to employment, releasing ourselves from the pressure of the status race, and allowing ourselves to become reacquainted with the landscapes, both natural and social, that support us. It means spending more time thinking about what we can do, rather than what we can acquire. As Thoreau warned, "Most of the luxuries, and many of the so-called comforts of life, are not only not indispensable, but positive hindrances to the elevation of mankind."[72] Unraveling these hindrances and opening the path to a sane home life may cause a reduction in our GDP, causing corporate-minded economists to wave their arms in alarm. But if this severance makes our community lives happier, if it means we are more secure, healthier, more content, better able to meet our needs, free to care for our family and neighbors, able to help restore our planet and live lives of creative fulfillment and dignity, then why should we care about GDP? Put another way, who is "the economy" for?

Our society is riddled with myths to suggest that anyone who foregoes a conventional career track and devotes themselves to sustainable home and community life is merely squandering their life. The first half of this book has worked to debunk these ideas. Committing her life's energy to an employer has not made a truly "liberated woman." A homemaker's primary job is not to be a consumer. The choice to cultivate self-reliance, curb consumption and live well on less money drains only the extractive economy, but feeds a life-sustaining economy. The pursuit of affluence, the ennoblement of excessive work and hyper-individualism are not manifestations of the American dream, but causes of a national nightmare.

In the remainder of this book, we visit the people who have peacefully and quietly rejected these mainstream mythologies and are learning how to create lives that honor social justice, ecological sustainability, personal creativity, true freedom and the joy of family and community. Far from a life of leisure, it is work that begins with overcoming or simply coping with the hurdles that keep Americans desperately punching the time clock in order to secure health care, provide for their children's education, pay for housing and child care, afford their transportation and still save for the future. But as they work to reclaim lost skills that enable them to live joyously with little money, they also work to find fulfillment in creating a better world beyond their own doorsteps.

Part Two
HOW

MEET
THE RADICAL HOMEMAKERS

AUTHOR'S NOTE: *The second half of this book is organized thematically around the different lessons and observations I gleaned from the twenty Radical Homemaker interviews I conducted across the United States. The coming pages are filled with quotes from these interviews. In order to help keep track of the different people speaking, I've provided a short "who's who" of the homemakers below, in alphabetical order according to their last name. Each homemaker is also profiled more fully in the back of the book. The page number on which their full profile appears is given in parentheses after their name.*

Susan Colter (p. 256): Susan was raised in a well-to-do suburban community and recently graduated from a prestigious college. At the time of our meeting, she was working on a farm and living with her boyfriend and two other housemates in an apartment in Durham, New Hampshire.

Kelly Coyne (p. 257): Kelly Coyne is married to fellow Radical Homemaker Erik Knutzen. She lives in Los Angeles and is coauthor of the book *The Urban Homestead: Your guide to self-sufficient living in the heart of the city.* She and Erik blog at homegrownevolution.com.

Maryann Heslier (p. 258): Maryann is raising her two children in a rural Mid-Atlantic village, where her husband is able to bicycle to work. She spent her twenties living out of a truck, working as a rafting guide, traveling, and earning a masters degree in poetry.

Julie and David Hewitt (p. 259): After exiting corporate America when it failed to help them cope with the needs of their first child, who was born with Down syndrome, Julie and David moved to a rural coastal community in the Pacific Northwest, where they now live with their two home-schooled children.

Eve and Paul Honeywell (p. 260): Eve worked as a school teacher in the same New England town where she grew up when she met her husband, Paul. After traveling and soul-searching, Eve and Paul moved back to his family's farm, where she operates a C.S.A., he operates his own garage, and they home-school their children.

Erik Knutzen (p. 257): Erik is married to Kelly Coyne (see above). A lifelong resident of L.A., he is the coauthor of *The Urban Homestead* and blogs at Homegrownevolution.com.

Deirdre and Rick Ianelli (p. 261): Deirdre and Rick live on his family's farm in the same rural Vermont village where they both grew up. Deirdre worked as a school teacher for three years before opting to leave work and start a family. Today they produce grassfed meats, help run an on-farm B&B, and Rick also works in his family's financial planning business.

Rebecca and Steve James (p. 262): Rebecca and Steve are living in a rural town in the Northeast, where he works for the local newspaper and she runs a three-acre homestead and home-schools their three children. Prior to leaving work due to stress-related health complications during her third pregnancy, Rebecca was a teacher for children with severe behavior handicaps.

Alise and Eduards Jansons (p. 263): Alise grew up fifteen miles outside of Manhattan, and Eduards grew up in Minnesota. They met as teenagers at a Latvian song festival, and maintained their relationship through college. Eventually they followed Alise's childhood dream and moved to Alaska, where Alise managed a brain injury program and Eduards worked as a temp. Today Eduards works for the fish and wildlife service, and Alise manages their Alaskan homestead and cares for their son.

Nance Klehm (p. 264): Nance lives, writes, does some remarkable community organizing and teaches about sustainable urban living from her home in a Mexican neighborhood on the southwest side of Chicago. She raises and forages most of her food in the heart of the city and keeps the world updated on some of her efforts at spontaneousvegetation.net.

Carrie and Chad Lockwell (p. 265): When Carrie and Chad met, the two earned very little money, but he'd bought some inexpensive land with an old barn a few years prior. Uncomfortable with excessive debt, the young couple borrowed $10,000 and converted a portion of the barn into an apartment, which has since been expanded to accommodate their family. The rest of the barn is used to support their farm. Carrie works full-time on the farm, and Chad works as a mechanic. They have one son, Shawn, who is home-schooled.

Stormy McGovern (p. 266): Stormy dropped out of high school and eventually earned a G.E.D. and associates degree during the down times between hitchhiking adventures. As part of her young-adulthood survival, Stormy learned a lot about cooking, food preservation and production. Today she lives in a mobile home on a homestead owned by some friends, where she helps with the food production in exchange for rent and partial board.

Michael and Sarah Mills (p. 267): High-school sweethearts, Michael and Sarah took turns working jobs and staying home over the course of their marriage as they built a home and raised a family (as well as nearly all their own food). Today, with their children now out of school, Sarah continues to work as a teacher and Michael hunts for their meat, manages their Christmas tree business, works with Sarah to manage their produce and fruit production, and keeps the home fires burning.

David Peterson (p. 268): David and his wife Janice met in Boston, where he was a woodworker and she was completing her residency for her M.D. They eventually moved to rural Vermont, where she worked as an emergency room physician and he stayed home with their son and built their home.

Anna Reynolds (p. 269): At the age of fifty-two, Anna Reynolds found herself divorced with three children still at home. She relocated to a run-down farm in rural Pennsylvania where she finished home-schooling her children. Today she gets help running the farm from her two sons, who are taking turns attending the nearby land-grant college.

Kelly Robideau (p. 270): When Kelly's first marriage broke up prior to the birth of her daughter, she moved in with her parents so that she would have the flexibility to care for her baby and complete her masters degree. She supported her young family by publishing a newsletter on children's nutrition and through teaching periodically. Remarried, she and her husband now live in a suburb north of San Francisco. She continues to teach two days per week, while she and her husband grow and process whatever food they can.

Carol Rydell (p. 271): Carol's husband passed away unexpectedly in 2006, leaving her alone to work her intensive backyard garden in their Midwestern suburb. A dietician and community activist, Carol joined forces with another homemaker, Amanda Shaw, to continue to raise much of her own food while she moved forward with her community organizing and teaching.

Amanda Shaw (p. 271): In 2001, just after her children were grown and out of the house, Amanda Shaw's husband left her. A long-time stay-at-home mom and avid gardener, Amanda moved into a trailer park, joined forces with Carol Rydell (see above) in her suburban backyard to raise food, and embarked on an educational and emotional journey to heal. Today Amanda teaches about locally based sustainable nutrition and continues to team with Carol in both community organizing and food production.

Holly and Brian Simmons (p. 272): Holly and Brian live on a ranch that is a team venture between her parents and most of her siblings. While each nuclear family unit has its own house and ranch-based business enterprise, the extended family works together to manage the land, share food and resources, and home-school their children.

Penelope and John Sloan (p. 273): After receiving an inheritance, Penelope and John invested it into certificates of deposit and decided that the relatively stable income of $20–22,000 per year would be ample for them to live off. While still in their early thirties, they sold their small urban home, bought a fixer-upper farm in rural Vermont, and continue to live there today, growing most of their food.

Sylvia Tanner (p. 274): While Sylvia Tanner was in graduate school, her marriage broke up and she found out she was pregnant. She worked both part- and full-time jobs as her single parenting situation allowed, with the goal of achieving partial financial independence and living in rural New England. She eventually bought a derelict cabin in Maine and, with the help of friends, was able to fix it up and raise her son while living off the grid. With her son now grown and on his own, Sylvia farms the land surrounding her cabin and works sporadically as her financial needs require.

Bettina and Justin Winston (p. 276): Self-proclaimed "poor artists" in New York City, Bettina and Justin moved to be near her family in upstate New York following the birth of their first child. Bettina and Justin team up with their extended family to share vehicles, raise their two children, and put up their harvests. Meanwhile, the couple continues to run a craft business and to create artwork.

CHAPTER FIVE

HOUSEKEEPING

"There's no use trying," Alice said.
"One **can't** believe impossible things."
"I daresay you haven't had much practice,"
said the Queen. "When I was your age,
I always did it for half-an-hour a day.
Why, sometimes I've believed
as many as six impossible things
before breakfast."

— Lewis Carroll

The cover story for the March 23, 2009, issue of *Time Magazine* was titled *"10 Ideas That Are Changing the World."* The first idea advanced as a way to help Americans cope with a downturned economy was that "jobs are the new assets." The story goes on to explain that each of us is endowed with a certain amount of human capital — the education, skills and training that we've acquired over our lives. Sadly, the piece suggests that the only mechanism for extracting value from that capital is *employment*.[1] But unless that job honors the four tenets of family, community, social justice and ecological health, most Radical Homemakers would view this concept *not* as an idea for changing the world, but rather, for protecting the status quo. Because this notion only equates "human capital" with earning potential, such stories, they might say, are little more than cultural propaganda intended to keep the would-be career employees scuttling for job "opportunities" to make the rich richer.

It is easy to believe this line of thinking, however, because our economic system has so thoroughly inculcated allegiance to the employer and the paycheck. "Modern economics grew as a handmaiden to the industrial revolution," explain social psychologists Ed Diener and Martin Seligman.[2] When Adam Smith wrote *Wealth of Nations* in 1776, meeting basic human needs for food, shelter and clothing was not universally assured, thus economic prosperity was directly associated with human well-being. Eventually, conventional thinking assumed that having options to buy many different things equated to a higher quality of life, because people could make selections to maximize their well-being. "Since income correlates with the number of choices," write Diener and Seligman, "greater income is equivalent to higher well-being" in the eyes of conventional economists. But, increasingly, research shows that the direct link between personal wealth and well-being is limited. Once that threshold has been crossed, the correlation between more money and greater well-being diminishes steeply, and income or gross domestic product is no longer an accurate measure of the welfare of a society.

Still, most Americans have not realized this. They continue to believe that more money equals more happiness and more security. When researchers Susan Fournier and Michael Guiry explored the aspirations of ordinary Americans, they discovered that 35 percent of their sample aspired to wealth that placed them in the top 6 percent of income distribution. Forty-nine percent aspired to attain the next 12 percent of income, and only 15 percent were comfortable being part of the middle class.[3] These aspirations keep many of us handcuffed to the corporate-driven powers and institutions that offer the salaries we covet.

Even if we don't aspire for more than a middle-class income, many of us live in fear of what will happen if we don't have a paycheck, health insurance, or the means to send our children to a good school. Paychecks, health insurance and the "right" schools serve as institutional benchmarks for success. But if we fixate solely on them, we run the danger of overlooking the *real* questions, such as whether we are enjoying our lives, whether we are healthy, and whether our children's emotional and intellectual needs are met. Distracted from the real issues, we become entirely dependent on entities outside ourselves, our families and our communities for determining our welfare.

This "falsified culture," David Korten writes, "induces a kind of cultural trance in which we are conditioned to deny the inherent human capacity for reasonable self-direction, sharing and cooperation that is an essential foundation of democratic self-rule."[4] This conditioning has so imbued our zeitgeist, that most of us never ask the fundamental question: how do we truly define *wealth* and *poverty*?

REDEFINING WEALTH AND POVERTY

For the Radical Homemakers, wealth and poverty are determined by a different paradigm. One of the first determinants of "impoverishment" was a lack of personally "owned" time — life-hours lost to participation in soul-sucking work pursuing excessive desires and, ultimately, leading to neglected and disintegrated relationships. Other signs of impoverishment included the inability to access nourishing food, to get adequate rest, to properly nurture their relationships, or to live an ecologically responsible life. Understanding this new view of poverty, it becomes clear that the definition of wealth is far more complex than the mere accumulation of cash. In fact, in the eyes of most Radical Homemakers, money had little, if anything, to do with their perception of enduring wealth.

Few of the homemakers interviewed for this study had family incomes that exceeded 200 percent of the federal poverty level (about \$10,000–\$12,000 income per person in the household, or about \$20,000 for a single-person household).[5] Despite their modest incomes, none of the Radical Homemakers pointed to more money as a way to improve their well-being. They were walking proof of Emerson's observation: "It begins to be seen that the poor are only they who feel poor, and poverty consists in feeling poor."[6]

Yet, feeling poor happens very easily in our mainstream culture, due to our perpetual desire for more. Juliet Schor explains that Americans' over-reaching aspirations are a recipe for mass frustration, and as we fall short of them, we become increasingly dissatisfied with our lives. While Radical Homemaker Sylvia Tanner as a single mom was raising her son, she witnessed firsthand how the insatiability of neighbors quickly translated into feelings of "impoverishment":

A friend of mine . . . had a kid, and her husband worked, and they had this beautiful house. She lived a few blocks away from where we lived, [and they had] the nice swing set in the backyard and . . . they bought this . . . brand new Volvo station wagon . . . But anyways, [comparing herself to how I lived with my son], she would [say], "Oh, wow. I wish I could stay home with [my son.]" She was working full-time. And it was just so crazy because here her husband was working and making really good money, but they wanted to buy all this stuff. So I guess I just sort of traded buying all that stuff for having time with [my son].

"I think that we're losing and risking emotional connectivity in the pursuit of stuff constantly," says Rebecca James, who grew up in a series of suburban neighborhoods and now lives with her family on three acres of land in the rural Northeast. "It's a sickness, and so many of us don't even realize how much we're doing it, how ubiquitous it has become." Rebecca talked about how she sees cultural pressures encourage senseless and damaging acquisitiveness:

I think that we all grew up with this sense. I mean, [my husband and I] got married and we had a wedding registry and we were getting these ridiculous things, like grapefruit spoons. . . . We had this idea of an outfitted kitchen, or the correct sort of family room . . . that comes from this suburban model that is about other people making things for you and telling you what you need . . . I'm so tired of being told by the radio, by the television, by the mass media what we need, and then running like an idiot trying to get to it. I don't think that's sustainable, I don't think it's practical, I don't think it's a good model either for us or for our neighbors overseas, in terms of having to deal with us as these people who just consume, consume, consume. Our actual needs are so much larger emotionally and so much smaller [materially] than we have come to describe them in American society.

Bettina and Justin Winston echoed these sentiments and were thankful for the freedom they gained from shedding excessive materialism. "You don't need all the stuff that advertisements say you need, and you can have less stuff, but have a much more fulfilling life," commented Bettina. "You don't need as much money," adds Justin. "You could work less and have a lot more free time and you'd be a happier person."

Justin is keenly aware of the impoverishment that results from marriage to a job. He grew up in a Midwestern suburb, where his father worked for a large corporation. When his parents visit him and Bettina, "they think [our life] is absurd, luxurious and self-indulgent." Today the couple earns money for their family through their small craft business and their artwork. Justin is proud that they don't have to work for a corporation, nor do they log sixty hours per week in order to make ends meet. "I always quantify it in terms of quality of life," he explains. "We spend tons of time with each other and with our kids, and doing what we want to do . . ."

Rebecca James reaffirmed that time poverty resulted in increased consumption. Recalling the days when both she and her husband worked, she notes, "Although we tried to be aware of our family's footprint and make ecologically sound decisions, we consumed very actively in order to support our working lifestyle." Indeed, in the 1920s, Harvard economist Thomas Nixon Carver cautioned, "There is no reason for believing that more leisure would ever increase the desire for goods." Working from the paradigm of an extractive economy, he speculated that leisure was bad for business, lamenting:

> It is quite possible that the leisure would be spent in the cultivation of the arts and graces of life; in visiting museums, libraries and art galleries, or hikes, games and inexpensive amusements. . . . it would decrease the desire for material goods. If it should result in more gardening, more work around the home in making or repairing furniture, painting and repairing the house and other useful avocations, it would cut down on the demand for the products of our wage paying industries.[7]

Beyond accelerating consumptive habits, Rebecca James continued, when she and her husband both held jobs, it was draining the family's health. "We were also sick often, and generally stressed. After having stress-related birth complications with my youngest son, we decided we'd had enough."

Carrie Lockwell operates a small farmstead and home-schools her son while her husband, Chad, works as a mechanic. They feel that a lack of time impedes access to good wholesome food. Nutritional deprivation, to the Lockwells, is a form of poverty that leads to poor health. Having never earned more than $40,000 in a year, Carrie and Chad have come to view conventional, high-salaried jobs as a cause of food and health impoverishment. "Is making $75,000–$100,000 or more a year and being stuck in an office the best thing? Is it really the best thing for families?" she ponders. Chad tells of his brother, who earns significantly more money, but works long hours: "two out of his three kids have asthma —"

"And allergies!" chimes in Carrie. They believe that a poor diet, resulting from a lack of time to prepare good food, contributes to these health conditions.

The price of his brother's job, in Chad's eyes, is greater than the lack of time to prepare decent food. Lowering his voice he adds, "He's going through a *divorce* right now because of his job. . . . He's in a management position, but . . ." Looking away from my recorder he finishes his thought: "but it cost him his wife."

"But he's got a lot of money," admits Carrie.

As David Korten reminds us, "money is simply an accounting chit created out of nothing, without substance or intrinsic value, which has value only because we believe it does and therefore willingly accept it in exchange for things of real value."[8] At the heart of Radical Homemaking is the quest to identify those elements of life that have tangible value, that deliver genuine wealth, and then make a beeline directly for them, relatively undistracted by the intermediary of money.

Because Radical Homemaker families work together toward common goals, a primary asset the couples identified is the strength of their marriage. Referring once more to her brother-in-law, Carrie Lockwell drew a comparison:

> He works 60–70 hours a week to make more money for [his family], and [his wife] was . . . stuck home with the kids, being a single parent. . . . They never really worked together. With Chad and I, we just kind of thought, "Well, we're a team, or a partnership. This is the way it's going to be." [A marriage] shouldn't get worse, it should be better and improve. . . . Chad calls us soul-mates. . . . [We're] partners. You make a commitment and stick with it and improve on it.

Bettina Winston expressed a similar teamwork approach to her relationship:

> I can't hang out with women and bitch about my husband. . . . He's my best friend, and I really have nothing to complain about. . . . That has so much to do with why we're able to do this. He's my business partner. We're always together and he doesn't drive me crazy.

Beyond having a solid marriage, family cohesion was critically important. Many of the homemakers counted the ability to provide their children with stable, peaceful home lives as a central feature of their wealth. Reflecting on this, Maryann Heslier felt that even seemingly mundane actions of her daily home life are tied to the health and welfare of her children, her community, and the earth. "If I choose to make bread . . . then I'm choosing to . . . be a bigger part in both the health of my kids, the life of my kids, of my community. . . . I just feel like I'm part of something bigger." Deirdre Ianelli, who was pregnant with her second child when we spoke, left her job as a teacher before her first pregnancy and, with her children's developmental needs in mind, chose a home-centered life. Referring to her first child, she explains:

> I feel like I'm providing for him a good, stable home life. I
> feel that it's wonderful to be able to raise your own child and
> not have to fight with a child after they've come from another
> place that doesn't share the same morals. . . . And that's really
> important to both [my husband] and I — that he's raised by *us*.

Equally important to relationships with spouses and children are
friendships beyond the family. Sylvia Tanner didn't have a husband
when she embarked on a Radical Homemaker path with her son. She
attributes her ability to build her solar-powered home, raise her child,
maintain her small farm and live free of conventional employment to
the support she has garnered from her friends. "You have to invest in
your friends," she says. "If you don't, they're not going to be there for
you . . . It's just always been really important to me." Sylvia explains
further how her friendships substitute for financial wealth:

> Money is just an agreement by people to treat this dollar bill
> for what it stands for. . . . it has come about just because it's an
> easier, cleaner way of doing things, rather than strict barter. . . .
> [But barter] works if I needed something that you had and you
> needed something that I had, and we could come up with a
> swap — and I do that with friends.

A keystone attribute of Radical Homemakers' version of wealth
is a passionate appreciation of good, clean, nutritious food. Typically,
organic, sustainable, local cuisine is presumed to be a specialty luxury, available only to the high-earning epicureans. To the contrary,
because Radical Homemakers either pay a higher percentage of their
lesser income for the premium price, or because they invest the actual
labor to grow it for themselves (and often, their community), they
actually show a *stronger* commitment than the moneyed set to local
and organic food. For many, the decision to pursue this lifestyle was
a decision to guarantee their access to wholesome, nourishing food.
Rebecca James made just such a choice:

What I decided is, "Okay, we'll be poor and I'll do sweat
equity." We don't make money off of the chickens; I sell
[enough eggs each week] to pay for the feed. That's the way it
is, and we get free organic eggs out if it and, hurray! We probably couldn't afford organic eggs every time we went to the
store otherwise.

Michael and Sarah Mills view as part of their affluence the plump
organic blueberries that filled their yard as we spoke on a July afternoon. "The quality of food is really important," says Michael. "When
you get two gallons of blueberries a day, you feel rich!" Carrie Lockwell notes that it is not just the presence of good-quality food that
contributes to a sense of abundance, but the ability to eat it with family members. "We eat just about every meal together," she explains.
"There's nothing more important."

Radical Homemakers gauge their "wealth" by their ability to
include in their lives such incalculable values as good relationships,
good food, or self-determination. But equally powerful in their
sense of fortune is their ability to determine what they can exclude.
Before the Lockwells decided to home-school their child, Carrie ran
a housecleaning business while their son was at school and Chad
was at work. "Shawn was becoming a latchkey kid," said Carrie, and
she herself was becoming overwhelmed with her workload and felt
depressed. Seeing her distress, Chad presented the argument that
they didn't need the money. "He said. 'We can make do. We've made
do with less money. We produce most of our own food, so we eat
beef three times a week (because we grow it for ourselves), you know
what I mean?'" While most count wealth as the presence of surplus
money, the Lockwells and many of their peers count their wealth
as the ability to live well without it. Sylvia Tanner gleaned lessons
about money and the power of not needing it from a book called
Your Money or Your Life, which she read prior to pursuing her Radical Homemaking path:

I realized that when I bought something, I was paying for
it with money that I earned with my life energy, and that
you only get so much of it. . . . and so when I spent money
on things, it needed to be worth it . . . And my whole drive
[toward achieving] sustainability and towards being really
cognizant about resources and our use of resources, putting
all that together just enabled me to . . . [not] need to impress
people with the car I drive. . . . I don't need to impress people
with the clothes I wear or my furniture, or I don't need to have
granite countertops or whatever, you know? And so to me,
there are things that are just a lot more important. . . . I don't
go into debt and I don't take on more than I can afford, and
[therefore, I have] the freedom to be able to do the things that
I really care about.

   Genuine, enduring wealth is not found in a stock portfolio (as
recent events have shown) or in gold bullion. It comes from the
ability to access those things in life that keep us happy and healthy
— fresh air, rich soil, clean water, sustained friendships, healthy relationships and time to rest and play. Money *may* be a way to acquire
different pieces of this equation, but it cannot acquire *all* of it, and
it may not even be necessary to acquire *most* of it. Thus, it is important to forever ask ourselves the question, "How much do we really
need?" By no means were there enough participants in this study to
accurately quantify just *exactly* how much money an individual or
family requires to live a happy and free life, and, of course, personal
circumstances vary. As I mentioned earlier, however, most of the families had financial incomes of about $10,000—$12,000 per year per
person in the household, with slightly higher figures for some people
living in more urban areas or for those who lived alone. Interestingly, these figures are consistent with the findings of Ed Diener and
Martin Seligman, who documented that, worldwide, there seemed
to be diminishing returns for increasing wealth above $10,000 per
capita income, an amount significantly below the median household

income in the United States.[9] If this is the case, then why are so many Americans in so much financial trouble?

THE IMPOSSIBLE DREAM

In 2004, Elizabeth Warren and Amelia Warren Tyagi published a book called *The Two Income Trap* in which they argued that families with two incomes, while they were bringing in 75 percent more money than their single-income counterparts from the previous generation, were financially worse off.[10] By the time two-income families pay for a home, health insurance, the second car, child care and taxes, there is very little money left over. Presumably, two incomes should double a family's standard of living and household security. But Warren and Tyagi argue that the reverse is true: if the family is relying on both incomes to afford their way of life, then they are twice as likely to suffer if someone loses a job. If someone in the family gets sick and needs care, then the family is financially brutalized; either someone must quit a job that the family was relying on, or the family must pay an outside caregiver. Whereas a second income was once used for family "extras" such as vacation money or toy money, today it has become part of the family's living requirements. "A big part of the two-income trap is that families have basically bid up the cost of living," says Tyagi, particularly in the areas of housing and education.

Harvard Professor Elizabeth Warren, who has spent her entire career studying personal debt, says the reason that American families are in so much financial trouble is because of what she regards as fixed expenses. "Where American families are getting ruined financially is in the areas of mortgages and health insurance. The fact that they've got to have two cars, the fact that they've got to put their children in child care, their taxes — the things over which they have no control," says Warren.[11]

Millions of Americans struggle for ever-higher household incomes because they believe that they simply cannot wriggle free from certain costs, namely transportation, housing, health insurance, child care, education, and retirement savings. Sidestepping these "fixed" costs is considered to be impossible. But, like the Queen of Hearts in *Alice in Wonderland*, many Radical Homemakers believe, and live, the impossible. They embrace a reality that is wildly different from conventional thinking, dubbed here, in the spirit of the Queen of Hearts, as the six "impossible" things:

- Nobody cares what (or if) you drive.
- Housing does not have to cost more than a single moderate income can afford (and can even cost less).
- Health can be achieved without making monthly payments to an insurance company.
- Child care is not a fixed cost.
- Education can be acquired and not bought.
- Retirement is possible, regardless of income.

Nobody cares what (or if) you drive.

In 2004, the American Automobile Association conducted a study and found that the average American spends $8,410 per year to own a vehicle.[12] That was just the cash out of pocket. The true costs of vehicle ownership are even greater. When accounting for the multitude of indirect costs associated with driving — not only the cost of the car, fuel, insurance, maintenance, and fees, but also infrastructure, congestion, pollution, parking, accidents, land value, and other indirect costs — according to commutersolutions.org, the average cost of driving 10,000 miles per year is somewhere in the range of $12,000–$13,000. National annual vehicle costs include 155 billion gallons of gasoline, 40,000 fatal car crashes, 6,000 pedestrian deaths, 50 million animal deaths, 7 billion pounds of unrecycled scrap and waste, $200 billion in taxes for road construction and maintenance, and $60 billion spent to ensure Middle Eastern oil supplies.[13] Each car requires one-fifth of an acre for roads and parking spaces, which means that every five cars requires that a chunk of earth the size of a football field be permanently smothered in pavement.[14]

Americans are famous for having a "love affair with our cars," but given that our societal and settlement patterns make it almost impossible to live without a vehicle, is this really love, or mere dependency? Marketing efforts have persuaded us that these costly hunks of plastic and metal will not only fulfill all our transportation needs, but they can define our personality, set us apart from the crowd, and contribute to our happiness. But the happiness research tells us otherwise. The things that we habituate to most easily are our material possessions, particularly our cars.[15] Thus, the delights of a new car seem exciting and potentially a source of happiness at first, but once we own it, the upholstery gets coffee-stained, the dog leaves "pup-kiss" smears on the windows, and the oil needs changing. Most of us return to our prior state of happiness, no better off for the shiny new vehicle and a lot worse off financially.

I would like to brag that the Radical Homemakers in this study were able to live car-free. I, personally, have tried to fathom myriad ways to accomplish this in my rural setting, but have found it, as yet, impossible. That hasn't stopped my hoping and dreaming. Of all the homemakers I interviewed, Erik Knutzen has come closest to living car-free. Living in downtown L.A., he has sworn off driving, insisting that foot and pedal power, backed up by occasional public transit, are the only forms of transportation needed in a city. In the book he wrote with his wife, Kelly Coyne, *The Urban Homestead,* the chapter on transportation begins with an "Axe-Grinding alert." "Be warned, we're biased towards human powered transit, specifically, we're bike obsessed (at least one of us is)."[16] Kelly, Erik's wife, does not share Erik's view that an automobile is completely unnecessary in Los Angeles. Thus, even their urban homestead has an old "clunker" car in the garage that Kelly pays for and uses on the rare occasion when her feet or pedals deem the distance too far (most of the time, in these cases, she leaves Erik behind to resort to his own devices).

Even if they have not been able to swear off automobiles completely, Radical Homemakers have found ways to minimize their use and associated expense. By one estimate, when the miles driven are divided by the time spent buying and maintaining our cars, the average speed comes out to five miles an hour.[17] By this calculation Erik Knutzen's view that bike power is more efficient is certainly valid. Several other Radical Homemakers have come to similar conclusions.

Sarah Mills hates driving, and rides her bike to work as much as possible. More than thirty years earlier, when she and Michael were dating, neither one of them owned a car. They would borrow one if they needed it. Nance Klehm uses her bike to get around Chicago, even during the winter, preferring to keep her truck parked unless she needs it to work on her house or to haul something for a friend as part of a barter exchange for electrical or plumbing work. Penelope and John Sloan own a car and a truck on their Vermont homestead, but they feel that leaving home is a dreadful inconvenience, and they avoid turning them on. They carefully organize their trips so that they don't leave home more than two days per week. Last year they put a combined total of 5,830 miles on their vehicles, and that included three out-of-state trips.

Several families have discovered that they can make do with only one vehicle. Bettina and Justin Winston are firm believers that they do not need more than one car. They drive an old car, and if they run into a situation where a more reliable vehicle or a second car becomes necessary, they can borrow her parents' hybrid. When Maryann Heslier's husband Thomas accepted a teaching job at a rural college, they opted to buy a house in town so that he could bike to work and they could get by with owning just one vehicle.

We have become so accustomed to the multicar family that even those who do not go off to work every day believe that a car must be parked in the driveway "in case of emergencies." This is symptomatic of an unhealthy American ideal. We are so fiercely independent that we shudder at the idea of asking a neighbor or friend for a lift, even if we are in trouble. Even if we don't want to ask for free help, often a trip in a taxi or rental car would be cheaper than the annual costs of owning an extra vehicle. In the case of a true emergency, it is probably more prudent to call for an ambulance, a taxi service or a neighbor than to drive oneself to the hospital. Furthermore, communities grow stronger when neighbors know one another and know that they can rely on each other for help.

Chris Balish, author of *How to Live Well Without Owning a Car*, advises readers when they are thinking about buying a vehicle, new or used, to take the cash purchase price and multiply it by two, as this is what five years of ownership of that vehicle will cost. A large part of this expense is financing. If a person is in her twenties and intends to finance new vehicles every five years for the rest of her life, she can expect to shell out more than $500,000 in interest and payments over her lifetime.[18] For most Radical Homemakers, owning a car might be absolutely necessary, but they will avoid, if at all possible, incurring debt for something that will rust, rot and depreciate. Accordingly, the purchase of a new vehicle is a rare phenomenon for them. Sylvia Tanner gets around in a 1994 sedan that gets over forty miles to the gallon; Penelope Sloan has similar luck with her 1997 Honda Civic.

Rebecca James and her husband have a newer used vehicle, a fact she deeply regrets. She explains that they made their choice because they did not have the skills to do their own repair work. "You wouldn't advocate for a car like that if you were somebody who was accustomed to fixing cars yourself, or who could patch things with gum and duct tape," she ruefully remarks. Indeed, this sort of ingenious ability is a fantastically valuable skill for Radical Homemakers. Eve Honeywell's husband is able to keep their vehicles on the road at very little cost and operates a garage off their farm, fixing cars and machinery for their neighbors. Anna Reynolds' two sons are both brilliant mechanics, a skill she pointedly encouraged from the time they were very young. She is never without a set of wheels, and keeping a car on the road has never put her in the poorhouse:

> We just found another car, which is a 1989 Chevy Celebrity.
> . . . It had 50,000 miles. Somebody hit a deer with it or some-
> thing. It was $500. So if I can drive this car for a year and put
> $300 worth of repairs into it — [actually,] $300 worth of parts,
> because they [my sons] can do the repairs. How am I not bet-
> ter off than if I were paying $350 or $400 a month for a car
> payment? . . . One of the cars out there [is] a Cavalier that [the
> boys] bought for $200, and [my daughter] was driving it. . . .
> it had a leak in the gas tank. But . . . there was one on the next
> road over that was about the same. My one son looked at it for

a while, the guy wanted $200. But after a while my son was
able to trade him a bag of hamburger (from our beef) for the
car [to be used for parts]. Looked like hell. But between the
two [cars], it ran for a year.

Keeping two new cars on the road is outlandishly expensive, particularly if money must be borrowed in order to acquire them. With
a little ingenuity and a willingness to forego the prestige so often
attributed to our vehicles, Radical Homemakers have found ways to
dramatically reduce their transportation expenses. Some use their
bicycles, others avoid driving. Most make do with older cars that
they can buy outright without debt. The fortunate ones are able to
maintain their vehicles on their own. But the cleverest of them all,
in my opinion, are able to score their wheels in exchange for a bag of
homegrown burger.

Housing does not have to cost more than a single moderate income can afford (and can even cost less).

When he wrote *Walden*, Thoreau observed, "Most men appear never
to have considered what a house is, and are actually though need-
lessly, poor all their lives because they think that they must have such
a one as their neighbors have".[19] From my earliest correspondence
with the Radical Homemakers, it seemed that they intuitively understood Thoreau's admonition. I was told stories of buying run-down
fixer-uppers, of sharing housing with relatives, and of taking up resi-
dence in city ghettos. With each home visit, I anticipated austere
conditions, monastic simplicity, and an emphasis more on utility
than comfort and coziness. To the contrary, I found myself sitting
in, beyond a doubt, some of the most beautiful homes I have ever
entered. While all were far from opulent, home magazine centerfolds
could never capture the feelings of warmth, creativity, the love of
beauty and the practicality that emanated from most of the Radical
Homemakers' abodes. These were the sort of domestic spaces one

wants to spend time *in*, rather than simply admire. Only time and love could create them; they could not be bought.

As I would first enter these beautiful spaces, I often doubted the financial moderation of the people who lived in them. Surely, I thought, they must have ample funds drawn from someplace to invest in the roofs over their heads. But as I sat at their kitchen tables and we ran the tape recorder, bit by bit the stories of their homes would come out. I'd learn about a chimney made from a mosaic of discarded stone, glassed-in mudrooms made from salvaged windows, a countertop cut from a tree on the property, a chair that was a year-long wood-working project, dish sets patched together from thrift stores, family rooms erected by friends, floors laid by moms and dads working together late into the night after the kids were in bed. The results were homes that had a deep, organic, natural beauty. They were not the product of some suburban arbiter of prefabricated taste. Rather, they were magical spaces that had clearly evolved from the creativity and spirit of family members who were present in them day in and day out, year after year. The inhabitants of these spaces did not require a finished, perfect home the day they moved in. Rather, they let time, ingenuity and the flow of their lives act as their interior decorators. In so doing, they sidestepped one of the biggest traps facing American families — overreaching housing costs.

Looking through my photos of these homes, I can't help but conclude that their beauty is owed in large part to the owners' lifelong commitment to being present in them. Most Radical Homemakers were not buying their houses with the intention of "flipping" them in the real estate market or in an effort to upscale their lifestyles. These homes were lifelong investments, lifelong creative projects, and reflected a lifelong commitment to "putting down roots" in a community. Most of them had very humble beginnings.

"A friend of mine described [our home] affectionately as a 'shit-box,'" said Julie Hewitt as she served me tea at her kitchen table. "It had blue shag carpet and old aluminum single-pane windows . . ."

"It was dated," David, her husband, diplomatically interjects.

"David did a lot of the work," Julie adds. "We had this piece right here, someone built that for us, and then we just created that little area. . . . he finished [the basement] with a friend." This theme repeats itself in most of the families in the study. Alise Jansons says she and her husband Eduards "are always fixing the house":

> We just don't have the budget to put in the kind of work we
> want to, and so right now he's putting in the new bathroom
> fan. We've redone every floor in this house. We've done it
> all ourselves. The house was just a mess when we got it, and
> everything had to be redone, new painting, new floors, new
> trim . . .

Home rehab work was not limited to those people who had prior experience, nor was it limited to the husbands. Nance Klehm bought a house in a lower-income neighborhood in Chicago because the price was right. She has since grown accustomed to "ripping things up and painting and repairing," and to working out elaborate trades with the occasional plumber, electrician or carpenter whose professional services she sometimes requires. Sylvia Tanner tells about the condition of the plot of land she bought in Maine, where she eventually raised her son:

> When I first bought this place, the cabin part was just totally
> derelict. . . . It was sold as a piece of raw land because there
> was no roof; it was just boards, no foundation, that all col-
> lapsed. You'd [fall] through the kitchen floor. . . . water was
> pouring through. There was no driveway, there was no water,
> there was no power, there was no anything. So I started by
> trying to take this cabin and trying to turn it into something
> that was tight. So I hired someone, and then I hired myself on
> as his assistant to jack it up and put piers underneath it . . . and
> then I put a roof on.

When she was ready to add a living room to her one-room cabin, Sylvia hired a carpenter friend; then, in order to pay for the work, she advertised throughout New England for a building workshop, recruiting people to *pay* for the privilege of learning carpentry. Once the main construction was complete, she continued doing the rest of the work herself and continues to tinker and work on her home to this day.

House-building was how two of the men in this study found themselves to literally be filling the role of full-time home*makers*. When Michael and Sarah Mills bought eighty acres in the northern Catskills, Michael quit his job and Sarah went to work as a teacher's aide. They took their time on their building project, taking care not to incur debt as they worked. "I continued to work on this house while we lived next door," Michael explains. "Then we bought a camper and we lived in a little tiny camper here for the next building season . . . we had a two year old and a four year old [in that space]." "And a big dog!" adds Sarah, smiling. David Peterson worked as a chair maker prior to becoming a full-time homemaker, and he gradually made the transition to carpenter to realize a personal dream of building a post-and-beam saltbox home on Vermont land once owned by his ancestors.

> The idea was that it made more sense for me to work at home, building the home, than it did for me to go out and get a job. . . . So I said, "I'll build a shop the first year," because I'd never built a timber frame . . . "then I'll build a garage the second year . . . and then I'll build the house the third year." I had done some carpentry before, but I'd never built a whole house. The first year was pretty much on schedule.

As he says this, David looks around his kitchen that, years later, still has sheetrock on the walls and wood shavings in the corners. Smiling, he remarks, "In retrospect, I would've modified [my plan] a bit. . . . I also wouldn't have moved in before we were done."

Regardless of its unfinished state, the home is filled with light, warmth, comfort and joy. It seems a mystery, how a home can look nothing like those on the pages of a magazine, how it can have children's art projects spread out across the kitchen table, unwashed dishes in the sink, plywood floors, no trim, unfinished walls, and maybe even sawhorse tables, yet still feel like an embracing refuge from the world. Part of the warmth comes from the presence of human beings constantly inhabiting them, keeping the living systems within them vital. But Rebecca James put her finger on another interior decorating trick — lose the "ridiculous crap." She highlights novelty candles as a case in point:

> You know, people buy them now, and their purpose has been
> lost. Now candles are to make your house smell good. That's
> not what candles were originally for; they had a purpose. But
> now [people think] we have to have fifty candles in every room
> in a house to make it smell good. . . . And they're expensive.
> Just dumb stuff like that.

Aside from the straightforward (but apparently forgotten) strategy of buying a home that can be afforded within one's means, the Radical Homemaker often devises innovative ways to pay for it. Nance Klehm laughs as she recalls her own personal strategy for acquiring a home, which was creative and unconventional, indeed, if a bit extreme:

> I was squatting in this building, and I was like, "Oh my God.
> I can't believe I'm squatting in this building, and I'm thirty-
> three years old, I can't believe I'm doing this." But I was, and
> I did that for about six months, and I made a huge amount of
> money that year. I might have made $40,000, but all that went
> to my house [that I was planning to buy].

Once she acquired her home, Nance made sure that it worked for her economically.

So my mortgage now is $450, and everybody I know who's living in a cheap one-bedroom apartment is paying $700, so I'm paying very little. And a lot of people use it. It's where I teach all my classes. I have a community seed archive. I have bread classes in my house, and I have people come and live in my house in exchange for helping work on something.

Carrie and Chad Lockwell had a different, but equally innovative, strategy for acquiring a home and making it work for them, allowing their patience and creativity to supplant a sudden infusion of cash. Chad had acquired a barn and surrounding land years earlier when the price was very cheap. Carrie explains:

Our house is in the barn . . . It was a 100'-by-33' dairy barn. . . . There was two feet of crap on the floors that the previous owners hadn't cleaned out, and then horse apparatus and haying equipment in the upstairs. . . . When we got married, we had no place to live. Chad said "Well, we could live with my parents," and I said "there's no WAY! I'm not getting married to move in with someone else's parents." . . . so we took out a $10,000 loan and we built a little apartment [in the upstairs of the barn], 30-by-30 . . . and lived in that for a long time. Shawn came along, we built into a bay and made him a little room, and then five–six years ago, we finished the main living room, a two-story living room, and we finally had a little more space.

As Carrie's resistance to living with in-laws indicates, young couples often feel a stigma associated with drawing upon resources that might be readily available within the extended family. Compelled by our cultural provenance of adherence to "fierce independence," couples typically borrow from banks to recreate and replicate everything a new home needs; this lends only a false sense of independence, since families, now saddled with debt, are thereby doubly dependent on their jobs. But this illusory independence can make way for genuine *interdependence*, where family ties create genuine security. Making prudent and mutually beneficial use of assets within the extended family was among the most important strategies Radical Homemakers used to start their families, reduce their reliance on the extractive economy, and begin the shift to the life-sustaining economy.

To secure their housing, homemakers capitalized upon many forms of family resources. Maryann Hesliere used an inheritance to buy a home debt-free. Penelope and John Sloan received an outright gift from his parents to help them buy their first home without having to take a loan from the bank. Eve and Paul Honeywell, with his sister and brother-in-law, have made arrangements to buy the family farm from Paul's parents. Everybody lives on the family land, and Paul's parents will hold the mortgage, benefiting from the sale of the property and an interest payment that will serve as part of their retirement. Alise and Eduards Jansons borrowed money outright from Eduards' family to make the downpayment on their homestead in Alaska. The logic is simple: if assets are readily available, it is far better to retain that wealth within the family and community than to turn it over to lending institutions that profit from one's debt.

Another equally important option is evaluating whether independent home ownership is even necessary. Stormy McGovern, in her mid-twenties, lives in a mobile home on a picturesque farmstead in a coastal community in the Pacific Northwest. In exchange for rent and food from the farm, she helps the family with child care, tending the livestock, gardening and preserving the harvest. "A lot of us are going to be landless, and we're going to have to learn to cooperate together," posits Stormy:

> I mean, certainly there are little parts of me that are like,
> "Wow! It would be so amazing to have something that was my
> own," but then there's so much of me that says, "What about
> property taxes? What about eminent domain?" . . . You just got
> to think about the energy input and the energy output, and if
> there's wonderful people that want you to be there on the land,
> and you have the energy to work and they've already gone

through [the trouble of acquiring the land], they have that headache, you can just come be.

Stormy sees the world as a changing place, where people will have to work together in more cooperative arrangements in order to deal with climate change, peak oil, economic collapse and a deteriorating national infrastructure. The new world, in her eyes, is very different, albeit very hopeful:

> It's just all about energy exchange and helping people pro-
> duce food on their land, helping people preserve their harvest,
> helping people fix their bathroom or whatever it is, chop their
> wood. . . . Everybody can use a little help . . . and I just think
> there's good partnerships to be made out there all over. . . .
> I see some of my peers purchasing land, and almost all the
> young people that I know that purchased land, they really have
> that approach. Like, "Please come be part of this." [They are]
> putting it out to all their close friends and community: "Please
> come help us live, help us." Obviously, it works better when
> you're not alone.

Deirdre Ianelli would agree with her. She and her husband Rick live on his family's farm in rural and stoic Vermont, but they have a similar outlook about cooperative living. Deirdre and Rick are raising their family in one half of a duplex house that sits on the family's organic farm. She "pays" part of the rent by cleaning the other side of the duplex for guests who come to stay at the farm's bed and breakfast, and by helping at the farm's inn. Deirdre is proud that she and her husband still live in their home community and are deriving their security from their family's pooled resources. "I think it just builds stronger communities. It makes people happier," she says. Deirdre reflects on her own foray from her home town and even overseas:

> I think a lot of people, once they leave and then go back to
> visit, realize "I miss my family, I miss my home town," and

we've seen that here, because we've been here [all along]. . . .
people think there are bigger and better things out there, and
that they need to go away and prove themselves for some
reason. . . . I wanted that too, I think, but I think it's nice to be
able to accept help from family. . . . your family is always going
to be there for you, and your family can pull together.

Famously flinty New Englander Robert Frost once quipped,
"Home is the place where, when you *have* to go there, they *have* to
take you in." Such sentiment notwithstanding, it is, indeed, *possible*
for family unity to be "nice," as Deirdre says, in many ways. When
families live near each other, or even in the same house as in Eve
Honeywell's family, provided there are some basic allowances for privacy and autonomy, everyone may be better off. Beyond the comfort
of family support, there are practical benefits as well, such as shared
transportation, shared labor, shared tools, etc. Assuming the extended
family agrees on child-rearing philosophies, young families have support raising their children, and elders have support as they age.

Undoubtedly, there are truly "lone wolves" amongst us who will
likely experience deep anxiety at the following suggestion — But
human beings, for the most part, are social creatures. It is *not* unnatu-
ral for people to share roofs and resources. Indeed, there are some
good reasons in favor of it. A 1997 survey of mental illness in Great
Britain found that the highest rates of mental problems were found
among unmarried people, single parents, and people living alone.[20]
Women who have confidants or partners are less likely to suffer from
depression and are more likely to be satisfied with their lives.[21] When
men and women lack confidants or companions, they report lower
overall well-being.[22] Research has shown that loneliness increases the
risks for psychological problems, physical impairments and dissatisfaction, and that when excluded from social groups, most people are
more likely to experience negative emotions.[23]

Since we are social animals, the ideal of generational independence is a cultural myth that is reinforced by television shows and
movies forever mocking the tensions between spouses and their in-

laws, stigmatizing parent-adult child interdependence, and perpetu-ating the notion that family dysfunction is normative. The elderly person who winds up living with his or her children is regarded as a "burden." The young men, women or couples who live with the older generation are pegged as "losers." The media-driven idea that we can-not get along with or trust our family infuses our psyche, ultimately convincing us that our trust is best placed not in our relatives, but in banks, long-term-care insurance, credit card companies, and an extractive economy.

Of course, some people do come from genuinely dysfunctional families with unreliable ties or even unsafe relationships. Some have gone through a divorce or have lost a partner. Some simply find more peace living alone. As we will see later on, those people need not count a lack of formal ties as a barrier to the Radical Homemaker lifestyle. Five of the homemakers who participated in this study lived alone for varying reasons. Some relished it, others did not. All of them, how-ever, created their own families from their friends and community. In the end, most of us need to create some sort of dependable ties, whether the roof is shared or not. To regard ourselves as emotional and financial islands is simply untenable for the vast majority. To set up housekeeping for each of these islands can put excessive strain on our natural resources, can be cost-prohibitive, and a heck of a lot more work.

Health can be achieved without making monthly payments to an insurance company.

Of the twenty households participating in this study, seven had health insurance provided by an employer of one of the spouses. A few of the remaining families who could afford it had chosen to purchase private insurance or had taken out high-deductible ("catastrophic") health plans with health savings accounts. Others adopted views that may seem difficult for many Americans to accept, starting with the baseline conclusion that Bettina Winston expressed: "What I know is that if we were to pay for health insurance, then we would be poor. And that's just kind of crazy."

Several of the families qualified for government-subsidized health insurance for their children, or short-term Medicaid insurance for catastrophic medical conditions or pregnancies. Most agreed that, once enrolled in these programs, they were a wonderful service. At the bureaucratic end, however, it was another story. Dierdre Ianelli, who was pregnant for her second child and enrolled in her state's temporary Medicaid insurance program for pregnant women, talks about the emotional strain of "accepting a handout":

> I think when people walk into our home, they think, "You guys are fine." That was really hard for me, because I feel like we do have some nice things, and we do keep a clean house for the most part . . . and I think I always associated Medicaid or assistance with people who are very, very, very, very poor, not just at this level. I don't feel poor, and I . . . felt bad because I thought people might be thinking, "Oh gosh, they're taking advantage, and they're fine!" . . . People might look down on me because I have an education and because I could go to work, but I choose not to. We're in this position because I've chosen to stay home, and it was a choice. It was not something that "just happened" to us.

There is a sad double-standard at work in our culture — parents with spouses who garner high salaries and health benefits are fully entitled to stay at home to raise their children, while families that opt to earn less in order to have the same stay-at-home choice are stigmatized as "a burden on the system" if they seek income-qualified assistance for health insurance. "In my mind I say to myself, 'I am doing something good for society,' and I really truly believe that," says Deirdre, "but it's really hard for me to try to justify that to others."

Bettina Winston refuses to feel guilty about her choice to accept government-subsidized medical insurance for her children. "We do pay taxes in many different ways," she explains. "I would like to pay something [for insurance], but I don't understand why it has to be

$500 a month or nothing. That's what I find frustrating." Bettina adds, "I've never felt guilty about having that [assistance]. I have felt very *embarrassed* about being on it, for sure, because you are treated differently if you are on it at the doctor's offices." Bettina wonders if her perception of how she is treated when she takes her children to the doctor "is in my head," but she feels as though she is treated differently. "They sometimes will whisper to me, 'So, are you still on the same insurance?'"

Stormy McGovern feels very strongly that she is treated differently because of her inability to afford health insurance. In the past, Stormy had been very casual about health coverage, explaining, "I didn't have health insurance . . . I was like, 'oh, I'll be okay, we'll see what happens.'" Now, suffering with a chronic health condition she contracted while volunteering in the Hurricane Katrina recovery effort, Stormy has a different story to tell. "I'm not being treated like a citizen of the United States. I'm being treated like I am indigent, and I'm basically not receiving good health care because of that."

The problem lies in the paperwork generated by the application, qualification and approval processes for the services. It is particularly grueling for those without a conventional income stream, who are unable to produce such documentation as pay stubs from low-wage jobs that do not offer health insurance. Bettina and Justin, who were attempting to enroll in one of the government-subsidized health plans for themselves, dropped out of the process because of the stress it induced. She explains:

> We felt just absolutely harassed by our county office. I mean,
> really, it felt like harassment, and that's why we eventually,
> before we were even out of the [qualifying income] bracket, we
> quit. We pulled ourselves out, because I could not handle the
> stress of it anymore. We were like, audited, practically. I don't
> have a better word for it. I mean, never in my life have I had to
> give every scrap of my existence to somebody. Photocopies of
> every receipt, everything, everything.

Thus, while government-subsidized plans can be helpful tools for Radical Homemakers, they come at a cost to the applicants' privacy, their emotional well-being, and to the time they must invest to successfully complete the paperwork and defend the documentation they provide. Assuming the family's income is not simply a paycheck from an employer, applicants must carefully document all their sources of income, attend repeated meetings to review their eligibility, obtain personal letters from income sources that may not offer conventional pay stubs, respond to repeated inquiries for further documentation of their financial and legal status, adjust their record-keeping to reflect changes in documentation requirements, and then do it again each year they are enrolled.

Indeed, if it were affordable, it would be easier to simply send a check to a conventional insurance company every month. However, for many reasons, a number of the homemakers pointedly refuse to participate in this system. In a sense, they have become conscientious objectors to the conventional health-care industry. They might not find it hard to pay affordable health insurance premiums if they felt assured that the money was used to help those in need. It is hard paying exorbitant premiums, however, knowing that a significant portion is used to employ a staff whose job security relies upon denying claims by its policy holders. It is also hard to pay high premiums knowing that a portion of the money also goes to support a powerful lobby effort in Washington to fight comprehensive health-care reform. Further, it is ethically challenging to support the for-profit health-care system, because it handcuffs so many Americans to jobs that do not honor the four tenets of family, community, social justice and ecological health. Dr. Suzanne Schweikert, an MD practicing obstetrics and gynecology in California, sees how this system of ensnaring a labor pool creates a circle of destructive living patterns among her patients:

> . . . when I ask my patients who are obviously suffering from
> the stress of overwork why they don't cut back their hours, I
> am not surprised when their reason is "to keep my benefits."

Ironically, the one thing they believe is there to protect their
health is the same thing that hurts it in the long run. It pays
for visits to the doctor, but all we can tell our patients is that to
decrease the stress in their lives, they may need to seek another
job with shorter hours and no benefits.[24]

Some Radical Homemakers object to the current system because
they feel it does not accommodate their personal views about what
constitutes good and appropriate health care. "I've always pretty
much been skeptical of medicine, of the way modern medicine and
pharmaceuticals have been going on," says Nance Klehm, who feels
that living a life in touch with the earth has more health implications
than an insurance policy. Carol Rydell, a retired registered dietician,
feels that the health-care industry "is missing the point of what really
constitutes good health." Amanda Shaw, her friend who is also a
nutrition consultant, echoes her view:

I have issues with carrying health insurance . . . do you know
what I could do with that [money]? Do you know how much
good food that would buy, and how much alternative health
care I could do with that? So that's the thing. People pay all
this money for this "security" . . . when they could be feeding
themselves. They could have true health insurance that would
be good, quality [local, organic] foods.

"Manipulating matter is not our gig," says Holly Simmons. She
and her family are Christian Scientists and feel that most medical
interventions are violations of spirit-given health. Brian, her husband, explains their philosophies further:

We have a real strong spiritual sense and practice. Our health
is more than what you eat or [medical interventions]. It's how
you live your life. . . . We have a lot of friends that we love
dearly who are physicians, and others that rely a lot on the
medical world . . . They are very successful at living their life

the way they are, [but] we want to just avoid all the little traps
that are part of that life.

Not all the homemakers shared Holly's and Brian's exact philosophies, but several expressed reluctance to pay money into a conventional medical system that they did not trust. There is some good
data to back them up. Fifty-eight percent of family practitioners in
one study reported that the source of information for the last drug
they prescribed came from the pharmaceutical sales representative.[25]
In the 1950s the United States was one of the healthiest countries
in the world. Today, it ranks below every other industrial country,
despite the fact that we have the highest expenditures on health care.
According to the United Health Foundation, Americans now have
a healthy life expectancy of sixty-nine years, putting us on par with
Portugal and Slovenia. Our infant mortality rates are more than
double those in Japan, Sweden, Finland, Singapore, Slovenia, Italy,
Norway, Denmark, Portugal and the Czech Republic. The Common-
wealth Fund ranked the United States' health-care system last when
compared to systems in Canada, the United Kingdom, Australia,
New Zealand, and Germany.[26]

According to Families USA, 61.6 million American families
spent more than 10 percent of their pretax income on health-care
costs in 2008; more than 82 percent of those families had health
insurance.[27] High health-care costs are not simply a problem for the
uninsured; Families USA says the data now shows that more than
one in four people *with* health insurance report that they are having
trouble paying their medical bills or that they are in the process of
paying off medical debt. The for-profit health-care companies simply
are not providing the service they promise. This system doesn't work,
many Radical Homemakers feel, so they simply refuse to buy into it.
Justin Winston is among them:

> The health insurance industry is a scam. It's a rip-off. It's
> not worth it. It should cost a tenth of what it costs. So many
> people I know have taken jobs just so they can qualify for their

employer's health plan, and it's ridiculous. They've become a slave. And we're unwilling to be slaves.

Justin has a different idea about how the system should work:

> We WANT to pay for our health care, just not $500 a month. I think the big problem with our system is that all health care is lumped into one package. A better idea might be to treat it like any other insurance, such as car insurance — it doesn't pay for the tune-ups or maintenance, only for accidents. Ideally, there would be a) health care and b) health insurance. That way, we could have general practitioners seeing people regularly for a reasonable cost without all the HMO B.S. And health insurance would be for extreme situations. In theory, that's how it's supposed to work, but it doesn't.

"I think the insurance is all based on fear," says Holly Simmons. She elaborates further:

> Fear is a marketing tool. . . . We don't want to be run by fear, we're not going to let fear take over. We just believe that there is a principle of love that's guiding us all, and fear gets us off track from listening to that principle of love.

This fear-mongering has penetrated across the political spectrum. Whether the message comes from the left or the right, we are convinced that families cannot make it on a single income and that losing a job that offers health benefits will plunge us into poverty and homelessness. This is a hegemonic assumption that keeps us powerless to create momentum for change. As long as we continue to believe that money and health insurance are our only sources of security and self-reliance, then we are enslaved by those that provide them. Our bowing to this belief has led us to tolerate billions of dollars in governmental bailouts for corporate recklessness. We grudgingly shoulder the economic (and moral) burden of wars contrived to plunder the natural resources of other nations to feed corporate enterprise. We abide expenditures of all sorts to uphold corporate-commandeered power structures. Viewed through this lens, it seems a poor trade to submit to onerous employment for insurance while foregoing the hope for egalitarian health care, remaining complicit in a precarious and ecologically devastating "cheap" food system, and watching our planet and her inhabitants slowly simmer in the pot of climate change.

Money and health insurance suggest security, independence and power, but are theoretical concepts. True power is the collective ability to restore and sustain the living systems of our planet. True independence is the ability to live free from enslavement, which can only come about by creating true security, which in turn comes from honoring the necessary interdependence of family, friends, community, fertile soil and clean food, water and air — all of which play critical roles in creating a healthy life. This is the health insurance policy ascribed to by the Radical Homemakers who resist our current corporate insurance paradigm.

Several years ago Deirde Ianelli's family began seeing a naturopathic physician, who they could afford to pay without having to rely on health insurance (which would not have paid for such preventative health care anyway). "That just sparked a lot of interest about herbs and alternative ways of healing," says Deirdre. Today, her outlook toward caring for her family has evolved to include a repertoire of remedies and practices that work far outside the coverage of conventional health insurance. Deirdre now spends time reading books about nutrition, maintaining health and alternative ways of healing. She is conscientious about providing her family with a wholesome locally based diet, and like many of the homemakers, she and her husband work to grow most of the food they consume. She has also trained herself to use herbal remedies that are growing in her own backyard, free of charge, in place of visiting the drugstore:

> I don't want to give my kid something that comes off an
> apothecary shelf . . . I'd rather be able to make something,

like if he [my son] cuts himself or gets a bruise, I know that I
can use arnica, and I know I can get mullein outside here for
swelling . . . I know that I can harvest nettles and make a tea
that's anti-inflammatory, and it's really good for kids because
it's so mild.

Healing remedies were once standard knowledge for homemakers, right up until the industrial revolution. "Early in the nineteenth
century most cookbooks or advice manuals had contained lengthy
chapters devoted to the preparation of medicines and foods for the
sick," says historian Ruth Schwartz Cowan.[28] By mid-century, however, entrepreneurs saw an opportunity to make money and began
manufacturing and mass marketing the remedies, sparking the
pharmaceutical industry. "By the end of the century," says Schwartz
Cowan, "the patent drug business was so active, and so many varieties
of remedies were available . . . cookbooks had stopped giving recipes for preparing them at home." Reclaiming the lost knowledge of
health maintenance and self-healing is central to those who must live
without a health insurance plan. Many uninsured homemakers have
worked to reclaim these skills and use them in tandem with seeking care from affordable alternative health-care practitioners such as
chiropractors, naturopaths, kinesiologists or homeopaths, who they
believe are more effective, less invasive and less toxic than their conventional allopathic counterparts.

Thomas Berry observed that "no amount of medical technology
will enable us to have healthy humans on a sick planet."[29] This idea
is a driving force behind many people's decisions to pursue Radical Homemaking. The ability to provide ourselves and our loved
ones with quality, earth-sustaining, nourishing foods drives many
homemakers to garden extensively, raise grass-fed livestock or pastured poultry where space allows, and to learn ways of preparing and
preserving their harvests. For many of the homemakers, locally produced, organic and nutrient-dense foods were more reliable guaran-
tees for health than medical insurance. "The way that we eat . . . keeps
us healthier, so we're not spending a lot of money on doctor's bills

. . . or medicines," says Eve Honeywell who, along with her husband, became so passionate about good food that she began farming.

The decision for many homemakers to forego the expense of a conventional health insurance policy in favor of affording a "nourishing food policy" makes sense; between 1950 and 2000 the United States managed to achieve the distinction of having the cheapest food in the world, while at the same time it managed to have the highest health-care costs per capita.[30] The correlation between the two is too striking to dismiss. Americans are more at risk for obesity than starvation, and about 400,000 of us die each year from complications related to unhealthy diets and inactive lifestyles.[31] Radical Homemaker Amanda Shaw, who devotes much of her energy to offering nutrition consulting, feels that the symptoms of poor diet are manifested in more ways than our waistlines:

> We are a culture being dumbed down . . . We're so nutrient-
> deficient that a lot of us can't even think anymore. It's literally
> massive malnutrition, and [most Americans] are not even able
> to make conscious, well-thought-out decisions.

Carol Rydell agrees with her. She places more faith in a sound, local diet than in conventional medical treatments. "The thing is, the [conventional] doctors don't understand how important nutrition is," she laments. If they did, our society might be more aggressive about combating the massive consumption of sugar, high-fructose corn syrup, and highly processed foods. Instead, in the past twenty years, childhood obesity has doubled and adolescent obesity has tripled.[32] Aware of these problems, Radical Homemakers also believe that a critical part of a home-based health plan is not just *what* is eaten, but *how* it is eaten. Most of them are passionate cooks, and they are emphatic about the family coming together at meal times. Evidently, this can have an effect on kids' health. A study reported in the *Journal of the American Dietetic Association* reported that kids from families that regularly ate meals together had diets that were higher in calcium, iron, folate, fiber and several other vitamins.[33] A nationwide survey of adolescents found that those who took their evening meals with their parents ate more fruits, vegetables and dairy products than those who did not.[34] But regular home-cooked meals help more than just children. Now in his sixties, David Peterson is trim, robust and full of life; as he returns from feeding table scraps to his pigs, he talks about the next building projects he will do around his home. Apparently his vitality, though normal compared to prior generations, is an anomaly in his extended family:

> I look at my sisters . . . several of them work in office jobs
> . . . and I look at people . . . on the bus younger than me, and
> they're not going to last another ten years. . . . My grandfa-
> ther grew up on a farm and was active all his life, and he was
> ninety-four, I think, when he died, and that wasn't unusual.

David observes that good food alone will not guarantee good health. A sound home-based health insurance policy requires living a joyous, fulfilling and consequential life. Indeed, in their research on well-being, Ed Diener and Shigehiro Oishi have found that positive states of well-being correlated with better physical health.[35] Several Radical Homemakers intuitively discovered this and have opted to pursue lives they enjoy more, rather than work stressful jobs in order to have conventional health insurance. With more time to have fun and rest, there is less cause to be ill.

Psychologist Bruce Levine observes that the American ethos, with its misplaced reverence for work, sets the stage for people to actually require an illness in order to gain a culturally acceptable respite from the unrelenting drive for productivity. "Despite American advances in medicine and public health, Americans are often sick," says Levine. "Unless we are ill, it is not socially acceptable in our society to be non-productive or inefficient. Our culture, unlike many traditional ones, does not encourage a regular withdrawal to reevaluate our lives."[36] He points out that our consumer culture is more interested in selling products to divert people from their pain, rather than actually healing it. "The natural crafts of transforming emotional pain to energy and healing emotional wounds are not great consumer products because they are available to us without money," says Levine.

The Radical Homemaking path identifies that sound health can be had through a way of life, rather than through costly prescriptions and doctor visits. "I have different ways of insurance," says Nance Klehm, living in Chicago. "There's edible insurance, I've got that going on. And herbal insurance. But there's also community insurance, and I'm working on those things all the time. I'm trying to deepen those things." She explains:

> I've been practicing yoga for fifteen years and I meditate and I ride my bike most places. . . . that's part of my health insurance, as well as how I eat, and working [with] plant medicine, and . . . working with animals, and just, how I am in my space. . . . Every once in a while I'll take a yoga class and all these women are just completely, perfectly lycra-ed up, and they're doing their yoga, and then they jump in their SUVs and they go off on their way, and you hear about what they do for a living, and it's just counter to their spirit. . . . How do you do that? . . . Everything I do is my life, is my work, is my being, so I don't make that distinction. Work, non-work . . . I don't make that distinction between leaving this behind and doing this now; it's all kind of fluid. And I feel like that's part of my mental health, and just general health insurance.

Holly Simmons takes a similar view, focusing on living her spirituality as a path for healthy living:

> In a way, we feel like matter — our bodies — just react to our thoughts. And so, when we are healthy in our thinking, and we're working with the spiritual concepts of the universe — basic things — like life is a spiritual concept — then we are living our truth. . . . Those things that are strong, basic principles that we *can't* see . . . invisible things that we all live . . .

if you're tuned into that stuff, then our bodies and our relationships and our financial situations, everything that we *can*
touch, are like little roll-offs, and they just go on in harmony.

Agreeing with her, her husband Brian adds that, in their spiritual practice, "health is not something that there's any fear associated
with." Further, he feels that if it is not something to fear, then it is
hard to justify purchasing a product based on the fear of ill health.
Stormy McGovern, though her views are decidedly more secular,
echoes a similar sentiment:

> I definitely believe that there is an amazing cosmic force that
> you could . . . flow on and embrace. And it's hard to really put
> into words, but when you spend your life in fear and in need
> and in regret and guilt, then it doesn't work. There are block-
> ages, and the walls come down. You're unable to really just be
> an animal on this planet.

This reflects a broader benefit of finding personal health through a
self-determined, spiritually harmonious lifestyle. Using this interpersonal way to attend to bodily health, we must connect our individual
well-being to the integral health of our families and even our communities. The fears that we associate with ill health may be misun-
derstood. "Perhaps the greatest fear any of us can have is that no one
will care enough to be with us in our time of need," remarks David
Korten.[37] None of us is invincible or immortal, and at some point,
our bodies will tire and we eventually move on to another realm. As
Holly, Brian and Stormy suggest, fearing this natural progression of
our lives is fruitless. The core of our fear may not be our own mortality, but rather, loneliness. And that is easy and cheap to overcome.

Deirdre Ianelli sees her own family as her life insurance policy.
"It's a different kind of safety net," she says, one in which everyone is
assured that they will be taken care of in their time of need by those
who love them:

I think that everybody [in the extended family] . . . in the back
of their mind — feels that way, that they're safe here . . . that,
I think, is really important . . . I feel really safe knowing that
we're here, and there is somebody always going to be here to
take care of us.

Stormy, who no longer lives near her own family, creates a different social safety net, capitalizing on her skills to weld, garden, put up food and house paint as a way to garner health-care services. "I painted a woman's bedroom . . . She's a reflexologist, and so I'm going to get a few reflexology sessions." Stormy has found that, while she has had difficulty accessing conventional health care, she has been able to easily procure services in the alternative medical traditions, which she refers to as "Eastern." She finds opportunities to access care outside of medical conventions, but she adds, "you just have to take the time in the community to nourish the relationships and find out if that kind of relationship is possible."

Sylvia Tanner saw the profound importance of the social safety net as she participated in the palliation and ultimate loss of her long-time friend to breast cancer:

I was her medical proxy. . . . She was really afraid of being in
pain, and she was really afraid of losing her dignity, and she
was really thinking at some point of, like, some sort of suicide.
. . . and so she could explore those ideas with me. We'd have
these outrageous conversations on the phone. She'd be like
"Okay, I'll come up there to visit you, and we'll all go off into
the woods together, and you'll just leave me there and I'll just
be in my underwear or something" [she laughs]. [I told her] "I
think we're going to have a hard time explaining to the Maine
State Police that we didn't notice that you were in your underwear when we left you in the woods." So you know, it was
really weird to be having these conversations with this person
who was your friend, but what she was gaining from it was the
strength of knowing she had options, that she was taking back

control of something that was robbing her of control. . . . And
in the end, we kept her pain as well controlled as we could,
and friends came in from all over the place. She was a musi-
cian, and friends came in and played music and danced . . . I
remember the week before she died . . . we were all there, her
boyfriend and a whole bunch of us, and her daughter, and we
just all piled into her bed and took pictures.

A joyous, contented, love-filled life is as critical to our health as
it is to our peaceful passing. In a measurement of longevity called
"quality-adjusted life years"(QALY), which discounts time spent
in ill health, depression ranks above cancer, stroke, diabetes and
obstructive lung disease as the third-leading cause of reduced QALY
scores.[38] The key to sustained well-being is supportive, positive relationships and social belonging. "People need social bonds in committed relationships, not simply interactions with strangers," say social
psychologists Ed Deiner and Martin Seligman.[39]

I asked Sylvia if she thought her friend died happy. "Yeah, she
did," she says, smiling. While they *might* cover a few doctor bills,
health insurance, life insurance or long-term-care insurance policies don't offer joy, love and companionship as part of their benefits
package.

Given the state of our health system, the choice to forego health
insurance coverage does certainly entail an element of financial risk,
and such a decision cannot be made lightly or without family participation. For at least some of the tens of millions of uninsured
Americans, the price tag is simply out of reach; for others, the sacrifices entailed in affording it simply outweigh the prospective benefits it may (or may not) deliver. In my own family, we were faced
with exactly this choice. As our costs rose 18 to 25 percent annually, my husband and I had to forfeit either our way of life or our
health insurance. For all of the reasons above and more, we chose
to forfeit the health insurance (except for our children). That doesn't
mean we would reject it, if we were able to participate in a plan that
didn't counter our philosophical and ethical objections against the

for-profit health-care industry. Equitable access to health care is a universal need, and the lack of it can be a major stumbling block for enterprising Americans seeking to lead a more healthful, simple, ecologically and socially responsible life. But universal health coverage is not an option for Americans yet. And to surrender a fulfilling, joyous and, most likely, a healthful life in the interim seems a shameful and a perverse sacrifice.

Child care is not a fixed cost.

With annual costs ranging anywhere from $4,000 to $14,000 per year, child care for infants, toddlers and preschoolers can be a serious burden for any family. But while it may be a fixed cost for some two-income families, it needn't be an expense at all for Radical Homemakers. When David and Janice Peterson's son was born, they did the math before enrolling him in day care:

> I said to Janice, "Well, if we put him in day care, we have to
> buy a second car." I had an old beat up truck, but it was going
> downhill fast. "We have to buy a second car [and a few other
> things] . . . then that would mean I'd have to earn this much
> before taxes to have this much money left over after taxes to
> pay those bills." And we looked at it, and [realized] . . . I'm not
> going to make enough money to even break even doing that.
> So we'd be financially ahead of the game to have me
> stay home.

While investigating work and family issues, sociologist Pamela Stone reviewed research dating back to the 1940s exploring whether mothers' employment out of the home had an impact on children. "People have always looked to working mothers as the cause of problems, but it always came out a wash," Stone argues. She adds, however, "what's more important is other things, like the *quality* of child care."[40] Despite the sophisticated day-care options available to families today, Mom and Dad are still usually the best candidates for raising their young child. For young children, quality care is not necessarily the number of enrichment or developmental activities that are packed into a day; it is about the love they experience. David Korten discusses the emotional development that takes place during a child's earliest years. "The ability to accurately communicate one's emotions and to read the emotions of others through verbal and nonverbal cues — is only partially formed in humans by the time of birth," says Korten.[41] He explains that the "limbic brain" is the portion of our brain that gives mammals the unique ability to experience and interpret emotion, socially bond, nurture and cooperate. "The limbic brain of the newborn represents a potential that must be cultivated into a usable capacity through emotional exchanges with a primary caretaker," most often the mother or father, someone who will have a deep emotional connection and long-enduring relationship with the child. Says Korten, "Practice in such exchanges activates the neural connections essential to the intuitive reading of emotional states." He adds that the broader and deeper these exchanges are between the child and caregiver, the more the child's limbic brain develops. The result is greater emotional intelligence, greater capacity for empathy, bonding, nurturing and responsible moral function.

Of course, professional child care cannot be universally dismissed; used appropriately, day care has a valuable function. But there has arisen a troubling trend whereby the nurturing home is routinely supplanted by the child-care industry, on the rationale that parents are thus enabled to bring more money home. Radical Homemakers have used day care for a needed break, to periodically free themselves to engage in some form of creative or productive work, to help during periods of single parenting, or to introduce their children to others in the community. But they use it infrequently, sort of as a dessert or a snack. In most situations, it is not the main meal, the substantive nutrition on which they raise their children. No matter how qualified and loving the available professionals may be, Radical Homemakers feel that they, as parents, can offer the best care and the best opportunities for sound emotional development in their own homes. Many of them designed their vocations to accommodate this role in their children's lives. "I love being able to know that I'm raising my children myself," says Bettina Winston. "I really don't like the idea of day care. . . . I guess my take is that I brought these kids into the world, I'd like to raise them. And I really think that if your kid is at day care all day long, then that is who's raising them."

Kelly Robideau enrolled her daughter in day care for a period while she had to juggle single parenting and work. Comparing the at-home and the day-care experiences, she observed that her daughter was able to learn to be more self-directed in her home environment, where she had to learn to occupy herself without the perpetual line-up of activities that took place in the day care:

> I noticed that in day care, what she learned was to be entertained. Out of day care, she had boredom. And when she had boredom, she got creative and she thought of things to do, and went outside and climbed the tree. . . . At day care, there was always an activity, one thing after another, and so she kind of got used to being entertained. I don't think that's necessarily a good thing.

Kelly's comments underscore another important issue for many of the stay-at-home parents. Radical Homemakers were very sensitive about over-scheduling, and for many of them, stay-at-home parenting did not mean they must become chauffeurs and personal planners for their young children. They did not feel that a hyperabundance of early enrichment activities would somehow secure their children's future or benefit their family's well-being. Further, such "hyperactivity" can be costly, can infringe on the child's need to learn independently or play imaginatively, and can incur an ecological cost. Deirdre Ianelli, a former teacher who was parenting her two-year-old and expecting her second child any day, observed a lot of pressure to have kids enrolled in lots of activities in her community. "There are some moms with two-year-olds who I've met whose kids are busy *every single day* . . . and I think that's really . . . a lot for a two-year-old . . . and the ecological footprint is definitely much higher."

Some stay-at-home parents, agrees Kelly Robideau, are simply "over-involved." She cites as an example an acquaintance who felt she was a "neglectful mother" because she had only four professional photography sessions with her three-year-old son. Eve Honeywell, a former teacher, has intentionally avoided enrolling her children in enrichment activities. "I think they need this time just to be kids," she says, "to play, to use their imaginations, to run around naked outside if they want to. I think now's the time to just be kids." Radical Homemakers' unwillingness to redirect their lives for the sake of the early-enrichment craze is sometimes at the center of self-deprecating humor. Off-handedly describing themselves as "the world's worst mom" in their e-mail correspondence, their brand of humor communicates both the compulsion to participate in the frenzy and their commitment to instead provide a nurturing environment at home for their children. Eschewing "enrichment" centered around Suzuki violin lessons, pre-K soccer teams, ballet, karate and play groups, these families value the ability of kids to just "be" and to learn how to truly play. Plain and simple.

Stuart Brown, founder of the Institute for Play, feels that plain old-fashioned play is critically important and the lack of it can lead to depression.[42] Jack Wetter, a clinical psychologist in west Los Angeles, suggests that these Radical Homemakers may be tapping into something important. "Children being pushed too hard may not be able to articulate their feelings, but the signs are there," he says. "They become emotionally volatile, or complain of aches and pains. They can't sleep. They lose touch with their friends." Wetter argues that the popular diagnosis of attention deficit disorder may really be a symptom of children who "just don't know how to express their frustration. By the time they are 16, many are burned out, antisocial, and rebellious."[43] Betsy Taylor, founder and president of the Center for the New American Dream, cites renowned pediatrician and author T. Berry Brazelton in her argument for reducing the scheduling of our children, pointing out that "unstructured play," such as the type offered in the homes of many of these Radical Homemakers, "encourages independent thinking, creativity, positive social relations, and connection to nature."[44] Other researchers point to the role of free play in the development of critical cognitive skills, including "executive function," a key to controlling emotions, resisting impulses and exerting self-control and discipline.[45]

Moreover, the ability to keep families at home, together and connected has important implications for reducing the rates of mental illness, behavior problems and emotional distress in the children. The Commission on Children at Risk asserts that these complications are an epidemic and that numerous studies are linking the nationwide increase in depression, anxiety and social dysfunction among our youth to a decline in social connectedness within families and their communities.[46] Even though the expression has become cliché, it still takes a village to raise a child, not a day-care center or a nanny.

The Radical Homemakers embrace this concept. Stormy McGovern, child-free and single, enjoys her youthful freedom, but still sees herself as having a role in raising the children in her community:

> I'm so lucky that I'm still free. I don't really have things that
> tie me down; I can just go, and I love that. . . . But also, I love
> children, and I love helping raise children. I spend time with
> kids all the time. I babysit a lot. I babysit [in exchange] for
> coconut oil and honey.

One day, while walking her own daughter home from school, Kelly Robideau noticed one of her six-year-old child's classmates walking alone across a four-lane highway, outside of the crosswalk. Feeling that, as an adult in the community, she shared a responsibility in the welfare of this child, she called the boy's mother:

> I called his mother, and I said, "Is it all right if I walk him
> home?" . . . She was at work and he was going home to a teen-
> age brother, and I just felt, like they say, it takes a village to
> raise a child, but it takes more than that. I mean, there has to
> be somebody around to make sure a six-year-old isn't cross-

ing the street in a dangerous way. . . . She was a little put off; I think she felt that I was saying that she wasn't doing her job, or that she was neglectful . . . but this was a single mother with four children. . . . I just said that "you know, I want to make sure he's safe," and it actually all worked out, and I see her regularly, and it all worked out fine in the end.

The Radical Homemakers' willingness to pitch in and help other community members with their children created a mutually beneficial resource: reciprocal child care. Homemakers like Rebecca James, who have no family nearby and who couldn't afford a babysitter, networked to find other families with whom she could leave her children when she and her husband needed occasional "alone time." Eve Honeywell takes her two children to a friend's house twice each week so that she can work on her farm. Each mother then returns the favor when the other parent needs it. Maryann and Thomas Heslier, also raising their children without the aid of extended family, periodically use professional day care for relief, but they have also nurtured relationships within the surrounding agricultural community, providing their children with experiences that foster a connection to the earth while simultaneously broadening their own food production skills:

> The fact is, there are so many friends, people we've met, who have their farms, who love for kids to come over. And that's what I've done. I go over [with the kids] and learn from them [the farmers], and basically work for my produce, and this year they're going to help me set up two raised beds to do the stuff we want to be able to pick every night.

Child care can be costly, but as the Radical Homemakers have shown, there are many inexpensive or costless ways to raise children in accordance with their beliefs and values — provided, of course, that there is a vital community and social cohesion. Most American families are familiar with the irreducibly simple tactics the Radical Homemakers employed, but few find the community infrastructure

— the social capital — available to them. Creating this social infra-structure is part of the great work these homemakers are performing for our culture.

Education can be acquired and not bought.

The expenses associated with education can be among the most sig-nificant financial stumbling blocks for any family, but especially for those living at or below a middle-class income. Nonetheless, few have questioned whether it is, in fact, a necessary expense.

It is hard to delve into a critique of the American education sys-tem when I personally have benefited from it. Having gone through public school, then through the Land Grant education system, I acquired high school, baccalaureate, masters and Ph.D. degrees with-out incurring one dime of debt. Nevertheless, the best educators are keenly aware that they have not proffered a true education if their scholars do not engage in critical thinking. My graduate school-ing ended almost ten years ago, primary and secondary school long before that. Much has changed since that time. Many of the Radical Homemakers who were interviewed have incisive assessments of a system that they feel has personally troubled or financially burdened them, interfered with their children's development, or offered only an incomplete education. Consequently, they ascribe to alternative methods to teach their children, believing that a true education is procured by the active learner, not delivered by the tenured professor.

For most Americans, education for their children incurs extreme costs beyond tuition fees. Concerned about the increasingly com-petitive global marketplace, parents want their children to succeed in the race for the top schools and jobs with the best employers. Sociologist Juliet Schor argues that this translates into high housing costs in areas surrounding the best schools, as well as greater finan-cial outlay to buy kids any other items that might give them a leg up over their competition, including tutoring, extracurricular activities, personal computers, or private school tuition.[47] This drive to help our children compete leads to the need for two or more salaries, as well as all the additional costs associated with the employed household, such as child care, multiple cars, time-saving conveniences, career wardrobes, etc.

Despite the financial investment, our public education system is not making the grade. Whereas an American public school education once had a premier reputation worldwide, it now ranks thirteenth among the eighteen developed countries in fundamental literacy skills.[48] In 2008, *The New York Times* reported that the education advocacy group Common Core conducted a survey of American teenagers and found that 25 percent of them could not identify Adolph Hitler, and 33 percent were unaware that the Bill of Rights guaranteed freedom of speech and religion.[49] The same article reported that an American high-schooler drops out every twenty-six seconds, adding up to more than a million dropouts every year, one of the highest dropout rates in the industrialized world. Those kids who manage to graduate are the targets of corporate marketing efforts that have succeeded in getting product placements in curriculum materials and programming, as well as plastered throughout sporting events. David Korten argues that, with the exception of a few extraordinary schools, the majority of American students are confined to institutions where their daily task is "to fight off boredom while mastering the mechanics of reading, writing, and arithmetic and memorizing large quantities of information unconnected to any other aspect of his or her life."[50]

There is ample evidence leading to the conclusion that the current school system is dysfunctional. Julie Hewitt enrolled her children in public school when they first moved to their new home and found that the system just made them too anxious and detached from their family:

> Both of them would come home, and they were so unhappy
> at the end of the day that we couldn't have any meaningful
> family time, because they were a mess. I mean, they were just
> really crabby, and Rachel would just lock herself in her room. I
> noticed that when we had conversations at the table at dinner,
> she wasn't really coherent; she wasn't plugged into what was

happening. By Sunday, they were great. And so then on Mon-
day it would start all over again. Of course, summer was always
wonderful, because we were together all the time.

"Shawn was falling behind in class," says Carrie Lockwell, who
felt that the pace of the conventional education and college-prep
system was deleterious to her son. "The testing, and the evaluation
in school, and the peer pressure, it was just really bad for him," she
explained. She wanted to create an environment where he could learn
at his own pace without the pressure to participate in the multitude
of extracurricular activities that Shawn's peers were committed to:

> I have friends that are running their kids all around. . . .
> They're going to gymnastics and Girl Scouts and soccer and
> lacrosse and their kids are Shawn's age, eleven, and they started
> when they were six! They are constantly going every night.

This phenomenon of over-involvement is so widespread, social
critic Jonathan Rowe claims, that "kids today are getting day planners at age six. Their days consist of a sequence of lessons and super-
vised sports, all governed by the clock. Unstructured outdoor play has
dropped by fifty percent since the late 1970s."[51] Since the 1970s, children have lost twelve hours per week of free time.[52] Family advocates
William Doherty and Barbara Carlson feel that the current generation of parents is so preoccupied with the visible signs of success of
their children that they insist that they read earlier, compete more,
and begin preparing their college resumes by the sixth grade. The
result, they say, is a loss of family time for dinners, outings, vacations,
or simply being together. The pressure to succeed has made American families overscheduled and under-connected. The nearly obsessive fixation with early success lays the groundwork for a status race
in adulthood, where the grown-ups are perpetually driven to out-
compete everyone around them. Economist and happiness researcher
Richard Layard points out that this is a self-defeating effort, since if
someone else does "better" as a result of a perceived competition, then

someone else must necessarily do "worse."[53] It is hardly a constructive ambition for a society.

The worst victims of the status race are affluent suburban kids. As was mentioned earlier, in a longitudinal study where students were followed through high school and beyond, researchers found that affluent suburban kids were less happy and suffered lower self-esteem than their peers from middle-class neighborhoods and inner-city slums. They had higher rates of depression, anxiety and substance use.[54] These kids suffered from high-pressure expectations for achievement and isolation from adults as a result of all the family members being over-scheduled.

Many kids, affluent or otherwise, are investing more than the equivalent of an adult workday in school, extracurricular activities, and homework. A University of Michigan study reports that kids are spending eight more hours per week in school than kids twenty years ago, and the homework load has nearly doubled.[55] Unfortunately, the time invested does not seem to be as much about genuine learning as it is about getting a good grade. Denise Clark-Pope from Stanford University intensively studied five successful high-school students for one year and determined that they felt stuck in a "grade trap," where they believed their future success in life would be determined by their grades, test scores and advance-placement programs. While these achievements may help kids get into good colleges, Betsy Taylor argues that they come at the cost of healthy daily rhythms and the emotional and physical well-being of our children. Perhaps it should come as no surprise that drop-out rates are so high.

Julie Hewitt experienced the compulsion to push for achievement and to over-schedule her daughter, who has Down syndrome, through the pressure to participate in what she describes as a "disability culture." Julie felt that excessive "special needs" interventions disempowered her family, and underscored to her family that they would perpetually require the help of experts. Julie talks about Rachel's first five years of life, wherein she felt, as a parent, that she was subjected to "brainwashing:"

Then there was another sort of . . . how would I say it, *brain-washing*, I think, that occurs when you have a kid with special needs. You're told "we have all these specialists. You need to bring her to special schools, you need to hand her over to us to do special therapies with her. It's not a cure, but if you don't do it, she's going to be, well, you know (seriously dysfunctional). . . . It's this subconscious . . . sort of disability culture. When she was three years old I was told "Well, there's a special school you should send her to, the bus will come and pick her up." I put her in a car seat on a bus by herself with some strange man who drove her to a school and . . . at some point . . . I just went, "this is wrong!"

Julie eventually tapped into an alternative network of people with experience raising children with Down syndrome. She learned a different, more empowering way of raising Rachel:

You don't have to buy into the whole disability culture. These are people who make money. Therapists, all these, they all make money from your kid basically, and you don't have to buy into that. Let her have a normal childhood. . . . Instead of therapy, go to the park. You're not too dumb to realize that running and jumping and those things develop muscle tone, etc. . . . [Eventually] I decided to home school, and now she's testing twenty points above her IQ, and they [the "experts"] are all scratching their heads, going "how can this be?" . . . Well, I'm paying attention to her!

By keeping her daughter in a comfortable home environment where she was able to attend to Rachel's needs, Julie was able to accommodate some things that many Radical Homemakers feel have been abandoned in the conventional education system — tolerance and encouragement of individuality. Psychologist Bruce Levine points out that healthy societies should be made of neither isolated nor conformist individuals. Rather, it should consist of "voluntary cooperation among non-standardized personalities."[56] From the Radical Homemaking perspective, the American school system often seems set to squelch the notion of individuality, opting instead to "normalize" our children so that they can all accept an industrialized, standardized education. When William H. Whyte wrote *The Organization Man* in 1956, he shed light on American culture's increasing insistence on uniform personalities, which best served the corporations and bureaucracies that were wielding increasing influence over society. Perhaps predicting a future of epidemic depression and mental health crises, he warned, "The quest for normalcy . . . is one of the great breeders of neuroses."[57]

The intent of our modern education system is to create "productive" members of society, which are seen as people capable of extracting resources, manufacturing, distributing, or marketing products, overseeing the process, managing the money or legal matters involved, or buying the stuff that has been manufactured. The student who resists the standardization is filled with the fear of an "unpromising future." Not long out of post-secondary school, Stormy McGovern remembers being just such a student. The pressure eventually drove her to drop out and run away, eventually opting to acquire her G.E.D. and take a two-year college degree on her own terms:

> I like not being scared to live in the world we live in, however we want to walk in it. I think that . . . I just saw this fake lifestyle. . . . I'm sitting there in early high school and going, "Okay, you want me to graduate and you want me to find a college, and go to that, and then you want me to pick this career, and then have this career and make this money . . ." And it seemed . . . too cookie-cutter.

Stormy, and many of her counterparts in the study, felt that the school system was not only too conformist, but also that the skills taught seemed increasingly irrelevant. Graduates of the conventional school system lack much of the knowledge required to engage in the traditional crafts for cultural survival, such as farming, food

preservation and preparation, intimate knowledge of the Earth's natural systems, and an awareness of how to live joyfully within their
limits. Rebecca James explains her frustrations with how conventional education has moved us away from practical, resourceful living:

> . . . it used to be a one-stop shop, and the shop was your
> house, and other than going to whatever small general store
> was available in your town, the buck stopped here. You made
> it, you grew it, you bartered for it; that was how you got it.
> And people don't think like that anymore. They don't think of
> themselves as being able to procure or make or grow what they
> need. But you know, we're not all rocket scientists, and every-
> body used to make or grow or barter for what they needed.
> So these are skills that we can learn, but there has to be this
> mentality of education not being something that happens in a
> building. . . . [You] need to be able to pick up and learn any-
> thing you want to learn, whenever you want to learn it, because
> it's relevant to you at that time.

At its root, to educate means "to rear." Wendell Berry points out
that education means, quite literally, "to 'bring up,' to bring young
people to a responsible maturity, to help them to be good caretakers
of what they have been given, to help them to be charitable toward
fellow creatures."[58] He goes on to argue that when an education is
used well, it is brought home and applied where one lives. It comes
with a sense of obligation that it should be reinvested in the community. "When educational institutions educate people to leave home,"
he asserts, "then they have redefined education as 'career preparation.'
In doing so, they have made it a commodity — something to be
bought in order to make more money." The transgression here is that
a true education should be free. "What is taught and learned is free
— priceless — but free," says Berry. "To make a commodity of education, then, is inevitably to make a kind of weapon of it because, when
it is dissociated from the sense of obligation, it can be put directly at
the service of greed."

Rebecca, who had an intense career in the conventional education system, claims that the career preparation skills taught in the schools supplanted an enduring education and were ultimately not useful:

> We got into a lot of automation [as a culture]. ... I think a lot
> of the problems in our education system come from the same
> kind of thinking, and we're all cogs and we all have our specific
> little function that we're supposed to engage in, but we don't
> know anything outside of that sphere, and I don't feel like
> that's helpful.

Bruce Levine suggests that the deficient school curricula are not only unhelpful, but damaging, because students are motivated by fear to memorize information that, for them, is meaningless. He concludes that most people learn one basic lesson from their schooling: "the belief that surviving depends on motivating oneself with fear so as to succeed at tasks that are meaningless." Levine sums up that "this is nothing short of a blueprint for a depressing life."[59] This is also arguably a blueprint to support the existing power structure that keeps an extractive economy in place.

Education was not always designed this way. Prior to the industrialization of the 19th century, education more closely followed the model that Wendell Berry advocated. Parents reared their children to take a place in their communities and to survive within the resource base. It was not until the industrial revolution hit the United States that the culture changed its child-rearing philosophies so that our youth were socialized and trained for the role of employees (or factory owners), rather than stewards of a home and members of self-sustaining communities.[60] This post-industrial system is no longer relevant, argues Julie Hewitt:

> I just want them [my kids] to be able to be self-sufficient and
> solve problems and get information. To be able to retrieve
> information. I think those are things that are missing in the
> public school . . . being independent . . . being resourceful,

and being a thinker ... [not] just a receptacle for information without really knowing what to do with it. . . . School doesn't necessarily teach people how to think. It just gives them information, and they have to spit it back out.

There is an old maxim that says if you are "against" something, it is because you are "for" something else. While many of the Radical Homemakers offered critiques of the conventional education system, they were mostly conversational bridges for passionate discussions about their visions for their own children's education. For Alise Jansons up in Alaska, it all starts outside:

> Our natural resources are going to be our biggest commodity in the future. The ability to understand natural cycles, to know the difference between a birch tree and an oak tree . . . to appreciate nature, to want to protect it, to understand it. And I feel I'm giving him the best education possible. We're outside all the time. . . . I mean, how hard is it to teach your kid how to play a video game? I feel like this background will hopefully help him continue . . . to want to protect it.

Rebecca James hopes to raise her children to be self-reliant and to happily live in opposition to the consumer culture:

> I think it's important for us to raise self-sufficient individuals who know how to make and do things, as opposed to simply consume things. . . . I feel like we're not going to solve the problems that face us by watching the news and trying to consume differently. We're going to have to be original thinkers, and we're going to have to have capabilities that we are able to employ, and we're going to have to say to ourselves, "I can learn this; there isn't any reason I can't learn this."

For Radical Homemakers, the brick-and-mortar institutions associated with school districts and high property values have little relevance to their children's education. Rather, they feel the most critical skill to cultivate in our youth is the ability to self-educate. Education has nothing to do with what money can buy; it has everything to do with capitalizing on children's innate inquisitiveness and desire to learn. For Eve Honeywell, it is about encouraging her children to be independent thinkers. "I want them to be able to make their own decisions, not follow the crowd, to be able to resist media," she says. Her idea of success has nothing to do with a job placement:

> I think for them to really be successful in life and to do what
> they love . . . they have to be able to think independently to
> make those kind of choices . . . to be able to live the way we do
> . . . outside the norm.

Eve, who like Rebecca, also had a former career as a teacher, is not encouraging her children to enter the competition for a position in the global marketplace, and she is adamant that this is best for their development:

> I think that having this time just to play and use their imagi-
> nations is going to prepare them more than pushing them
> into reading earlier, excelling at piano or whatever. I think that
> just letting them be kids is going to give them far more of an
> advantage. . . . I really think that it changes what's going on
> in their brains if you're pushing them into these really struc-
> tured activities before they're really ready. I think as far as how
> their brain develops, you're following a more normal course
> of things in allowing them to develop at their pace by letting
> them play.

By reassessing the compulsion to prepare their children to compete in a global marketplace, Radical Homemakers are avoiding ambiguous anxieties and apprehensions; further, they avoid many of the expenses associated with conventional education. They are also unwilling to allow a calm and harmonious home life to be superseded by domestic planning and over-scheduling. Carrie Lock-well is unapologetic in her approach. "I'm there [at home] most of the day, and I'm not shuttling my kid all over. And he likes to be home." Rather than raising their kids to be competitive, their goal is to raise children who are independent thinkers, resourceful and self-reliant. These children are not being prepared to live in a world where everyone must fight for dwindling resources. Rather, they are being prepared to live in a creative world, where resources are replenished and abundance is shared.

When their children are raised with full participation in home life, there is a natural flow between play, work, learning, community, spirituality and family. In many cases, this means schooling at home, but this was not always the case. Some families worked to ensure a strong link between home and the school. Alise Jansons will be enrolling her son in a charter school next fall, where the parents themselves determine the education model. She feels her son will learn better in this environment than at home, and since the charter school is technically a public school, the family will not incur any tuition expenses. David Peterson felt it was critical to enroll his son in the local public school. "I think the school community is really important," says David, "and it turned out the school was wonderful. We couldn't have paid a private school to be better than that." He and Janice did, however, make a point of staying involved in school functions by volunteering with an environmental learning program, then in subsequent years coaching children's reading practice. Years later David would go into the school to help students do their library research, and eventually he became a substitute teacher.

For the primary and secondary school years, there are many alternatives to conventional education. But college can present some hurdles. The Radical Homemakers I interviewed had deftly accrued skills to enhance their self-reliance and reduce their need for a con-ventional income. They came up with clever living arrangements to keep housing costs manageable. They gave up extra cars, reduced the miles they drove, eschewed credit card debt and skirted around health insurance. But for many, the one financial burden hanging over their heads was a vestige of their past life — the debt many of them incurred while pursuing their college degrees. Some found their way around it. Carrie Lockwell was leery of taking on school debt when she graduated from high school, and thus opted for a career in the military for a few years. Michael Mills went to college, he says "because there was no other plan." Soon, however, he questioned whether it was an appropriate use of his time:

> It was all paid for; I had scholarships. It wasn't costing any-
> body a dime, and I just really was not interested at the time.
> I really wanted to be outside. I really wanted to be living my
> life; I was very curious, but not curious about studying things
> in books. . . . After I quit college I enjoyed reading Homer and
> Plato and all kinds of stuff, but I just did not like the whole
> structure of the whole college experience.

Michael illustrates the fact that college may not be for everyone and that the years immediately following high school may not be the best time to attend. Indeed, there are countless college graduates in this country who have emerged with degrees, only to question the choices they made. Erik Knutzen and Kelly Coyne both earned advanced degrees in the fine arts, but ultimately questioned their value in the life they were visioning for themselves. "I really didn't find what I was looking for there," admits Erik. "We had these kind of fancy degrees that prepare you for nothing but being academics, and neither of us were going to be an academic." The decision to forego college altogether does not have to mean that a person will sacrifice a life as a well-read, informed and educated citizen; indeed, this is at the core of the homemakers' intent — to raise confident, inquisitive, autodidactic thinkers.

Susan Colter, the young woman we met in the introduction to this book, had just completed her four-year degree at a prestigious private school, and was finding herself completely lost as she tried to apply her education to her desire to lead an alternative lifestyle. When she and her peers considered lives that included farming or arts or any vocation that didn't fit the parameters of a conventional workplace, they felt lost and bewildered about how to move forward. Susan felt that her education did not adequately prepare her for the life she wanted to pursue. While she knew she could acquire the agrarian skills she lacked, she felt stymied because she had no sense of her options, no vision of what such a life might look like, and no idea if it was even possible:

> I never sensed that I had an option other than working for someone and working up in salary, and working up in position. That was always the ultimate [goal]. . . . Everyone on that campus and on every other campus, it seemed to me, is absolutely focused on graduation and then continuing, whether it be with more education, or stepping into a job that's going to get you on a track to status, to some sort of position where you will be admired, or where your work will be lauded. . . . Working on a humbler scale couldn't be considered successful.

The failure of some universities to accommodate, let alone encourage, pursuit of a humbler, more creative and ecologically conscientious living is symptomatic of a prevailing assumption that humans hold dominion over nature, that the planet is here exclusively for human use. Such a view fails to acknowledge the interdependence of all the living systems on the planet and lays the groundwork for ecological abuses. "As now functioning," says Thomas Berry, "the university prepares students for their role in extending human dominion over the natural world, not for intimate presence to the natural world. Use of this power in a deleterious manner has devastated the planet."[61] Berry views this problem as a cultural disorientation that is intellectually sustained by the university. He underscores his critique by pointing out that education largely prepares students for a place in industry, commerce and communications, and that much of it is underwritten in some way with corporate dollars.

Corporate funding notwithstanding, college degrees are costly. In 2004, Warren and Tyagi claimed that college tuition was increasing at three times the rate of inflation. They argued that student loans are not an appropriate solution. "We need to start thinking about other ways to make college more affordable," said Tyagi in an interview with *Mother Jones* magazine. "What we found is that colleges often increase tuition just because they can. When you look at what universities are spending money on, they're spending far more on sports programs, far more on administrative overhead, far more on food services."[62] Not surprisingly, some Radical Homemakers have questioned whether a college education for their own children is an appropriate expenditure. "I've seen kids pressured to go to college, but they don't know what they want to do," observes Carrie Lockwell:

> Then they come out and they're so in debt and they're bogged down and they're . . . stuck in a rut. . . . Maybe [people] shouldn't be pressuring their kids to do certain things. Maybe they should be looking at . . . is making $75,000–$100,000 more a year and then being stuck in an office the best thing?

Not all Radical Homemakers are turning their backs on post-secondary education. But they are using alternative tactics for affording it. Holly and Brian Simmons are hopeful that their sons will go to college, but they are not intending to pay their way. The decision to go, says Brian, "will be based on what they're interested in and what their merit is." The cost of college tuition beyond their local state school is simply unfathomable to them. Rather than incurring excessive school debt, "you could apprentice yourself to somebody," argues Brian, "you could learn a life skill." When Anna Reynolds became a single mom, she still had three children at home. She relocated her family on farmland within a short commuting distance from a state land-grant college, and allowed her kids to make up their own minds about whether or not they wanted a college degree. Her daughter opted not to attend, and the two boys have decided to take turns. One has taken over the bulk of the farm responsibilities while the other commutes to school. When he is finished, they will switch places.

Their family income level also qualifies them for grants and scholar-ships. Susan Colter, now out of college, is working to catch up on the education she feels she missed. At the time of our interview, rather than pursuing graduate school, she was planning to travel around, seeking experiential learning opportunities to glean more skills for living off the land.

Rebecca James still winces at the cost of her college education and expresses gratitude that her family is helping manage some of the debt for the time being. The debt, along with her current views about education, has led her to question the assumptions her own parents made when they encouraged her to pursue a college degree:

> I don't think I look at college as the brass ring anymore, in the same way that they [my parents] did. I think education is won-derful, but once you started thinking of education outside the box and you've stopped thinking of it as something that some-one hands down to you, it opens up a lot more possibilities.

Pulling from her own background in education, Rebecca argues that the world has changed. Educational and career models are no longer satisfactory platforms for visioning a life:

> There has been a lot of talk in our society about how people used to work for the same company for fifty years, and then get their brass watch and retire. . . . Everything is changing now, because we work for "this.com" or "that.com," and we're going to switch jobs again and again. It's so different. But I don't know if I think that either one of those models is neces-sarily [ideal]. I don't know why we're always painting pictures of what model is going to be THE model that we're all going to work toward within our generation. . . . THE model that will work for all of us. I think people want someone to just hand them a solution that's easy, and life's not like that. It's messy and it doesn't always go the way you expect it to go.

Free from presumptions about what will and what won't work for her children's future, Rebecca no longer sees learning as confined to the classroom. Thus, in her mind, there are ample opportunities for her children to gain an education without having to purchase a college diploma.

> I want the kids to be doing something that serves their needs and that is fascinating to them. And I expect that that is going to evolve and change over time. . . . There are so many things that are so interesting out there. I think with home schooling, I'm really trying to set them up for mentoring relationships later in life. I'm trying to set them up so that they will learn to participate in internship-type experiences, and I think that that's going to become more valuable over time. We've got a society now that . . . perceives college as the thing that you should do, but if we are all going to college, then what differentiates us from each other?

Rebecca makes critical points — there may not be a competitive advantage to a college degree if everyone holds one, and our individual educational needs are not all the same. Institutions may be valuable for some of us, but they are not necessary for everyone, and they are not the only means through which a person may become educated. I personally enjoyed much of my own formal education, yet I've met many people who, while they possessed fewer or no degrees, struck me as far better educated than myself. For many Radical Homemakers, the goal of one's education should be to contribute to human communities that might become a beneficent presence on the planet, to learn how to support rather than destroy our ecosystems, or how we may, in Thomas Berry's words, learn to "exist for the integrity of the universe and for the earth," as opposed to asking how they may exist for our own purposes. In that case, brick-and-mortar institutions may not always satisfy our needs, particularly if they require so much money to attend that we are obliged to subjugate ourselves to the extractive economy for the privilege of their degrees.

Retirement is possible, regardless of income.

The final impossible thing to consider is that a family on a reduced income can save money for the future. We have come to assume that the American middle class must earn two incomes to accrue adequate funds for retirement. Even when the extractive economy was purportedly doing well — before the economic collapse of 2008 and the sad loss of many Americans' retirement savings — those two incomes weren't getting us very far. Prior to that period, as more Americans used their houses as collateral for bank loans, home equity values reached an all-time low. In 2004, the average debt liability Americans held for real property was more than $290,000 per household.[63] In the autumn of 2008, a story in *Yes!* magazine reported that families were carrying an average of $5,100 of credit card debt.[64] In 1980, U.S. household debt added up to 65 percent of disposable income.[65] By 2005 it stood at 125 percent. Between 1997 and 2005, more Americans declared personal bankruptcy than graduated from college.[66]

All this points to a mysterious paradox that several of the Radical Homemakers identified — the more money brought in, the more money goes out. For Deirdre Ianelli, earning money and going to a job every day exposed her to a certain level of peer pressure that encouraged her to constantly be spending her earnings:

> I was definitely sacrificing a lot having been in that job.
> Money–wise, too . . . I think you're around other people who
> might be spending money in different ways than you are, than
> you would like to. . . . You might be thinking, "Wow, I don't
> want to spend my money that way," but then you do, because
> everybody else is. When you are removed from that situation,
> it just doesn't happen any more. So I probably was spending
> money that I wouldn't spend now, just being in that situation
> . . . [for example] clothing, just wanting to dress a certain way,
> professionally. Certain books, because people want you to read
> this or that or the other thing . . .

For Rebecca James, the presence of a readily disposable income distracted her from being more resourceful:

> I put in lots of rose bushes [as opposed to vegetables that would provide food]. I had a perennial herb garden, but you know . . . I wasn't getting [seed] starts from friends. I wasn't getting books through interlibrary loan. There are so many places where I could have been doing the same things I was doing, and economizing, but I wasn't. And then, whenever I was too tired to cook, we ate out . . . at least twice a week, because we didn't think anything of it. All our friends did. Everyone blew off steam every Wednesday, because the weekend was coming, and so we'd all go out and we'd have a couple of drinks, and we'd buy some appetizers. . . . You know, hindsight is 20/20, but I could've set myself up much better to be home with my kids [today], and I didn't.

For many Radical Homemakers, the income ultimately came at too great a cost. Rebecca describes her return to work after her second child was born. During that time she became pregnant for her third. She explains:

> I made "Teacher of the Year" the second year . . . but wound up having an emergency C-section because I had polyhydramnios. I had all this extra fluid; my body was dealing with the stress by creating this buffer for the baby. They said the day that [my son] was born, they could have taken two two-liter bottles of fluid out of me and there still would have been enough for the baby. So he wound up being a C-section, and I just said, "I've had it."

Sylvia Tanner tells how she and her son paid the price for her commute to a job out of state:

[I would] leave in the afternoon and get home here, and usually come home to total chaos, especially in the winter. You
know, a frozen water pump, the driveway not plowed, just
everything was happening. Pipes were freezing, and it was just
bad. . . . [The next winter] I just couldn't bear the thought of
driving down there, and it was really hard on my son, too. He
was having a really hard time when I would take off, so then I
left. I quit, and just said, "Okay, I'm going to wing it here."

If there is a fundamental financial planning lesson to be taken
away from this lifestyle choice, it is this: it matters not what you
earn; it matters what you save. Eve Honeywell acknowledges that
finances are tight in her household. The reason is because their first
priority is contributing to their savings account. "We're not touch-
ing that money." she says, "There's no way we're going to touch that
money." She explains that, living this way, "our spending habits are
certainly different. . . . I see brand-new cars and brand-new houses
and brand-new clothes, and I wonder how that can be maintained.
. . . I don't think we would choose to do that anyway. I think we're in
pretty good shape."

With three fast-growing boys, Holly and Brian Simmons do not
see this as the time to be padding their retirement accounts. They feel
their first priority should be toward seeing to the needs of their kids,
that earning extra money can come later when they are more independent. Nevertheless, they are still building their savings. "We have
savings and IRAs and things like that," says Brian. "We contribute to
them when we can," but, he adds, "We'll continue to generate income
as long as we're alive." The reason is that their labors on the family
ranch are a source of joy, and they do not anticipate leaving or totally
abandoning their endeavors. In fact, when the boys are older and more
independent, Holly and Brian plan on investing more of their energies into their family enterprises. "We're not in want," says Holly. "We
have an incredible lifestyle. So when the boys go and they're on their
own, then we can concentrate more [on] making some more money."

When reporting on his research on happiness, Richard Layard remarked, "When they are asked how much income they need, richer people always say they need more than poorer people [claim to need]."[67] The ability to live happily with less reflects a deeper wealth for Radical Homemakers, because it frees them from working longer to attain more money. Penelope and John Sloan felt they had this genuine wealth while he was in graduate school. They lived on very little money, yet had a joyous time:

> We lived on something crazy, like $15,000 a year. I didn't make
> very much because I was temping, and he made $6,000 for his
> T.A. assignment. But we lived a really good life. We had good
> food, good wine, and we hung out with our friends . . . and
> once a year we'd go on a little trip somewhere . . .

When they unexpectedly received an "early inheritance" from John's parents, the couple opted to maintain their modest lifestyle. They purchased a series of certificates of deposit from their bank, and live off the interest. Today the couple lives on $20,000 per year. Michael and Sarah Mills, nearing retirement age, demonstrate a similar wealth. "My accountant tells me that he knows doctors our age who have less net worth than we do," notes Michael. Despite their modest earnings, they have accumulated wealth. But an important distinction has enabled Michael and Sarah to keep their savings goals realistic. "It is very important for me to be financially secure," he explains. "I have absolutely no desire to be rich."

One of the traps of income is that we attribute more meaning to it than simply the ability to buy things. In our culture it has become a measure of how we are valued personally and, ultimately, our self-worth. Sidestepping this misconception and detaching self-worth from a paycheck can be extraordinarily liberating. Once that myth has been shattered, we can confront our deeper desire for money — to buy security. Unfortunately, David and Janice Peterson, like so many other Americans, have recently discovered that security cannot always be bought with money. Describing their retirement planning, David notes:

> We've done it in a very traditional way, or the current tradi-
> tional way, which isn't so traditional — the IRA-type thing,
> and you know, we've watched our money go. . . . We were told
> that this was the way to do it, and I've learned not to believe
> that anymore!

One thing that David observes, however, is that, had he left home and gone to work and saved and invested some extra money, he and Janice would have fared no better; they simply would have lost more savings in the economic meltdown of 2008. Thankfully, security can be acquired in more ways than simply with money. When his son came home from college at Christmas time, David came face to face with a critical part of the security system he and Janice had worked so hard to build — family. In a letter to me, David writes:

> Before going back to college after his Christmas break, our
> son told me, "I'm so proud that you make things, chairs!" He
> is frustrated that most careers he is exposed to have less obvi-
> ous rewards to show for their efforts and lead to less stable and
> self-sufficient lives. With crying and hugs he urged me to keep
> working in my shop and offered me his unused bedroom as a
> warm winter shop space. He cleared a space for me and helped
> me move a small bench upstairs.

At age 61, David has realized that the security for his and Janice's future will be drawn more from their relationships, their connections to the community, and their self-reliance, than from their IRA. In her mid-twenties, Stormy McGovern has already seen the wave of the future and embraces a similar lesson:

> I don't like to live in fear, so I just tend to make simple goals.
> I want to eat well, I want to see my family happy, and I know

that can't always be up to me. . . . I have no interest in piling
money up for my future. . . . You know, you can't eat it. And
who knows what it's going to be worth some day. . . . I think
it's a good energy tool, you can use it for different things, but
it would sure be a bummer to work your ass off all your life
just to have money, and just depend on buying everything, and
then, all of a sudden, see it be worth nothing.

These observations about the limited power of money to guarantee a secure future harken back to an observation made by Gandhi: "I
do not want to foresee the future. I am concerned with taking care of
the present. God has given me no control over the moment following." We do have control, however, over the quality of our relationships and the ability of our communities to be self-sufficient. And
that, in turn, builds security. As our extractive economy falters and
our fossil fuels deplete, Bill McKibben notes, "comfort will come
less from ownership than from membership. If you're a functioning
part of a community that can meet at least some of its needs — for
food, for energy, for companionship, for entertainment, for succor —
then you're more secure."[68] Maryann Heslier's quest for security is
directly linked to self-sufficiency. But, like McKibben, she sees self-
sufficiency as a community goal:

I would say if the "self" in "self-sufficient" is community, if
that's what that's representing, then we're more sufficient, sustainable in our place. But our place is not this house; our place
is this community, and the people in our church, the people
that we know on the farms right around, things like that.
. . . What makes it sustainable is that we've developed those
bridges, and we know they're there for us.

Another part of the goal for building security is investing in family. Rejecting the uniquely American notion that members of families
should seek to be independent of one another, Eve Honeywell sees
her investment in the family farm as an investment for everyone's

future. "We feel like we're really building something for our future
and for our kids' future," she says. "We hope that they'll want to be
here as adults and do something that they really want to do on the
farm. If that doesn't happen, that's okay, but we want that to be an
option for them." Deirdre Ianelli is on a similar path with her family. While her husband is a financial planner and works to build a
monetary nest egg, she sees their ultimate security in the family and
the land:

> I say, "Honey, that's just paper. Money doesn't mean anything
> to me." It's just in cyberspace somewhere, and what happens if
> . . . everything falls apart? . . . At least we have some land here,
> and family. . . . As far as retirement goes . . . mutual funds and
> that sort of thing . . . It's nothing tangible. But I think what
> we're doing here, that helps. If anything were to happen, we
> can at least support ourselves and teach our children how to
> support themselves, too, without money.

Sylvia Tanner considers her friends a critical part of her retirement plan and ponders whether co-housing might be how she
spends her later years. She feels that the secret to enjoying a sustainable future lies far from the paycheck or the pension fund:

> [We need to be] . . . shedding the whole notion of what it is
> you're supposed to be doing, and what everything is supposed
> to look like. I just think we have a lot of [mistaken] ideas . . .
> like "money in the bank is security." So a lot of people are
> working really hard at trying to accumulate it . . . and then
> [the bank fails] or the stock market tanks, or money becomes
> so devalued that it's worth hardly anything.

In short, the rules we have followed as a society since the industrial revolution have not benefited everyone, most especially now.
Thus, the Radical Homemakers would argue that building security
through skills, relationships, family self-reliance and community

self-sufficiency are far more prudent investments than a 401K or paycheck. Stormy McGovern sums it up best. There is a life to live without money that is defined by impoverishment, a lack of safety, and potential violence. On the other hand, even with low funds, there is another path that is surrounded by abundance and community:

> That's the path I want. . . . Money is just, I think if you have a good relationship with it, it's fine. But my security is not lying in a big stack of cash. [You can have a good relationship with money] if it doesn't worry you and . . . you're not afraid to receive it, not afraid to let it go. Not afraid to give it away . . . You can definitely be mindful about how you use it, but I think that once you let it damage your emotional and spiritual body, once you let it start taking over your life . . . I just couldn't imagine how horrible that would be, and you see so many people caught up in it. It's this wicked game that distracts us from being real and being human and from interacting with each other, sharing.

"Being real and being human" is the name of the game for the Radical Homemakers. Stormy's vision regarding a life unencumbered by money might go farther afield than many would be willing to venture. But freedom from enslavement to careers, freedom to make a sustainable life at home and to nurture family, friends and community, and freedom to pursue fulfilling life challenges are core goals that cannot be traded away. They are the goals that will move us away from the extractive economy and immerse our nation deeply in a life-serving economy. As Confucius observed, "The strength of a nation derives from the integrity of the home."

CHAPTER SIX
RECLAIMING
DOMESTIC SKILLS

"Let your life be a counter friction
to stop the machine."
— *Thoreau*, Civil Disobedience[1]

In the previous chapters we've considered the rationale of recentering our lives around the domestic sphere as a way to bring about social transformation, reclaim personal power, build security, heal the planet, and create a better life for ourselves and our families. But abandoning a job and returning to the home and garden is not a simple matter of making up our minds, submitting a two-week notice and living happily ever after. Building a successful career as a homemaker takes time (considerably more than two weeks!) and requires a set of skills that must be learned and cultivated. Understanding *why* we should reorient to the home, we now need to find *how* this switch is made.

There exist countless volumes that outline the myriad techniques that might play a role in designing an ecologically sustainable, self-sufficient, home-centered life. There are books, manuals, magazines, videos and Web sites that discuss planting a garden, using the harvest, building a chicken coop, cleaning without chemicals, making herbal remedies, raising livestock, growing food in the city, designing gray water systems, managing our money and time, repairing equipment and educating our kids. Rather than cataloguing the *how–to* of homemaking, the "*how*" I was seeking from these homemakers in my research was of a different sort. I wanted to discern the deeper skills that they possessed — those abilities that enabled them to brave the perceived risk of sidestepping conventional employment and to transition their homes to units of production, and that made them able to secure contented lives for the foreseeable future. I was looking for those nontechnical skills that are easy to overlook, but impossible to live without, and that cannot be simply outlined in a technical manual.

Over the course of visiting with the twenty families and individuals who participated in this study, seven fundamental skill sets became evident in nearly every situation. Sometimes the homemakers were consciously aware of them, were able to articulate their importance, and describe how they went about cultivating them. In other instances they went unacknowledged, having become such a natural part of the homemakers' daily life that I had to read between the lines of their transcripts and review photos of my visits in order to detect them. But, in comparing each homemaker's story, a set of seven quintessential abilities emerged, giving a clear picture of the unseen tactics that make such a life possible.

Of these seven skills, three of them — **nurturing relationships, working with a life-serving economy** and **cultivating an ability to self-teach** — are recovered, by and large, from the toolbox that men and women drew upon when setting up their households in pre-industrial communities. Aspiring Radical Homemakers must regain facility with them to create a lifestyle that re-ignites community-based self-reliance. Beyond the age-old traditions, however, Radical Homemakers must also cultivate a new set of skills, in which they fundamentally change certain assumptions and ways of thinking and unlearn much of what our modern extractive economy has ingrained so powerfully into our cultural beliefs. These "new" skills include **setting realistic expectations and limits, redefining pleasure in our lives, rediscovering the taste of real food, and adopting a fearless attitude in withstanding contrary cultural expectations**. The composite of these skill sets is a new "toolbox" that, like so much of Radical Homemaking, is informed by our past to create a new modernity.

NURTURING RELATIONSHIPS

Contemporary consumer culture is organized around one single purpose — making money. But preindustrial cultures were typically organized with a different goal in mind — well-being. If we want to be "happy homemakers," yet avoid the condition of housewife's syndrome, and if we want to create a system that enables us to achieve well-being, but without requiring a surfeit of money, then the first skill of paramount importance is the art of building and nurturing relationships.

Solid and satisfying relationships are beyond a doubt the primary step in building a sustainable home. People are simply happier when they are not always alone. In their study of "very happy" people, Ed Diener and Martin Seligman found that every respondent in their happiest group had excellent social relationships.[2] Other studies have shown that the personal attributes most likely to predict life satisfaction are interpersonal skills.[3] Magnetic resonance images of people as they were forming cooperative alliances showed a strong positive response in the pleasure center of the brain.[4] When Richard Layard completed his comprehensive review of happiness research, he outlined seven factors that affect happiness: family relationships, financial situation, work, community and friends, health, personal freedom and personal values. "Except for health and income," notes Layard, "they are all concerned with the quality of our relationships."[5]

The value of good relationships is not just about the ability to call in favors. It is as much about the giving as it is about receiving. "People who care about other people are on average happier than those who are more preoccupied with themselves," reports Layard.[6] Diener and Seligman corroborate this. While receiving social support is typically acknowledged as a way of coping with life's stresses, research indicates that *giving* support to other people is probably just as important. Social connectedness for people on both sides of the give-and-take equation has been found to support better autonomic activity, improved immunosurveillance, and lower basal levels of stress hormones.[7] Back in the 1950s, Erich Fromm observed that fully functioning adults needed to love as much as be loved[8]; a 2003 study confirmed this, reporting that the opportunity to offer social support is more important to longevity than receiving it.[9]

We have every reason to gauge our wealth in life by the quality of our relationships rather than the number in our bank accounts. However, since relationships can easily provide a far more gratifying substitute for cash, the extractive economy often pooh poohs their potential. We are taught to strive for "independence," to leave home by age eighteen, to buy nursing home insurance so as not to be a burden on our children, to buy an extra car "for emergencies" so we don't have to ask our neighbors for a ride, to drive alone to work so we don't have to have conflicts with car-poolers, to buy copies of every book we read to spare trips to the library or the wait for a friend to finish reading it, to own our own lawn mowers and tractors and rototillers lest we should need to borrow one, to buy a TV for every room in the house so we don't have to watch the same thing other family members watch. The extractive economy benefits greatly when people can't learn to get along together. People, however, do not. Human beings do not fare well when they have poor relationships in groups.[10] Research has also shown that people who are ostracized from groups suffer from impaired cognitive functioning.[11] In *The Feminine Mystique*, Betty Friedan talked about countless housewives who found the isolation of their suburban homes unbearable. With family members gone all day, and each home its own island, the loneliness took its toll on these women.

Radical Homemaking is about building self-reliance, but it is not about becoming totally *self-sufficient* and living apart from society. "There really is no such thing as self-sufficiency," argues Sylvia Tanner. She makes the point that Radical Homemaking is not about independence; it is about *inter*dependence or, perhaps, "*inter-reliance*":

> You'd just about go crazy trying to do everything yourself, and
> I don't know that it's healthy or really possible. . . . I think . . .
> being able to share things with your neighbors and share jobs
> and share chores and skills and tools and other types of things
> is really where it's at.

The tactical first step toward breaking from the extractive economy and building a life-supporting alternative to the consumer culture is the ability to unite and to nurture relationships with **family, friends and community**.

Family

For Justin and Bettina Winston, interdependence begins with their family members who live in the same community. Justin believes that good relationships with his in-laws not only help him and Bettina safeguard their bottom line, but also help bring about cultural change:

> When you're not surrounded by like-minded people, your
> option is to spend all afternoon canning, or you go to the
> grocery store and buy. . . . by isolating families into their gen-
> erational units in houses . . . they lose their ability to think
> effectively and act effectively as a group. — Kind of like a
> corporate strategy for making sure that you have to pay out
> for as many services and as many things as you possibly can be
> made to pay out for . . . because you're all alone. You and your
> [nuclear] family are all alone as an island.

> If you have your extended family around you, and everyone
> is conversing on how best to do things and working together
> to accomplish things, you don't have to go out and buy this
> or buy that. You can all just get together one day and build it
> yourselves (or can, or make maple syrup, as they have all done
> together). That's money that doesn't get sent to corporations;
> that's money that stays within the family, and it doesn't neces-
> sarily get spent on other things. There's a reason that people are
> put into subdivisions. [It makes cooperation more difficult.]

Utilizing family relationships to share, rather than replicate assets is, beyond a doubt, key to unraveling the extractive economy and rebuilding a life-sustaining economy. Further, if the relationships are fulfilling, characterized by positive interactions, forgiveness and tolerance, then rebuilding the life-sustaining economy delivers other dividends. Layard's research indicates that family relationships (and other close, personal, family-like relationships) have been more important *than any other factor* affecting our happiness. Predictably, the more positive interactions, such as giving compliments, helping with tasks, engaging in interesting conversations or expressing affection, the more desirable the relationships will be.[12] But as anyone with a family can attest, that won't always be easy. Dierdre Ianelli, who lives and works with her husband's extended family on their farm says, "I think we're really lucky in that we can make it work here." But, she adds, "There are definitely glitches":

> It's not perfect. It will never be perfect, but I just don't think
> it's perfect for anyone, because it is just hard to work closely
> with people that you know that well. . . . That's understandable.
> . . . We deal with it because I think that there's also some-
> thing really positive that comes with working with your fam-
> ily, because you do know each other so well. And you can say
> anything, for the most part. . . . These people have known you
> for a really really long time . . .

Nurturing family relationships may be easier for the Winstons, Honeywells, Simmons or the Ianellis, because most of the extended family members share similar ideals and have the same goals. But even if they don't see eye to eye on everything, almost everyone can still help each other out. One night, while traveling outside her own Chicago neighborhood, Nance Klehm was attacked and brutally beaten by members of a gang. While her parents lead an entirely different lifestyle outside the city, seeing her need for medical care, they stepped forward and offered to purchase health insurance. Rebecca James' mother had always expected her to pursue a prestigious career and did not anticipate that her daughter would become a homemaker. Nevertheless, her parents, demonstrating acceptance or perhaps support for her ideals, are helping with her student loan payments. Alise Jansons and her husband had no desire to live anywhere near the suburbs of New Jersey, where she grew up, but when her mother suffered a brain hemorrhage, the newly married couple promptly returned to the East Coast and put their life plans on hold to give her full-time care in her final year. Maryann Heslier's mother-in-law lives nowhere nearby and no longer gardens or cans, but she agreed to visit the family during tomato season to help her daughter-in-law learn how to put up her first harvest. When Kelly Robideau separated from her first husband before her daughter was born, her parents promptly opened their home to her so that she could finish graduate school without having to leave her baby in day care.

Refusing to accept help that is offered rarely saves anything except, perhaps, a little personal pride. But when openly discussed, the stigma is defused. "Rick and I came to an understanding that we're going to accept help, and it's not a bad thing," says Deirdre Ianelli:

> It's not a bad thing to have parents help you. They're not help-
> ing us because they think we need a hand out; they're help-
> ing us because they want to; and we're helping them, and its
> reciprocal. . . . I think for me it was a little hard at first. . . . It
> was really hard for me to say, " Oh, they're going to do that for
> us, they're going to buy that for us, or they're going to help us
> with that for a little while." It was really nerve-wracking. . . .
> I felt guilty for not doing it myself, but then Rick said "You
> know, it's my family. That's what families do." . . . I think that
> was the ultimate goal for them, was to be able to have this
> cohesive family here and be able to help everybody and be
> together. I think once we got past [not] being able to accept
> help, it just made a huge difference. The weight is just lifted off
> your shoulders.

Interestingly, Deirdre felt that being able to accept help also made it easier to give it. "I feel much more generous than I've ever felt in the past," she adds. To accept shared abundance makes it more plentiful for everyone. The acceptance of family relationships and resources, however imperfect, also fosters a genuine sense of security. "I feel safe in life because my parents raised me," observes Bettina Winston, who feels that her in-laws perceive her and Justin's lifestyle without conventional employment as risky. "I just always feel secure. I never feel in danger because I know I have their love, just unconditionally. There's something about that. It gives you just — *bravery*."

The participatory presence of family does more than help a couple feel supported and safe; it typically helps them keep their own marriages intact. "If people live near where they grew up, close to parents and old friends," observes Layard, "they are probably less likely to break up. They have a network of social support, which is less available in more mobile communities."[13] This becomes especially important when pursuing a Radical Homemaking lifestyle. When a couple makes this life choice, and one or both of them opts to forego a conventional career, then their economic sustainability will rely very heavily on the success of their marriage.

For the Radical Homemaker, keeping the marriage nurtured and intact depends largely on an equal balance of power and a sharing of duties. As suffragist Antoinette Brown Blackwell proclaimed:

> Let no women give all their time to household duties, but
> require nearly all women, and all men also, since they belong to
> the household, to bear some share of the common household
> burdens.[14]

Despite two or three waves of feminism throughout our nation's history (depending on who's counting), this early feminist proclamation has yet to be fully inculcated into our culture. According to Scott Coltrane, sociology professor at the University of California Riverside, women continue to perform two or three times as much housework as men in our culture. Even in our modern, "politically correct" times, says Coltrane, "Men tend to perform less housework when they marry, and assume a smaller share of the household work after their wives have children."[15] Frank Stafford, an economist at the University of Michigan, argues that men do increase their household

contributions by 2.5 hours per week once they get married, but that
is still a paltry sum when compared to women, who, upon marrying,
typically increase their housework on average by 6.5 hours.[16] Even
if one person has an away-from-home job in a Radical Homemaker
relationship, maintaining the home is a constant venture, particularly
because it incorporates elements of sustainability and self-reliance.
Everyone must contribute to the family ecosystem. Julie and David
Hewitt are terrific examples of this balance of duties. The following
dialogue provides wonderful evidence:

> Julie: *I do most of the home-schooling, David is sort of the pinch
> hitter. . . . He's been helping more* [lately] *because . . . we can do it
> so much more efficiently and quickly if you* [to David] *just help me
> for an hour in the morning. And then I feel like I'm over the hump
> and I can handle the rest of the day on my own. . . . I usually make
> dinner, you do the dishes.*
> David: *I usually make breakfast.*
> Julie: *You usually make breakfast and then I do the dishes.*
> David: *Lunch is a free for all. I do a lot of the garden work as well
> as the farm work.*
> Julie: *He does a lot of the garden, yeah.*
> David: *Julie is the goat girl.*
> Julie: *And you do chickens. I don't do chickens.*
> Shannon: [to David] *And you do the fixing as well?*
> Julie: *Yeah, and then he works* [part-time, from home], *so he's
> always doing something.*

Rebecca James also feels her husband, though he is gone during
the day, helps share the load. "He's a 'sensitive new-age guy,'" she says,
quoting the Christine Lavin song, "and he's much more integrated
into the daily parenting and the daily routine of the household than
my father was, his father was, a lot of the fathers his age that we know
are, and we're pretty comfortable with that. . . . I mean, he absolutely
does take responsibility for the overall cleanliness of the house, the
care and education of the children." Bettina Winston says, "I don't

do nearly as much of the housework [as Justin]. . . . Justin is far more motivated to get it done. . . . I like cleaning, I like vacuuming, I like sweeping . . . but I hate doing dishes and I don't like doing laundry . . . so he does the dishes [and the laundry] . . . and he likes cooking."

Not all of the husbands are as adept at housework as the wives, but they still pitch in. According to Alise Jansens, Eduards "never learned how to do laundry." Still, he figures out a way to contribute when he's not at work by cooking on weekends, changing diapers and helping outside. Coming from a more traditional culture, Alise allows that "we do have our set roles," but he still participates.

"I get scolded for being lazy," admits Erik Knutzen. "I do most of the vegetable gardening; Kelly does a lot of the cleaning. I do most of the cooking, actually." At this point, Kelly chimes in the conversation, demonstrating through their comic squabble that not only are the duties shared, but the power is shared as well:

> Kelly: *If I lived by myself I would be eating, like, an apple and a cracker. . . . Erik has to have three giant meals a day or he withers away and expires . . . so I'm making him cook. If he wants to eat that much, he can cook. He claims to not know how to clean house.*
> Erik: *Yeah. When it comes down to it, we actually split the household duties I think pretty much, although there's some argument about that.*
> Kelly: *Well, it's like, he gets the more fun household duties. That, I think, is what we argue about. I get the scut work.*
> Erik: *I do a lot of the construction work, such as there is.*
> Kelly: *Erik wasn't raised to clean house; he was raised with, like, a fifties mom, you know? And men just didn't clean house.*
> Erik: *Right!*
> Kelly: *And though he's very clever about learning how to do all sorts of things, he can't learn how to mop a floor. It's kind of beyond him, for some reason.*

Without a doubt, a healthy spat is as much a part of a vibrant marriage as the periods of harmony.

Friends

The Greek philosopher Epicurus taught that "Of all things that wisdom provides for living one's entire life in happiness, the greatest by far is the possession of friendship." Friendships played a major role in the happiness that Radical Homemakers expressed with their lives. They were especially critical for those homemakers who were without extended family. As Rebecca James points out, in this lifestyle "it's crucial . . . to have either 'family of choice' or 'family of origin' somewhere around you."

As soon as Maryann Heslier moved to her new community, she promptly began reaching out to find a network of friends. "In college, I realized how good a really good girlfriend could be, by letting me learn things, and learning things together." Maryann knew very little about food and homemaking when she moved out of her parents' house; then, her mom and dad died when she was a young adult. She thus attributes the homemaking skills she has acquired to the friends she has made in her life. Prior to college, Maryann had very little interest in food or health. Her friends helped change that. "When I went to college, I saw the people who would live in the more homey dorms and would make their own food — the real hippies. And it was great, and so I loved food then. Then, food was interesting and creative." After graduation, Maryann had her first apartment "and no money," and through her interest in kayaking, befriended some women who were about ten years older, all of whom loved to cook. "I was on my own for the first time in my life and had to cook for myself," she says. "I just didn't have money to do processed food." These women invited her into their homes, where they spent a lot of time cooking and sharing meals together.

Carol Rydell and Amanda Shaw regard their friendship as a source of nourishment, both bodily and spiritually. Carol and Amanda initially met after Amanda's children had left home and she was going through a divorce and starting life on her own. The two women shared a common interest in nutritional research and nutrient-dense local foods, such as raw milk, grass-fed meats and organic vegetables. Carol had always grown much of her and her husband's food in her suburban backyard, and Amanda was growing her vegetables on a rented city plot. When Carol's husband passed away suddenly, she observed that Amanda was having a difficult time keeping up with her rented plot, and she invited her to unite forces in her own backyard. Now, Amanda visits Carol once a week; Carol prepares a meal while Amanda weeds, and then they share a meal together. "It's fun for me to have someone eat with me and share foods, since I've got lots of stuff in the garden," says Carol. Looking at the food before them on their dining table and at Carol's fruit trees growing right outside the window, Amanda remarks:

> She feeds my soul. The garden and this place feed the soul. I guess that's what I've learned, is that we think we're learning about nutrition, and we think we're focusing on our nutrition, but it's really about feeding our souls. When your soul is fed, you're well.

Sitting with them both over lunch, I witness a delightful energy that flows between them, a constant stream of give and take — offers and acceptance of favors, food, friendship. As two women who have had to learn to make it on their own after the departure of husbands and children, they have discovered that a willingness to share is key to their emotional and physical survival. But, remarks Amanda, "the sharing isn't about things, so much as it is about sharing who we are, and our essence, and sharing those intangibles in life." As an afterthought she adds, "It's not the *giving*, you know, like 'I've got to go out and buy this gift.' It's just giving *yourself*, sharing a meal, preparing food together and conversing."

When Sylvia Tanner learned she was pregnant after she had split up with her husband, she had no extended family to fall back on; her friends became a life support system. "I've built my own family out of friends," says Sylvia. She and her friends have built her home, taken care of each other's children, served as one another's therapists, made plans to retire together and even attended one's deathbed. She has deep emotional connections with these people, even friends from high school, and they sustain her both emotionally and economically. "I think you can either be dependent on having all sorts of money to pay people, or you can do stuff other ways," she remarks, as she points out some large fish tanks on her property that belong to a friend who helped her build her house and who is also a licensed trout propagator. "They [the tanks] take the runoff from my springs," she explains. Sylvia feeds the fish daily, watches over the nozzles on the tanks and calls her friend whenever there is a problem. She charges him nothing. "He helps me with stuff," she explains, "like my solar system when I added new panels, or installing these twelve-volt refrigerators. . . . He came over yesterday and helped me rip some pieces of wood I needed with his table saw." As Sylvia demonstrates, friends are more than simply people you meet for beers. Friendships are relationships truly worthy of her life energy. Yet, she adds, this is not a skill she always possessed. She had to learn it:

> A friend of mine has said to me, "You must've grown up in a
> family where everybody was really social and had friends over
> all the time," and [it was] totally the opposite! I didn't grow up
> like that at all. [These are] skills that I've had to learn and I'm
> still trying to learn. I think it's a life-long process.

Community

Community is every bit as powerful as friendships and family in keeping the Radical Homemaking lifestyle viable. Many lessons on this front can be gleaned from the countless small farm communities that once dotted our national landscape, where neighbors collaborated to plant and put up the harvest, then watched their way of life fall apart as, one by one, farmers either replaced people-power with isolating and costly machinery or went out of business all together.

Many community-supportive practices live on in the Old Order Amish in Pennsylvania. Bill McKibben notes that one study found them to have a depression rate that was one-tenth that of their "English" neighbors. "It's not that the Amish are trouble free," remarks

McKibben, "they have drug abuse, wife beating, and social tension, just like every community on earth. But that's the point — they have a community, something more than the individual self to fall back on, to cushion the blows that life throws."[17]

As a pastor's daughter with alternative views, Maryann Heslier wasn't sure if her family would find a church community with the right chemistry for them when they were new in town. "But I also knew what I loved about the church [while] growing up was community," says Maryann, "and I wanted that for my children." Though they weren't Episcopalian, there happened to be an Episcopal church around the corner from them and they visited there. They found it a wonderful entrée into their community:

> I met this one farmer there, some other families there, and
> the other thing is, they're just . . . kid-friendly. Kids can do
> basically anything during the service. So that's been huge . . .
> and the community of women at the church . . . we knit, we
> cook, we do things for the community . . . but if anything goes
> wrong, or anyone is having a baby or anything like that, the
> word is out and there's food, and people are taken care of, and
> you don't have to worry about anything.

Maryann is adamant that community-building is an essential skill for a Radical Homemaker. "Evolutionarily, it's the only way our species has survived," she argues:

> If you can call them "choices" way back when, we decided that
> being able to get less air in was worth it to be able to make
> more vocal distinctions so that we could communicate more
> complexly with our own species. . . . So we can't run as fast and
> things like that, but it was a good bargain.

Maryann's quality of life relies on her community, especially, she says, since she and her husband have no extended family in the area. She feels the community is essential for her family's health. "My marriage isn't taxed as much. . . . [There are] other people I can ask for things, whether its emotional support or anything else."

Sylvia Tanner's country road seems to be the potluck capital of the county. "We have an e-mail list and we just invite everybody, and everybody shows up with really good food, and the kids run around and play, and everybody eats and we hang out, and we talk. . . . We've had baby shower potlucks, potluck-potlucks, and for-whatever-reason potlucks." In her rural community, Sylvia says it is important for her neighbors to feel connected. "People have really been there for each other," she observes. "We've had some great things, like marriages and babies and things like that, and we've had some really sad things happen, or scary things":

> One of my neighbors, her son was born with a defective artery . . . and had to be flown to Boston. . . . Everybody just pitched in with their older kid and the house and everything, and with food when they got back. When I went to pick up my dishes, there was this whole table full of dishes waiting for people to pick up.

> My neighbors up the hill . . . she had a really bad, bad delivery. . . . She was laid up in bed for about a month and was a total mess, and . . . a bunch of us were just bringing food up and shoveling her walks and just doing whatever had to happen.

Sylvia feels that nurturing relationships within our communities is a skill that we need to reclaim. "I think we've gotten really bad at it," she notes. But, she points out, "one of the things that is really important is to realize that everyone isn't going to be your best friend, but you have to be able to get along with them." She continues:

> You're still coming up against human nature and all of the issues that humans have in terms of getting along, so I think people have to make a real protracted effort and sometimes, I think

people don't want to do that . . . They just think it's too difficult; they'd rather just buy their own lawnmower or their own
pickup truck or their own this or their own that . . . rather than
deal with co-owning . . . or sharing it, or asking to borrow it. . . .
People are worried about the interdependence, they're worried
about asking people for things . . . It's something we have to
learn how to do again, how to be okay with doing it — asking,
sharing, asking and receiving, taking good care of things.

Of course, not everyone in a community or neighborhood is an
angel. "Occasionally, you get to know people and you realize where
there are issues," Sylvia admits, and "you have to set up boundaries."
Still, while establishing limits may be necessary, passing judgments
is not. "I think you really have to take people as they are," says Sylvia,
"and you hope that they'll take you as you are. Because I'm a very
imperfect being, and so I can't really expect everybody else to be perfect. . . . Lord knows, I have my faults!"

While learning to grow food in a desert city, Erik Knutzen and
Kelly Coyne were definitely presented with many challenges. In
order to succeed, argues Kelly, "you need community. The best way to
do any of this is to have someone show you how to do it." Reflecting
on their experience, she says:

I think a lot of these skills are not easily taught by books,
and when you're a person who's not been raised doing any of
these things, whether it's preserving or growing or dealing
with small stock, it's all very mysterious. You spend a lot of
your time going, "Well, what is this?" Like, "What's this spot
on the plant, why is my chicken doing that?" . . . and you can
go on the Internet and post them . . . and hope for people to
help you. . . . You could spend ages looking through books to
answer these questions, trying to find, like, what's blighting
your cucumbers. But if you know someone else, you can just
say "What's this?" And they go, "Oh, yeah. That's the beetle,"

and they just tell you. It's so much simpler. You need people
around you to support you.

Support also comes in the form of a community's cultural tolerance. Erik Knutzen appreciates the immigrant communities that can
be found across Los Angeles. "Immigrants coming here bring traditional ways of keeping households and growing foods and things like
that," he explains. "In this neighborhood, there are a lot of Filipino
people. Filipino people grow food in their yard; it's just something
you do. It's also a way of bringing flavor and food from the homeland
here that you can't get in the supermarket." The cultural acceptance
of growing one's own food in an urban setting is very helpful for this
couple. It means that Erik and Kelly can keep a small flock of laying hens behind their bungalow without worrying that the neighbors
will be disturbed whenever the hens cackle.

Nance Klehm, who lives and grows much of her food in a
Chicago ghetto, extols the virtue of community networks because
it enables her to work "pretty regularly with a non-cash economy
through shared resources":

> I'm not a very good typist, so someone comes in and she'll
> work for $30, plus something. . . . Like, I'll give her fifteen
> pounds of pears. . . . This is her way of getting better food.
> . . . She'll say, " Oh, I have some time here. I'll give you some
> time." And she'll give me the time, and then I pay her with . . .
> garlic . . . something from my freezer, my refrigerator, cheese,
> yogurt. . . . I always have too much food, so I might as well use
> it. That's how things work.

Nance trades food and yard and garden consultations for countless things — plumbing, electrical work, carpentry. "I also have this
thing called 'neighborhood orchard,'" she explains:

> I've gone to people I have a relationships with in my neighbor-
> hood and said, "How about we do some planting in your back-

yard, and I'll come in and I'll turn the soil and bring in some compost. What would you like to see growing?" So I plant a bunch, they can't possibly eat it all, and then, because there's such an abundance, I share what they can't use.

Community remains important to the Radical Homemakers, whether they live in a suburb, on a rural dirt road, or in the heart of a city. It is not necessarily something that exists from the get-go. In many instances, they have worked to build it. It is formed through nurturing egalitarian, mutually beneficial relationships. When human beings are able to care for each other and be attentive to one another's needs, it is amazing how readily the sense of abundance swells with each concentricity of love and generosity.

WORKING WITH THE LIFE-SERVING ECONOMY

When Americans worry about impoverishment, we tend to focus on whether we have enough money rather than on whether we will be warm, dry, well-fed, healthy, loved and happy. That is because we are accustomed to functioning within the extractive economy, whereby all the basic necessities of life are presumed to be exchanged for money. The problem with this system, of course, is that only those people with money are able to have their fundamental needs met. In a life-serving economy, poverty and wealth are not merely defined by cash assets, but rather by ensuring its members equal ability to acquire basic needs and attain a level of comfort and satisfaction that is not strictly reliant on financial income. Inescapably, money still plays a role but, because — in Stormy McGovern's words — "you can't eat it," it takes a secondary position. In the extractive economy, money has become more than a mere token of exchange and simple commerce; somehow, it has become a yardstick by which we measure each person's personal value and, hence, our own self-worth. In a life-serving economy, money is simply a tool to draw upon when another direct exchange for something of actual value cannot be worked out.

Writing back in the late eighties, Wendell Berry examined the remnants of the old subsistence economy that used to exist in his rural Kentucky.[18] While they were by no means perfect, he argues that these locally based subsistence economies were a source of "local strength and independence." Back when those communities were still alive, incomes were very low — he estimates about $1,000 per year. But the local subsistence economy was "elaborate and strong." People were able to grow, harvest and store most of their food, cooperate with each other to complete tasks, support one another socially, and provide their own entertainment. As their local economy was supplanted by a consumer economy, the number of dollars entering each home may have increased, but the net change in the community households was what Berry calls "a helpless dependence on distant markets, on transported manufactured goods, on cash, and on credit." While the original subsistence economies may have been cash-poor, Berry explains, they were still rich in economic assets. However, because these assets could not easily be measured in dollar equivalence, their value was considered intangible. Berry lists these assets as "culture borne knowledge; attitudes and skills; family and community coherence; family and community labor; and cultural or religious principles, such as respect for gifts (natural or divine), humility, fidelity, charity, and neighborliness." These economies were powered by sunshine and water, the renewable resources present to all people, rather than by the extraction of nonrenewable resources.

Certainly, a complete reversal to a subsistence economy is not feasible or even completely desirable at this point in time. But the essential work of Radical Homemakers is to build a bridge that crosses us from the dominion of an extractive economy, which primarily serves its own perpetuation, to a life-serving economy, where commerce, regardless of its form, directly fulfills a material human need rather than generating wealth for its own sake.

But in order to successfully leave the extractive economy behind, Radical Homemakers have had to learn to work within a nascent life-serving economy. Virtually every one of the homemakers interviewed was intimately familiar with what is perhaps the best book written on the subject of evaluating and reshaping our strangling relationship with money, *Your Money or Your Life* by Vicki Robin and Joe Dominguez. First published in 1992 (and recently updated), its concepts are as salient today as they were eighteen years ago, and it is a "must-read" for anyone pursuing the Radical Homemaker path.

The simplest and most sensible start for Radical Homemakers departing the extractive economy and building the life-serving economy were the elemental practices of thrift, frugality and debt avoidance. Beyond basic economizing, other tactics for minimizing reliance on the extractive economy range from pragmatism to philosophic inquiry; some are predictable, others are serendipitous. But a pattern of tactical behaviors does emerge. The defining principles are: including everyone in the economic picture; capitalizing on available resources; minimizing waste; becoming net producers of goods rather than net consumers; bartering; spending money where it matters most; and understanding the concept of "enough."

Include Everyone in the Economic Picture

In the course of her interview, Stormy McGovern remarked, "My network of friends and family, and the food we help each other create and eat . . . that is my social security. My social security isn't some number or some fund or some tax money that's put away, that I think I might or might not see some day." By including her friends and family as part of her economic picture, she hits on a very important point. When venturing forth in a life-serving economy, everyone, even children, must be included — not simply the people who bring in the cold hard cash.

Looking at her own family farm, Deirdre Ianelli doesn't worry too much about the amount of savings she and her husband have squirreled away for retirement. While she feels saving is important, she believes cultivating the ability to live within her resource base on the family farm is more important. Even in the absence of a pension fund, "we can at least support ourselves and teach our children how to support themselves too, without money," she says. Teaching her children how to function in the new economy is a way of making sure that everyone in the family can thrive together. Anna Reynolds encouraged her children to participate in a life-serving economy from the time they were small children by cultivating skills that could help supplant their need for cash. Feeling that it was very important for them to learn how to fix things, she would go to her local thrift store, find items like old toasters, remove the cords, then urge them to take them apart and explore how they worked. Today, her sons are able to keep the family with a functioning vehicle at all times, have a local reputation for being able to keep the neighbors' farm equipment in working order and, as we've already seen, they're able to swap a bag of homegrown hamburger for an old run-down car, which they convert into a working vehicle.

Typically, the family's economic viability is a team effort. David and Janice Peterson trust their son so implicitly that they have included his name on all their bank accounts and assets. "If something were to happen to us," explains David, "then, that just makes anything, any transfer [easier]. He'll be able to take it over right away. . . . He takes that very seriously, and he really appreciates that." In the Simmons family, several branches of the extended family all work together on the same ranch. Each nuclear family unit supports itself from a different ranch-based enterprise. "We share a lot of the same land base," explains Holly, "so there's work. We orchestrate that." To do this, the family uses a practice called Holistic Management, which incorporates social and ecological analyses into their management decision-making processes. In this practice, "*Everybody* comes to the table," says Holly, "*not* just the papas — the kids, the moms, *everybody* is making decisions together, and it's huge." While the big extended family meetings happen four times per year, Holly and John meet with their three sons weekly. "Somebody knows they can always come if they are unhappy, or if they want to present a great idea," and they spend time talking about their goals, spiritual and physical, and their quality-of-life issues. In this way the next generation is fully aware of the thoughts and plans of the elders, and vice-versa. There are no surprises, and everyone is able to work together to manage the resource base.

Capitalize on Available Resources

"Moose meat is such a commodity, everybody is going to run for the roadkill," explains Alise Jansens without a hint of irony. Many of her Alaskan neighbors do not trust the grocery store food. Thus, whatever meat that can be foraged from the wild or, in this case, roadside — moose, caribou, fish, or just about anything that could be shot or snagged with a pole or net — are the most popular items on the family dinner menu. In her county alone, 350 moose are killed on the road each year. Fearing that some drivers were intentionally aiming for the animals in an effort to secure some freezer meat, the State of Alaska established the Moose Kill List, a roster of nonprofit organizations that send representatives to a kill site at any hour, field-dress the carcass, and distribute the meat among their low-income members at the top of the rotating list. The driver that hits a moose on the road cannot legally claim the animal. Seeing an opportunity for their families, Alise's local Mom's Club promptly enrolled in the program. As a result, her family is able to put a quarter of a moose in its freezer each year. Additionally, many children also learn firsthand the practical skill of field dressing and butchering an animal.

Many of the homemakers in the study confessed guilty feelings of having some sort of "unfair" advantage that enabled their transition to this lifestyle. The Honeywells, the Simmons and the Ianellis all had extended families with significant land resources. The Jansens get their free meat from the Moose Kill List, and their family helped them make the downpayment on their home. Penelope and John Sloan received an early inheritance from his parents. Bettina and Justin Winston have her parents around to help them. Maryann Heslier's husband is a salaried college professor. David Peterson and Michael Mills have wives with well-paid jobs. Nance Klehm's parents have picked up her health insurance tab. Several of the parents in the study had children enrolled in government-subsidized health-care programs.

Their "guilt" is indicative of a slippery double standard in our culture: those who garner exorbitant salaries by leveraging and manipulating all sorts of resources in the marketplace (including government funds and other people's money) are regarded as "successful," while those who use the very same skills — entrepreneurialism, acumen, opportunism, and efficiency — to live without profiteering are regarded as "ne'er-do-wells," "slackers," or "mooches." Further, those who achieve their wealth and success "independently" through the conventions of the extractive economy are ultimately reliant upon someone's labors or have exploited some other resource. By contrast, the Jansens' coup from the Moose Kill List reduces food waste and provides their family with nourishing, ecologically sound food. Penelope and John Sloan's opportunity to live humbly on the interest earnings from the certificates of deposit they bought with their inheritance is an opportunity to detach from direct involvement with the extractive economy. The loan from Alise and Eduards Jansens' extended family helped protect them from excessive bank debt. Choosing to live on one salary enables Maryann Heslier to devote her efforts to cultivating the life-serving economy. Making careful use of family resources or government programs is not a shameful sign of undo privilege or leeching off the taxpayers; it is a prudent effort to stretch resources farther, tighten family and local ties, build a culture of interdependence, and reduce reliance on the extractive economy.

Minimize Waste

"They haven't gotten any new toys in forever," says Rebecca James as she looks around her home, which is chock-full of games, projects and even a children's library — everything her kids could need for a fun-filled home education and the pursuit of personal interests. Every parent interviewed in this study was keenly aware of the waste surrounding children's toys and actively sought to eliminate it. The philosophy of aggressively reducing waste carried over to every aspect of the homemakers' lives. To cut food waste, Penelope Sloan donates surplus garden produce to a local food bank. Michael Mills salvaged discarded slate roofing and used it to veneer his chimney. Julie and David Hewitt reclaimed discarded tables and a bed from their local dump to furnish their home. Rebecca James and Eve Honeywell scour garage sales for clothes, appliances and gifts. Eve Honeywell,

Deirdre Ianelli and Maryann Heslier all take advantage of hand-me-down clothes and cloth diapers. An avid reader, Rebecca James has found that her local library doesn't always have what she needs, so she makes use of online free book trading sites such as *bookmooch* or *paperbackswap*. Anna Reynolds and her sons carpool to reduce trips to town. To ameliorate potential frustrations, they keep a bag of used books from the Salvation Army in the car; whoever needs to wait for someone always has something to read. Each little trick does far more than save someone a little bit of cash — it stretches existing resources farther, tightens local networks, reduces the need for more consumer products, and cuts down on landfill pressure. Every reused item, every bit of waste eliminated, is a step toward a life-serving economy.

Transition from Net Consumers to Net Producers

When Betty Friedan levied her critique against American housewives in the 1960s, she argued that they no longer performed any valuable functions in the home except to feed money into the consumer marketplace. There was no longer a need for homemakers to garden, preserve food, bake bread, educate the young or help care for the sick or aging. In Friedan's opinion, any woman who chose to do these things was trying to solve her deeper problems of seeking a meaningful life through mere superficial actions. She argued that modern culture could perform these tasks more efficiently, making any homemaker's choice to do them simply an exercise in futility.[19] The American household was no longer a unit of production. It had become a unit of consumption.

What we understand today that we failed to grasp back in the 1960s was how these "improvements" that supplanted the homemaker have failed us. We didn't anticipate the ecological and health problems associated with factory-produced and highly processed foods. We didn't recognize that our schools and televisions and consumer culture were separating generations of children from any sense or understanding of their relationship to the earth. We hadn't predicted how our health insurance industry would bankrupt us, while at the same time miserably fail to equitably and effectively deliver support in times of need. The experiment of converting the American household from producers to consumers has been largely a disaster.

What's worse, in the process our culture has nearly lost its production traditions. Without a supermarket, fast-food joint, gas station, prescription drugs, shopping malls and television, many Americans would be at a loss for how to meet their basic needs and live a pleasurable life. "If it is true that folk wisdom is our basic wealth, the chief insurance of a culture's worth," writes William Coperthwaite, "then we are nearly bankrupt."[20] Traditional knowledge to care for the sick, nourish our families, produce our own food, and entertain ourselves has nearly disappeared from our culture, with all of it being transferred to "experts" — factory farms, corporate health care, chain restaurants, media conglomerates — who are more interested in maximizing a profit than in conserving or replenishing our living systems. The American citizenry has been convinced that out-sourcing our craft traditions will somehow profit the general public.

Radical Homemakers are aware of the misplaced priority on increasing the bottom line. Quite often their incomes are significantly below the norm. But that is because they have learned that there are two ways to make a living. In one method, the convention of our culture, substantial money is earned and then spent on purchasing life's necessities. In the other method, significantly less money is earned, and basic necessities are produced or otherwise procured. Packages from the mall, plastic-wrapped food, designer labels and television sets are seldom seen inside these households. Rather, they are filled with books, simmering pots, some dirty dishes, musical instruments, seedlings, wood shavings, maybe some hammers or drills, sewing machines, knitting baskets, canned peaches and tomato sauce, jars of sauerkraut, freezers with hunted or locally raised meat, and potted herbs. Outside the door there are no multiple new cars or manicured lawns. Whether in the country or the city, one is likely to find a garden plot or potted tomatoes, fruit trees, bicycles, probably a used car, shovels, spades, compost bins, chickens, maybe a wandering goat or some other livestock, and laundry blowing in the breeze. These people are producing their life, not buying it.

"If you're creating more, you're not spending it," explains Julie Hewitt. "When we first got chickens and then we put in the garden, we realized we had all this food and we didn't need to go to the store anymore." The act of producing is creative and joyful. So much enjoyment can be had that there is no "time to kill" at a shopping mall or sitting in front of the TV. Thus, not only are they lowering their cost of living through producing, but they are also reducing their urge to spend on distractions, instead filling their lives with meaningful and pleasurable activity. These people do not see the performance of their own bread-labor (labor for basic needs) as a hardship. Sylvia Tanner defines her quality of life as "a mix of being able to do work that I really enjoy and that I find to be important or needed, or useful, or somehow fulfilling." The work of Radical Homemakers is, almost inadvertently, rich with meaning and purpose. As producers, they reduce their need for money from an extractive economy and they are building America's bridge to a new, life-serving economy. As Emerson wrote:

> I think it plain that this voice of communities and ages, "Give us wealth, and the good house-hold shall exist," is vicious, and leaves the whole difficulty untouched. It is better, certainly, in this form: "Give us your labor, and the house-hold begins." I see not how serious labor, the labor of all and every day, is to be avoided.[21]

Barter

Alise and Eduards Jansens pay nothing for their meat in Alaska. As we learned already, they freeze one-quarter of a moose each year through her Mom's Club's participation in the moose kill program. The State of Alaska issues subsistence permits to residents, who are able to dip-net a limited amount of fish each year. Last year the

Jansens caught forty pounds of red salmon and thirty pounds of halibut. A lot of it went into their freezer. The rest of it was traded with hunters for caribou, more moose, and homemade sausages.

"I trade eggs for a lot of things," says Rebecca James. "If I have a surplus of vegetables, I'll trade somebody for something that they have a surplus of." Rebecca's spare eggs and produce have earned her family honey and other food, kids' clothes, shoes, and child care. Stormy McGovern relishes the barter system and feels it allows for the genuine value of an item to be truly honored in an exchange:

> It puts a new value on things. There's not this set monetary
> value. . . . It's like, what kind of energy did you put into this?
> . . . You're able to learn about the food or the thing or whatever. I mean, sometimes it's [straightforward] like, "Oh . . .
> I'll take this . . . and we'll trade this," and it's no big deal. But,
> sometimes it's like, "This is the golden raspberry preserve that
> I made in Alaska, and it's really special," and you know that
> you are going to crack that, and you're going to share the story
> with whoever eats it with you. . . . It brings the culture back,
> and we're able to be human again . . . [instead of] just absent-
> mindedly picking something out of an aisle of a fluorescent-lit
> store that came from god-knows-where. . . . That history — I
> like knowing that. It's exciting.

Some communities have even institutionalized their local bartering. In Julie and David Hewitt's town, a group of people set up "The Trading Post," a ramshackle shelter just outside the town's waste transfer station, where people can leave their unwanted furniture, appliances, clothing, toys, tools, etc. A ramble through "the Post" for the newcomer could take hours. The first thing one notices, however, is that nothing has a price tag. If someone has some money, they pay whatever they feel the object is worth to them. If they have no money, they simply take it. If they have unwanted serviceable items of their own, they simply exchange them. Julie keeps her unwanted stuff in the back of her car. If she needs something, she goes to The Trading

Post first to see if they have it, then gives them whatever she happens to have in the back of her car.

In Kelly Robideau's suburban neighborhood, one of the neighbors organized a neighborhood food chain. Every two weeks throughout the summer, everyone on the street meets at the local park and trades surplus homegrown produce. Kelly's backyard growing space is perhaps ten feet by twenty feet, including the trees. She is an avid gardener, but is very limited in how much she can produce. Thus, she exchanges her surplus tomatoes, basil, peaches and pluots for the rest of the fruit and vegetables she needs for her family.

The old idiom, "One man's trash is another man's treasure," still holds true, making the barter system a golden opportunity to be effortlessly generous, and enabling everyone ample opportunities to satisfy their needs while directly recognizing that their unique contributions and skills have value to someone else in their community. It is more than simply a way to save money and reduce waste; it builds relationships, celebrates the serendipity of finding just the thing you need without paying into the extractive economy, and generates a new sense of worth.

Spend Money Where It Matters Most

"I try to support the businesses that I like here," says Stormy McGovern. Recognizing that she is not just purchasing an item, but also helping sustain her local economy, she adds, "I want to spend money on someone who I want to support." No family is an entirely self-sufficient island, nor should it be. Some people manage to produce all of their fundamental needs and enjoy good health, but to repudiate interrelations with family, friends and community throughout life is not only sad and lonely, but downright impossible. Radical Homemakers work to become *net* producers, but that does not mean that they produce everything that they need in life. Barter does not always work either; sometimes cold hard cash is the only answer. When it is exchanged, Radical Homemakers do everything in their power to make sure it creates an effect toward what they believe in. The Honeywells grow their own vegetables and beef, but they buy their chickens, raw milk and cheese from other local farmers. Maryann Heslier considers financial know-how more than just about budgeting. It is about understanding the social and political consequences behind every dollar spent. To her, that means staying out of Wal-Mart and other absentee-owned corporate chains as much as possible, and instead buying her goods from locally owned shops and local farmers. Further, it means looking at each product she considers spending her money on, and assessing the social, economic and ecological impact of her purchasing decision.

"Everything we do is a vote," says Justin Winston. "Everything you do is political." So every decision to spend money requires an evaluation of how most ethically to use it. While their income may be lower than the national average, Radical Homemakers do not see that as a rationalization for paying the lowest price on their purchases. Typically, low prices are almost always a clue that some other cost along the production line has been externalized — either a worker was not fairly compensated, water was polluted, or resources were unsustainably extracted and consumed. Knowing this, Amanda Shaw sees her dollars as an extension of her ecological impact. "I want to leave no footprints when I go," she declares. "I share with the world who I am, and it will sustain me on a level that's not riding off of someone else's back." These people endeavor to have every dollar they spend go toward rebuilding the life-serving economy. While it is true that they still need to put gas in their cars or sometimes can find no option but to purchase a product unscrupulously manufactured in China, the majority of their dollars are deliberately spent in a way that recognizes the power of the life-serving economy and the need to construct it. When that value is at stake, there's no quibbling over prices.

Understand "Enough"

Thoreau wrote that "my greatest skill has been to want but little."[22] That sentiment is at the heart of mastering Radical Homemaking. One of the most important determinations a Radical Homemaking family can make in their lives is identifying the point at which they have *enough*. We are forever cajoled by our culture to pursue more — a higher income, bigger houses, better cars, more stuff. But all that comes at a cost even beyond the monetary price and impact on our environment. To acquire more, we must surrender more of our life energy to earn the means to buy it or maintain it. In 1970, Swedish economist Staffan Linder predicted that we would soon become a "harried leisure class." His theory was that, "as the volume of consumption goods increases, requirements for the care and main-tenance of these goods also tends to increase, we get bigger houses to clean, a car to wash, a boat to put up for the winter, a television set to repair, and have to make more decisions on spending."[23] Thus, exces-sive aspirations are also very costly in terms of the time and effort invested in acquiring, maintaining or, more likely, *replacing* them. Thoreau pointed out that, "the cost of a thing is the amount of what I will call life which is required to be exchanged for it, immediately or in the long run." With this as a gauge, Radical Homemakers are reawakening the credo that emerged with the burgeoning eco-con-sciousness of the 1970s — less is more.

"Money means very little to me. I could lose $200 or I could find $200, and it's like 'Oh! Look what I found! Look what I lost!'. . . It's just numbers and money," says Sarah Mills. Despite her nonchalant regard for dollars, Sarah and Michael never want for anything. Sarah says it is simply because, "I don't *need* a lot." Michael echoes her point:

> If there's a lesson that people need to learn, it's that you don't
> need all that crap that they're trying to sell you. The basic
> things you need are really simple, and people have been taking
> care of their domestic lives for hundreds of thousands of years
> without those things [that we now consider necessary].

The concept of "enough" is easily applied to our home size (it takes too much effort to clean a bigger house anyhow) or our car choice (why pay a lot of money for something that will rust, rot or depreciate?) However, it is not as easy, though it is equally important, to determine how much "enough" is when considering earnings. In part, this is because we have firmly attached our sense of security to earnings. Moreover, we tend to believe that earning more money or achieving a certain status or prestige, will make us happier than it truly will. This is because of a phenomenon that social psychologists Ed Diener and Shigehiro Oishi call adaptation. "We often mispredict what will make us happy and unhappy," say Diener and Oishi. "We believe that if we become wealthy we will be happier than we will in fact be, and we believe that if we do not obtain tenure we will be more miserable than we will in fact be."[24] Radical Homemakers who have identified the "enough" point in their lives are able to live more simply, reduce their needs, and then have to work less in order to afford them.

The magical trick about "enough" is that it is not discovered by deciding what you must do *without* — that can feel like a form of deprivation. Rather, it is perpetuated more by feeling satisfied and fulfilled with what you have and jettisoning the burden of the excesses. Julie Hewitt genuinely relishes her daily homemaking lifestyle, to the point that, when she goes to a more populated area with its pulse for consumption, what she sees surprises and repels her. When she was a corporate employee, Julie says she was a habitual shopper. Now she finds she has no such compulsion and is disparaging when she sees mainstream consumer messages telling her that she should want more:

> [When you go into the city] you just see how much crap there is that people are constantly exposed to — billboards, media, "buy, buy, buy," big box stores . . . and then [you realize] how little you actually need. . . . I could go into the city once a year, and I still wouldn't feel like I ever needed anything, really.

Enjoying what she has, feeling as though she has enough of what she needs — enough *true wealth* (family, friends, community, nourishing food, interests, security — make the products and overtime work-a-day world seem repugnant and utterly unnecessary. As Ben Franklin once observed, "Nothing is cheap that we do not want."

CULTIVATING AN ABILITY TO SELF-TEACH

Over the course of two years, I came to know Radical Homemakers who were providing for an enormous array of their family's domestic needs. While no single family accomplished everything on this list, I came across homemakers who would: grow, can, dehydrate, freeze and lacto-ferment vegetables and fruit; harvest and store root crops; make wine, beer and herbal teas; press juices and cider; make jams and jellies; raise livestock and harvest meat; make patés and sausages; smoke bacons or fish; keep honey bees; milk a dairy goat or cow; make cheese, yogurt, butter and kefir; make soap or other homemade nontoxic cleaning supplies; keep chickens; forage through city parks and streets, neighboring backyards and country roads for wild plants and "feral" fruits; cut their firewood; set up water recycling systems; provide their own human-powered transportation; make toys, invent games and educate their own children; make medicinal remedies; fix their houses and cars; sew, knit and mend their clothes; create art, literature, music and crafts; graft fruit trees; build their own homes; build soil through composting; and, of course, bake and cook.

Anna Reynolds, one of the older Radicals I met, had learned a number of her skills in childhood from her mother. Subsequently, Anna discovered that when her own life swept the carpet out from underneath her through a divorce, she was able to fall back on these skills to keep her family of three children still at home afloat. Most of the other homemakers had to learn these skills in adulthood. To accomplish this, the homemakers had to become autodidactic, that is, self-learners. The tips for becoming a self-learner, as they reported them, were to **think independently, embrace general knowledge, work with what they had, make mistakes, find their own teachers, and muster the courage to start from wherever they were**. In the spirit of Mark Twain's famous advice, these homemakers never let their schooling get in the way of their education.

Think Independently

Reflecting on her own experiences within the conventional education system, Julie Hewitt feels that "school doesn't necessarily teach people how to think; it just gives them information, and they have to spit it back out." Michael Mills, who despite his scholarships eventually dropped out of college, would probably agree. In order to have a viable Radical Homemaking lifestyle, he feels that critical thinking skills are the most important. "I think that the first thing you have to do . . . is question *why* are you doing what you are doing?" Asking that critical question is what led so many homemakers, prior to choosing their current path, to ask themselves: who were they truly serving by going to a job every day; who was defining their parameters for success and happiness; who benefited from their daily labors away from home; and who ultimately suffered from their family's lack of self-reliance? This same line of inquiry is what also led several homemakers to take their children out of the school system. The most common reason they offered was so that their children could learn to think independently, as we've already seen from Eve Honeywell when she describes her own hopes for her children:

> I want them to be able to make their own decisions, not follow
> the crowd, to be able to resist media. I think for them to really
> be successful in life and do what they love and do what they're
> passionate about, they have to be able to think independently
> to make those kinds of choices.

Independent thinking also means perpetually challenging your own existing knowledge and assumptions. Keenly aware of environmental issues, Rebecca James is conscientious about minimizing her family's ecological impact. Toward this end, she grows as much of her family's food as possible in her backyard and carefully chooses the foods she buys. Challenging her own existing assumptions, examining her personal experiences, and committing herself to learning more about the issues has led her to reconsider which foods might be best for her family's table and for the health of the planet:

I felt like the most ecologically sound choice was to be a vegetarian, and you know, you read Frances Moore Lappé, and
the statistics about how many pounds of corn equals a pound
of beef, and then you [read] that this state could go from producing 30 percent of its food supply to 50 percent, if they just
grazed animals on the rocky uplands that are everywhere up
here. . . . If we had a moderate meat intake, we could make
a 20 percent difference statewide . . . and to me, that's huge.
Plus, at some point, some of my hens aren't going to be laying
as well, and what do I do? Do I continue to feed them? Do I
advocate . . . for their well-being and sell them to someone else
and be glad that I didn't have to see them die, or do I take care
of it myself? At the end of the day, I think I'm a take-care-of-
it-myself kind of person.

For Julie Hewitt, thinking independently meant tuning in to her
own intuition, particularly regarding ensuring the best care for her
daughter with Down syndrome:

I was really not happy with her school, and there was always
this feeling of "It's something everybody does, why does this
not feel right? Everybody does it." . . . It was intuition, and it
was probably through her, and realizing every time [there was
an interaction with the education or medical system] something didn't feel right, whether it was what a doctor was telling
me or whatever, that I got involved in figuring out what the
answer was. . . . [Before her birth], I was not a questioning
person, especially when it came to authority, when it came to
questioning a doctor.

That intuition led Julie to start educating herself about her daughter's needs, rather than demurring to experts. Today, as a result of taking the leadership role for overseeing her care and education, Julie's
daughter is now testing twenty points above her IQ.

Embrace General Knowledge

If there was one defining feature in all of the Radical Homemakers'
homes, it was the books. They were double- and triple-stacked on
floor-to-ceiling shelves, lay open on kitchen counters and tabletops,
stacked on the floor beside the couch, mounded high on coffee tables,
and teetered on the edge of bed stands. The subjects ranged from
geopolitical analyses, social criticism, do-it-yourself plumbing or
auto repair, cookbooks galore, wildlife, weed and herb guides, fiction,
essays, poetry, prose, history, agricultural yearbooks, gardening guides,
songbooks, veterinary manuals, multiple back issues of *Mother Earth
News* and *Wise Traditions,* children's literature, educational theory,
even volumes on mathematics. Thomas Berry predicted that the 21st
century would be the time when we recovered "many of the valuable insights and skills in the art of living," and the personal libraries
of these homemakers are encouraging evidence. Erik Knutzen and
Kelly Coyne both trained to become scholars, but grew weary of the
academic culture. Happily, says Erik, through their lifestyle choice,
"we sort of found our way to be academics without being academic."
However, whereas academia drives practitioners to develop increasingly specific expertise, Radical Homemaking cultivates ever-broad-
ening knowledge and skills. It requires that we be true generalists.
"We need specialists in the world, certainly," allows Erik, "but we
also need generalists, so I realized, actually, in home economics, [we]
found a way of linking all of our varied interests."

"We both like self-teaching," adds Kelly. "We're both most happy
when we're teaching ourselves new things . . . And we don't like to
be tied down to any one subject area. . . . Our lives together have
been just sort of moving from one fascination to the next." Justin and
Bettina Winston concur. With the loss of many of the art-of-living
skills from their own community, they rely very heavily on expansive
reading to reclaim these domestic traditions. To be a Radical Homemaker, "you have to be good at doing research and learning," says
Bettina. And, she adds, "you have to like learning, because it is just
constant."

Work With What's There

While all of the Radical Homemakers were incorporating enough self-reliance into their families to live off of one income or less, not all had a solar home, five acres of land, a supportive spouse and instant utopian bliss. Amanda Shaw is divorced from her husband and lives in a mobile home park. Carol Rydell is a widow and lives in a crowded Midwestern suburb. Erik Knutzen and Kelly Coyne live in a bungalow just off of Sunset Boulevard in Los Angeles. Nance Klehm lives on the Southwest side of Chicago. Stormy McGovern owns no property of her own. Anna Reynolds and Sylvia Tanner are both single mothers. Yet all of them moved ahead as homemakers.

Carol Rydell and Nance Klehm are walking evidence that we can raise substantial amounts of our own food without becoming full-time farmers with vast stretches of land. Carol has cultivated nearly every inch of her suburban backyard for year-round production of fruit and vegetables; Nance Klehm gardens in the lot next to her Chicago house, on her roof, and even in her basement. While their small spaces may not be textbook material for farm design, they probably produce more food per acre (or, more appropriately, more food per square foot) than what a conventional farm can grow. What agribusiness uses in oil to grow food on vast acreage, Carol and Nance can accomplish with time and attention to detail.

"If you follow what the seed packet says, you're doomed," warns Kelly Coyne of gardening in Los Angeles. Most generic gardening books are written for four-season climates, she points out, not for raising food in an arid city. Rather than concluding that "going local" in their backyard was impossible, or choosing to move to the East Coast, or going to extreme measures to procure extra water, she and Erik simply learned to work with their conditions. "It's like spinning plates, because you can always have something going," explains Erik. "And there's no [seasonal] rest period," adds Kelly. Thus, it is easy to exhaust the soil. The couple learned to stop relying on the classic garden texts and turned their attention to what has worked for growing and preserving food in the Mediterranean; now they enjoy a diet rich in sun-dried tomatoes, prickly pear cactus and figs.

Michael and Sarah Mills had little gardening experience and limited financial resources when they set up their first home, but they didn't let that stand in their way. In their first winter they lived off what they were successfully able to procure and put-up — venison and home-canned green beans. With no land of her own, Stormy McGovern has set up partnerships with other landowners to grow her food and support herself. Amanda Shaw joined forces with Carol Rydell in her garden. Radical Homemakers have learned that very few how-to prescriptions will work for all situations. Becoming a self-learner is one part "how-to" and two parts "can-do." It is largely a matter of taking what you read, the advice you are given, and the experience you encounter, then adapting the information to your unique circumstances. Naturally, this leads to the next important element in becoming autodidactic.

Make Mistakes

Learning to work with whatever resources you have means that your experiments will probably not all go well the first time. When Sarah Mills first tried gardening, she read that she should grow peas on wires. Not understanding that she needed a horizontal wire fence, she dutifully uncoiled a collection of wire coat hangers, stuck them vertically into the ground, then planted a pea seed at the base of each one. Carrie Lockwell grew up in a farming community and worked in agriculture as a teenager. Even still, she didn't know when her own hay was ready to bale. "We've made a lot of mistakes, but we've always come out ahead," she says. Carrie and Chad quip that whenever everything on their small farm is not dead or broken, sometimes that's enough for them to consider it a good day.

Kelly Coyne and Erik Knutzen sun-dried their entire summer crop of tomatoes, stored them in a big jar in their pantry, and didn't notice that a pantry moth had got in. They lost their entire harvest to the larvae. Kelly recounts the story:

> It was so disgusting. It was hidden; I had put it way in the
> back of the cupboard, because we still had lots of fresh toma-

toes coming in and I [knew we wouldn't] even need those 'till
spring . . . and I pulled them out when I wanted them, and
it had liquefied and was full of maggots. . . . I almost cried,
because it's work drying all the tomatoes, sheet after sheet, day
after day, watching it. And the other thing was that they were
so delicious, they were like candy, they were like tomato candy,
and we didn't get any. The moths got them all.

Erik believes that anyone who seeks to do things for themselves
must have fortitude and a high tolerance for failure. He and Kelly
keep an urban homesteading blog, called Homegrown Evolution,
and have found that their failures are their most popular entries:

People who are not do-it-yourselfers have a low tolerance. . . .
[They] screw up once, and they're like, " See? I told you I can't
grow anything!" or "I told you I can't cook!" The real do-it-
yourselfer is like, "Huh. Why did that go wrong?" And people
love our failures; when we blog about our failures, they are the
most popular entries. And I understand that, because if you
describe a failure, it's a "how-to" in reverse. You learn so much
from failures.

Find Teachers

When I last checked, there were no classes for grown-ups to learn how
to become happy Radical Homemakers, and books don't always hold
satisfactory answers. Gleaning your community to find a "teacher" —
anyone with experience or insights to share and who can show you
what you need to learn — can often save a lot of time, resources, and
frustration. Further, "putting out feelers" into the community often
spreads the word about what you're looking for and leads people to
find you. Deirdre Ianelli's sister and mother-in-law were both experienced gardeners. Since they knew the farm soil well, Deirdre had
them come over to her house to show her the best way to set up her
first garden. Thomas Heslier found a colleague from his university

who was raising his own poultry, then helped him with processing to learn the proper way to kill and dress turkeys and chickens. Looking for ways to learn more about producing grass-fed livestock, Carrie Lockwell left her husband and son at home while she took a few road trips to different conferences to get ideas on how to manage their farmstead more effectively. She brought back books and ideas for Chad, and now the family attends conferences together whenever they can.

Recognizing the occasional need for live help, a number of seasoned Radical Homemakers around the country have begun offering classes on various subjects. Many of the participants in this study do the same. Carol Rydell and Amanda Shaw offer classes on local-centered nutrition and backyard gardening and food preservation. Nance Klehm teaches bread making, pickling, and herbal remedies. Kelly Coyne and Erik Knutzen regularly offer workshops on urban homesteading.

The important distinction for a self-learner, however, is not to rely on conferences and workshops as the only way to come by their knowledge. They do not lay unquestioning faith at the feet of their teachers, nor rely upon them to impart everything they may need to know. Likewise, they do not consider the successful completion of a workshop proof of expertise. Self-learners bring to such programs their specific questions and a willingness to experiment with ideas and concepts, to learn more from their own home laboratories, and then to adapt as necessary, rather than just blindly applying whatever the teacher says. More importantly, they don't grow addicted to external instruction. They understand that the single most important step in becoming a self-learner isn't endless continuing education. It lies in application and experimentation. Thus, the most important thing they can do is . . .

Start

Kelly Coyne and Erik Knutzen started homemaking with a pot of tomatoes on an apartment balcony. Deirdre Ianelli says, "I always wanted to cook. I just didn't know what to do." Finally, she started with "a lot of experimentation at first, and just kind of coming up with the fortitude to just throw things together." Bettina and Justin Winston moved into what they call "a K-Mart remodel from the 1970s" with industrial drop ceilings, fluorescent lighting and bad carpeting. Neither one of them had any experience with home remodeling. They simply started pulling the house apart one room at a time. They took a few photos to remember the way it was, then never looked back.

There are times in life to be thoughtful and cautious. Then there are times when the only way to learn is to jump in and "go for it," take the mistakes as lessons, call for help when you need it, look in books when you can. Radical Homemaking is energy in motion — the active transfer of our culture away from the extractive economy to the life-serving economy, the active transition from a work-centered life to a home and ecologically-centered one. Every minute spent sitting, theorizing and pondering without embarking on the lifestyle, no matter how simple the initial steps may be, is more time given to maintaining the status quo of the extractive economy and employee-employer power structure. If you start by simply cooking a wholesome dinner for your family, then you've *started*. Gaining experience and skills is far easier once you've begun gaining momentum and building experiences to learn from.

Sometimes we just need a push to go a bit further. Maryann Heslier was comfortable cooking with local foods, but was "cutting herself some slack" about her Radical Homemaking efforts because she didn't have a farming background or extended family who could offer to teach her any traditional skills. Then she read Barbara Kingsolver's *Animal, Vegetable, Miracle*, went out that same fall and bought potatoes and apples in bulk from local farmers, and set up her fieldstone basement as a root cellar. "You don't have to have the know-how or the background," she now realizes. "You can come to these things."

SETTING REALISTIC EXPECTATIONS AND LIMITS

When many of us picture homes with a full-time Radical Home-maker, we may envision a lush garden devoid of weeds, accented by sunflowers. Maybe some precociously articulate and well-mannered children are gathered around a long harvest table, helping each other study their lessons while a few perfectly made toys wait neatly along a shelf or window sill. Chickens wander peacefully outside, keeping the lawn free of bugs. The house is kept secure and well-repaired by competent hands, there is something delicious simmering on the stove, the dishes are always washed, and there is *always* time to sit with a mug of tea, study the pristine landscape, and ponder the good life. If such an image inspires you to move forward, wonderful. There might occasionally be blocks of time (never more than about five minutes) where a Radical Homemaker life can look like this. The remainder of the day is a flow of contained chaos where we endeavor to play a deeper and more mercurial role in our family ecosystem. When working with an ecosystem (as opposed to an office system), the work is never done. Life is always going on. Weeds grow, children express their true nature, the pump for the solar hot water burns out, windows stop closing correctly, chickens wander in the road or poop on your porch furniture, and the best toys have a quirky trait of pre-ferring floors and kitchen tables to shelves or window sills.

While the work of homemaking (Radical or otherwise) is never done, a key to keeping pace with the lifestyle is to limit the amount of time spent doing it. As long as all people and critters are fed and safe, all other work will always be there tomorrow. When Wendell Berry explored the life of an old Appalachian community with a sub-sistence economy, he noted that "their work was in limited quantities; they did not work at night or away from home."[25] Our nation's cultural veneration for laboring has many of us convinced that we must be toiling from the time we rise until the moment we fall into bed. And if we are not collecting a paycheck for our efforts, often a sense of guilt causes us to log even more hours at our unpaid jobs, compelled to justify our salary-less days. Such overwork, however, doesn't make for a very fun way of life and, as such, it cannot be sustained.

One thing we must accept at the outset is that we simply may not be able to accomplish as much in a day as the members of an old Appalachian subsistence economy were able to do. Most of our communities have lost the supporting infrastructure these economies once had. Extended family helped watch small children. Neighbors worked together to bring in the crops. Preserving the harvest was not a one-person production. Neighbors helped each other with repairs, swapped produce and crafts, shared equipment, and set realistic expectations about what could and couldn't be accomplished in a day. While each home was more self-reliant, no home was a one-stop shop. It was the *community* that was self-sufficient, not the home. Rebuilding that collective strength will take time, but as the family home is the foundational social unit for rebuilding these communities, we must reconstruct that first. The rest will come with time.

Yet another challenge we face is that, unlike traditional agrarian communities, most Radical Homemakers face contradicting cultural expectations daily. The roadside billboards tell us that business suits, hot new cars and communications technology are accessories of the happiest, most successful individuals. We have a long way to go before those billboards show images of contented children eating home-made soup (and spilling it down the front of their hand-me-downs) while mother and father wipe chicken poop off the porch furniture. As we negotiate for a different way of life, we must be patient and accept not only the limitation of what we can get done in a day, but also the limits of our ability (or need) to meet these expectations.

First and foremost, we cannot give undue care about appearances. It was almost comical how, with each appointment I made to visit the home of a study participant, we were greeted by clipped lawns, clean kitchens, put-away toys and made beds. After a few hours in the home, the toys once more gravitated to the floor, dishes reappeared beside the sink, and the household slowly crept back toward its state of happy entropy. Once the tape recorder was turned off and I complimented them on how beautiful and orderly the home was (such tidiness was far different from my own home), I was flooded by confessions of how hard the entire family had labored to have everything look perfect for my visit. Carrie Lockwell confessed, "I've been cleaning house for two days, because it got so messy! It was like spring cleaning [preparing for the visit]!" While we can all pull our homes together for a visitor, in general they will have dust and cob-webs, laundry may be on the floor, and dishes will clutter the kitchen. It is pointless to ruin our days over this natural fact of life. "You don't grow up in a spotless house without some sacrifices having to be made . . . that are not necessarily about what's best emotionally for the child," says Rebecca James. As Emerson noted, "a house kept to the end of display is impossible to all but a few women [and men!], and their success is dearly bought."[26]

"We all have this idea that your house is supposed to look like something out of Martha Stewart," observes Sylvia Tanner. "Well, you know, it's home. I'm happy with it. I like it. It keeps me warm; it keeps me dry."

Having small children understandably slows down the progress of our work. Without grandparents, aunts and uncles next door ready to step in, the calculation on progress must be readjusted. "With a six-, four- and a two-year-old, I have to make the baby steps and be okay with that," explains Rebecca James. "I think every mother that has any occupation that she pursues looks at it and says, 'How much faster could I get this done without this kid attached to my leg?' I mean, at the end of the day, you really say to yourself, 'Wow, I could've really knocked it out.'" Coming to terms with this is a daily struggle. Rebecca explains further:

> I think the hard thing for me is that, as adults, we have a ten-
> dency to set goals in our heads, and then life conspires to make
> those goals impossible, and then that's when my worst days
> are — when I get up and I have a mindset of what I was going
> to try to accomplish, and everything goes wrong. . . . The kids'
> needs are diametrically opposed to mine. . . . somebody's teeth-
> ing . . . [or] the kids are sick. That's it. Everything goes out the
> window. . . . There are days when they want to be inside and
> they want me to read to them, and I know that it's going to
> rain tomorrow, and if I don't get out and weed, or I don't get
> out and plant . . . [Or] a day when sibling rivalry has reared
> its head and they are going to argue all day, and it has nothing

to do with me, but I'm not going to be able to move them to
save my life . . . and I'm exhausted! And the baby is tired and
he wants a drink, and I've got another two hours of work to
do, and I could do it if I was by myself, and I can't. Because I'm
the only person who's gonna come in and attend to this child's
immediate biological need right now. So [the garden work]
has to wait.

Though children's needs might keep us from meeting our immediate goals, advice columnist Amy Alkon once observed that "Your
family is better served by a stay-at-home mother than a stay-at-home
martyr."[27] Being a Radical Homemaker does not mean being a perfect parent. It means doing your best and allowing both you and your
kids to have a life. In their letters to me, those Radical Homemakers who signed off as "the world's worst mom," simply chose not to
devote their lives *solely* to their children's needs and agendas. Radical
Homemakers limit the amount of chauffeuring to activities and play
dates, will not always sit and read the same board book fifty-two
times in a row, and typically refuse to prepare special foods in addition to the family menu for the sake of accommodating finicky eat-
ers. Sometimes kids are shooed outside and told to go play on their
own, rather than expecting mommy or daddy to be an on-demand
entertainment system. "My parents are dead, and my husband's are
divorced and live ten hours away," says Maryann Heslier. "Trying to
be everything to and for my kids would make me a worse mom."

Good parenting also means that, as the children of Radical
Homemakers get older, they are expected to help out. "We have a
little chart now, and we change jobs," explains Holly Simmons, "so
they're very capable." In addition to outside work, her sons play a part
in keeping the house clean and getting meals on the table. Rebecca
James' children are much younger, but even then, she finds ways to
elicit their assistance. "They're pretty good at helping with cleaning,"
she observes, and "they're getting better at helping each other out.
If you hit them at the right moment with a job that they think of
as grown-up, they love it." Rebecca has also figured out that getting

the help may require some strategic thinking: "They'll help me cook; they'll help with dishes. . . . I tend to set them on tasks as a gang as opposed to individually, because then they race each other and they get things done."

Even when children are not on the scene demanding our constant attention, we must develop a tolerance for imperfection. John De Graaf, David Wann and Thomas Naylor argue that a root cause of many of our ecological problems is "high-impact thinking," which includes "a compulsive need for spotlessness and tidiness." "The cleaner our houses, the more toxic our environment, from runaway chemicals used to overpolish, oversterilize, and overdeodorize our homes."[28] Likewise, the more pristine our lawns, "the browner our streams," say De Graaf et al, "from all the nutrients and pesticides that run off." Indeed, the typical suburban homeowner in the compulsive pursuit of visual perfection uses six times the pesticides and synthetic fertilizers per acre that a non-organic farmer would apply to his or her crops.[29] The obsessive manicuring also incurs an ecological cost — a power mower emits more exhaust in thirty minutes than a car driven 187 miles.[30]

"Our yards are not beautiful, our crops are not well-tended. But it works," says Kelly Coyne. "We want to get the most out of our yard with as little input as possible." In promoting this way of life, Kelly Coyne is very conscientious about encouraging people to establish realistic expectations. "I tell people you don't have to do all of this stuff, just pick a little — whatever interests you the most — and do that." In order for the lifestyle choice to work, it must be fun and rewarding. Moving our culture from an extractive to a life-serving economy should not necessitate that our days be all toil and self-righteous drudgery. If they are, then the life of a Radical Homemaker will seem like a stark diet — something that one pursues in order to absolve guilt, then abandons when the need for rest and pleasure becomes too overpowering. The lifestyle itself should bring contentment, defined outside the parameters that the consumer culture has established. Kelly explains that, for most of our society

. . . the only options in life [for fun] have been consumerism.
That's . . . our primary form of entertainment and satisfaction.
. . . You're bored, [so] you go to the mall. You expect other
people to do things. You go to the movies so other people will
entertain you. You buy music online so that other people can
sing to you, and you don't do anything yourself. . . . So you let
the specialist entertain you, and then as a consumer, you buy
things to pleasure yourself. . . . We [Kelly and her husband
Erik] found that the things in life that are pleasurable and
satisfying are the things you do for yourself. . . . [Anyone] can
do this. We are not special. We are lazy, we are unskilled, and
we can do it. You can do it, too.

One key to doing it, even imperfectly, is having adequate rest.
Without it, we begin to feel frantic, exhausted, even depressed.
Rebecca James says that, in order to fully enjoy this life, she had to
learn to discern her natural requirements for rest and replenishment:

What I've noticed is that I'm beginning to be able to feel
out the cycles. . . . My activity level drops somewhat. I have a
tendency to be a lot more fault-finding with myself and with
others . . . and I say to myself, "Okay, you're going to cut yourself a certain amount of slack for X amount of time. If you get
less done, that's fine. If you need to spend more time doing the
things that nurture you when you feel like this, reading books
that you don't have to read in order . . . to learn something for
a [task] that you gotta go outside to do tomorrow, that's okay."
And I give myself a certain amount of time to be babied, and
then I ramp back up. And that seems to work. . . . I go through
these periods where, literally, I could lift your car off of you
if you happened to be under it, and then I go through slower
periods of less activity. So I just run with it. I sort of say to
myself, "Wow! I can feel that superwoman cycle coming on,
so I'm just going to get a mountain's worth of work done, and
then when the slowdown comes, I'm going to let it happen."

Setting reasonable limits is not restricted to housekeeping. Sylvia Tanner explains that sometimes we have to set boundaries with family and community as well. "I think we have to also decide what's important to us and be okay with saying no when you can't do something." When a person doesn't have a formal job that calls them away each day, Sylvia warns, it is actually "easy to end up being overcommitted to too many things. . . . You just have to basically say, 'Okay, I'm here to work on things that are really important to me.'"

Understanding that true wealth is not measured in dollars but in time and self-direction, there is a financial advantage to allowing the time to rest and replenish our souls. De Graaf, Wann and Naylor argue that this wealth includes friends, skills, libraries and, most especially, afternoon naps. The more of this true wealth we have, the fewer dollars we require in order to make us happy. The minute we start to fall short of these assets, however, we start requiring money to buy help, buy relief, and buy entertainment. Psychologist Bruce Levine argues that one of the reasons Americans are so often sick is a cultural incentive to be ill; unless we are sick, it is not considered acceptable to be nonproductive or inefficient. He adds, "in a culture where there is a taboo against nonproductivity and inefficiency, what strategy do increasing numbers of us employ to withdraw? Illness."[31] Sylvia Tanner went through a period where she had become a homesteading superwoman, then realized she had lost the true wealth she was seeking in her lifestyle choice:

> I cut back on the farm dramatically. . . . It wasn't fun anymore. I realized that I had no time to do anything. Literally, I wasn't cooking, I wasn't canning, I wasn't putting away all the stuff I was growing. I mean, I was going into the winter and having to buy tomato sauce [even though] at the time [one] greenhouse was full of tomatoes. The other greenhouse was all eggplant and peppers, and I had two smaller greenhouses as well, and the lower field was all vegetables. . . . I had a lot more going on than now. Even with all that, I had no time to put anything by. I had no time to do anything. And I had an

injury. I had a hamstring injury, and I couldn't heal it, because I couldn't get off my feet. So I was limping around with a knee support all summer, and I realized that I hadn't been canoeing or biking or hiking or anything in ages. And I was like, "God, there's no quality of life in this." So I had fallen into that trap.

Sylvia cut back her production, reduced her marketing efforts, and made more time for herself. The reduced income didn't matter when she had rest and pleasure. That ability to find pleasure, incidentally, was yet another critical skill each of these homemakers possessed.

REDEFINING PLEASURE

Emerson once commented, "I honor that man whose ambition is, not to win laurels in state or the army, not to be a jurist or a naturalist, not to be a poet or a commander, but to be a master of living well."[32] Presumably, Emerson would not describe "living well" as being passively entertained by electronic media or recreational shopping; he was referring to the person who is able to take joy in life and find pleasure in daily existence. Like so many things for the Radical Homemakers, pleasure is not something to be bought; it is derived from intentional and conscious experience, and the skilled homemaker is adept at finding it. Rather than seeking inert distractions, they find pleasure in activity that, in the words of author Jerome Segal, "brings us more fully and deeply to life."[33] True pleasure comes from creative fulfillment, self-expression, self-realization, discovery and growth.

Pondering the topic of pleasure in her life, Kelly Robideau commented on an article she'd recently read in the dentist's office. "It was about a guy who has a business in San Francisco, where he'll come in and plant a vegetable garden in your yard, and then come every week and harvest it for you and maintain it for you." Kelly shakes her head at the story. "On the one hand, that's great. People are getting their fresh produce," she explains, "but they're really still not involved in doing it." Despite the benefits of fresh food, the idea of having a personal gardener to grow vegetables misses the point of having a backyard garden, Kelly argues. "It's a matter of being involved in your life!" A few moments later, Kelly explained her ideas further:

> People have gotten away from the creative parts of life, and have gone to the consumption parts. So people listen to music, but they don't create music. And they go out to a restaurant, but they don't cook the meal themselves, or grow the lettuce themselves. . . . There's something fundamentally *satisfying* about being involved in your life, whether it's making music or making food or whatever.

"I don't need to leave my house and yard very often," remarks Nance Klehm. Her urban home life is too entertaining for her to feel drawn to go out to seek amusements:

> I have my sewing machine and my power tools and my hand tools and my piles and piles of books all over the place, and I have clay and paint and wood and food in various forms, doing various things. I have this amazing garden. I have a still! I have all sorts of things to do. I have a solar dryer; I built a green-house on my roof from a bunch of doors and windows I found in the alley, and I think about . . . oh . . . maybe I can make my own underwear!

Being involved in her own life, in her own home, is a form of artistic expression for Alise Jansons who, when we talked, was par-ticularly enjoying doing tiling work in her house, as well as several other projects:

> I love fixing house stuff. One thing I do is when we find used furniture, I'm the one who sands, varnishes and paints every-thing. I also do the floors, I do tile work. . . . I had a minor in art, so that kind of brings out the artist in me. I find it incred-ibly fulfilling. And I do have to do side projects. I'm writing

goofy stories about our adventures in Alaska, trying to put
together a book with those goofy stories.

"I love plumbing and electricity, and he loves working with wood,"
says Bettina Winston, who regards homemaking as an expression of
her and Justin's creativity:

> Every few months, we'll pick up something [new] . . . like
> adding a new vegetable to the garden that we didn't do last
> year, or some task that we would otherwise have required help
> for. It's really endless, the amount of things that I would love
> to just learn about. And for me, it's also like a human history
> lesson. . . . I love making things.

For Kelly Robideau and her husband, the pleasure of creating
comes out on her table, where they serve, among many homemade
foods, their own homemade pancetta and wine. Aside from the fact
that theirs is the best pancetta they've ever had, Kelly says they make
these things for more than just ecological "local-vore" reasons. "It's
really enjoyable and satisfying. I guess it's a creative outlet. . . . It's
a way you can get really messy, and you have something delicious
to eat at the end, and I just really enjoy doing it." Talking about the
experience of making her own wine, Kelly explains the pleasures even
further:

> It's a feeling of connection to what you're putting into your
> body. . . . Knowing that I picked these grapes, that I stomped
> them with my feet . . . that I crushed them in the crusher, that
> I took care of them, that I racked them and got covered with
> wine and I bottled it myself and with our friends, and there's
> just something much more satisfying to me about that wine
> than it would be if I just bought a bottle.

Whether it is playing a guitar and singing songs with kids, tor-
menting the cat with hackneyed Irish tunes on a penny whistle (one

of my personal pleasures), figuring out how to fix an engine, making your own wine, knitting a sweater, tending a garden, making strawberry jam, repairing the floor or rewiring the bathroom, the pleasure is in the *doing*, not necessarily in having it done (although leaving projects unfinished for too long will surely annoy any of us). Buying a television and staring at it, buying a new couch and sitting on it, buying plug-in chemical deodorizers for the bathroom, or buying a new car deliver none of these deep, creative, fulfilling pleasures. Kelly argues that our national confusion over what constitutes pleasurable activity contributes to our unhappiness. Without the joy of becoming fully involved in our daily lives, "things are less meaningful," she says. Erik Knutzen says, "For me, it's the difference between being a citizen and being a consumer":

> A citizen is someone who is self-actualized. A citizen is
> someone who can do things themselves, maybe not be self-
> sufficient, but can actually make something or manipulate
> something, and I take a lot of joy out of being able to do
> things myself . . . Being a tinkerer.

Of course, tinkering, fixing and making stuff is not the only way Radical Homemakers define pleasure, nor do they feel the need to be producing at all times. While everyone confessed to loving a good movie now and then, most of the homemakers talked about the joy of recreation outside the consumer culture — camping, canoeing, hiking, ice skating on a back pond, attending contra dances, listening to public radio programs, going to concerts, observing nature, listening to music, creating artwork, devouring books, huddling by a fire in the winter while putting together puzzles with family members, or reading stories aloud to each other.

As much as these activities may be pleasurable in and of themselves, the joy they bring often comes from sharing them with others. Relationships were, in fact, the most significant and deepest source of pleasure for the Radical Homemakers. Holly Simmons says that cultivating relationships, whether with the land, the community or their

family, was a primary reason she and John chose their life path. Given
the option, she says, "We're going to invite a friend to dinner instead
of working late; we're going to have seasonal work and home school
so we can build deep, lasting relationships." When Anna Reynolds
talks about what she does for fun, the lines around her eyes deepen as
she smiles and talks about her life with her sons:

> I enjoy them. We laugh at each other's jokes. A lot of times
> one person will say something, and two or three others will
> come up with a line that feeds into it and it's the same line.
> You know, one of the things we enjoy is playing bridge. We
> like to do that a lot together. . . . [Or] we can go to the straw-
> berry farm and get the strawberries . . . and we bring them
> back and we all sit around together and we make these straw-
> berry preserves. . . . They taste better, and we have fun doing it.
> What more could you ask for?

Alise and Eduards Jansons rely upon their relationship to survive
the long Alaskan winter, and make deliberate efforts to maintain it:

> [We] have romantic dinners once a week. It's a set thing in our
> schedule. We have them at home. We put my son to sleep . . .
> and then we cook something really nice and put on the music
> and the candlelight. That's something we both really enjoy —
> to savor our food, and have some wine and just talk to each
> other, then sit by the woodstove. It's really the best entertain-
> ment I can think of. . . . Tonight we're having smoked salmon
> risotto.

Of course there is no single formula for finding pleasure in life,
but at its core, the concept is irreducibly simple. Whether it is sharing a smoked salmon risotto, homemade wine or brandy, a game of
bridge, music, a garden harvest or a chat beside the woodstove, the
lives of Radical Homemakers are rich in pleasures that they themselves have created.

REDISCOVERING THE TASTE OF REAL FOOD

"Shawn wouldn't eat the food at school." Carrie Lockwell recounts one of the issues that came to the fore as she evaluated whether or not to home-school her son. "He didn't even like the cakes and cookies the parents would bring in, because they were store-bought. They went to the grocery store to buy the birthday cake instead of making cupcakes or cookies." Carrie was not the first Radical Homemaker to comment how far from the national palate her own family's tastes have deviated. Seeing how the single mom living next door struggles with all her duties, Amanda Shaw longs to help her out by bringing over some home-cooked meals now and then as an alternative to the family's daily McDonald's fare. "The bump in the road . . . is, if I took something nourishing over, they would look at me like, 'you want me to eat this?'" There was a time, Amanda argues, when everyone understood what real food was, how it came to us, and what it was supposed to taste like. Today, she argues, "there's no connection." Food writers John and Karen Hess ardently concur that Americans have been "weaned on junk foods and soda pop," and that "their palates have been numbed."[34]

In our mainstream culture, "you get trained that certain tastes are what things are *supposed* to taste like and what's supposed to taste good," explains Justin Winston. When making this lifestyle change, "you have to learn what something tastes like when it hasn't been genetically modified or it doesn't have chemicals in it." Justin observes that, since Americans are now preconditioned to super-sweet, salty and chemical flavorings, wholesome food "doesn't necessarily taste better" at first. Making a commitment to cook sustainable local foods for one's family, rather than relying on processed foods and take-out menus, entails re-attuning our palates and tastes. We must learn again to discern genuine flavor in food. Once that switch has been made, however, it is impossible to go backward. Many Radical Homemakers find the idea of returning to mainstream American culture unimaginable if it requires that they must rely on the conventional food system for nourishment. "I don't really go to normal grocery stores," explains Kelly Coyne. "I just walk into them, and there's just nothing to eat. It's awful." Nance Klehm expresses the same feelings:

> When I walk into a grocery store, I am so offended by what
> they're representing as something that might taste good — I'm
> so offended by the packaging, and then knowing what's going
> on in the food industry, and knowing what's going on with
> the labor. . . . All these things kind of flood me at once, and
> I'm just . . . offended by what they're representing as choices I
> should make. And I don't want to make those choices.

At the core of the Radical Homemaking social movement is the rebuilding of a food culture based on principles of ecological sustainability and social justice. Barbara Kingsolver argues that this is something that we have lost in our nation's love affair with commerce. "A food culture is not something that gets sold to people," writes Kingsolver. "It arises out of a place, a soil, a climate, a history, a temperament, a collective sense of belonging."[35] Reclaiming that lost culture starts with understanding the relation to climate and the landscape. As Nance Klehm puts it, "I have a land-based diet."

Like all the study participants, Nance doesn't pass judgment on people's dietary choices, whether they are vegetarian, vegan, omnivores, carb-loaders or meat lovers; what mattered most was that they were eating in harmony with their regional landscape. What all Radical Homemakers eschew is processed and heavily packaged foods, foods that are transported excessive distances, or foods that are produced with ecologically damaging farming practices. Families like the Lockwells, Honeywells or Ianellis raised their own meat animals on pasture or had relationships with grass-fed livestock producers, and so had more meat-heavy diets. Others, like Kelly Coyne and Erik Knutzen, who have difficulty finding a source for sustainably raised meat in urban Los Angeles, opt for more vegetarian fare. The typical fare in each family differed greatly across the country, as well as from season to season. A late-October lunch in the Midwest included ingredients like homemade yogurt, salad from the yard, fresh raw milk, and cream. In the Southwest, it was homemade chili made with wild elk meat, lots of local cheese, and freshly picked pears and apples. In mid-coast California it included a locally grown pastured pork roast, homemade wine and a plate of persimmons from a backyard tree. Southern California had sourdough bread and butter, prickly pear cactus, figs, and eggs. The Pacific Northwest offered up root vegetables, fresh goat milk, applesauce, homemade jam, pumpkin soufflé and meatloaf of grass-fed beef.

When the growing season is over and the harvest has been preserved, there is still plenty of wonderful food to eat. Homemakers made sauerkraut and kimchi; canned green beans, salsas, tomato sauces, relishes, cherries, pears, applesauce, plums, peaches and pickles of all kinds. They froze summer corn, blueberries, raspberries, blackberries, broccoli, beans, cauliflower, meat and fish. They dried and cured tomatoes, bacons, hams, sausages, figs and many other fruits. They put up honey, jam and maple syrup, made kombucha, brandy, wine and beer, baked with regionally grown grains, and filled cellar bins with potatoes, carrots, beets, turnips and rutabagas. Everybody's cuisine was different based on locale, but nobody was going hungry.

As Stormy McGovern and I talk over a pot of herb tea from her garden, one of her friends is washing and stemming grapes in her kitchen. Once I leave, they will make wine together. I ask her what she feels she is accomplishing by her lifestyle choice. She smiles and grabs her stomach. "I got a little bit of a belly and I see a lot of happy, fed friends."

ADOPTING A FEARLESS ATTITUDE

So . . . you've thought it over, gone over the numbers, inventoried your material and social resources. You're anxious to clear out your desk, thumb your nose at the boss and drive out of the commuter parking lot for the last time, and revive and start using those skill sets. But, then again, *what if* . . .

Even if we are able to keep the bills paid and terrific food on the table while finding time to enjoy and nurture family, friends, community and the Earth, there may still be those bumps in the night that

cause fears to rear their pernicious heads. The home life doesn't readily provide benchmarks for gauging success or a built-in system of
praise and encouragement. It is very difficult to reverse a decision to
leave the workforce (particularly if you actually *did* thumb your nose
at the boss). It is hard to imagine having an enjoyable life without
being able to indulge in material purchases on a whim. It becomes a
challenge to uphold self-esteem when we don't have a profession to
tag onto our name when we meet people. To lead a life of one's own
design takes courage.

When Pamela Stone researched the lives of high-powered career
women who left the workforce to become stay-at-home moms, she
found that they missed the structure, rewards and camaraderie that
their jobs provided.[36] It bears mention that the Radical Homemaker
life carries the risk of this phenomenon as well. If we are used to
viewing authority as external to ourselves, then it becomes difficult to
validate our own personal successes in an environment that doesn't
come with a boss, job reports, annual performance reviews, salary
increases and myriad "way-to-go" rewards. Though Rebecca James
still found ample intellectual stimulation when she left her profession as a teacher, she did experience some of the other losses Pamela
Stone described:

> At school you had this compartmentalized list of things that
> you had to get done, and you knew when they were done
> because they weren't on your desk anymore. . . . I have lost
> that sense that someone is going to hand me a piece of paper
> and say, "Here's what you said you were going to do this year;
> here's how you're doing." When I went back to work when
> my daughter was small, I said to myself, "If I have to leave my
> kids" — and I'm crying in the car on the way to work — "if I
> have to do this, I'm going to make 'Teacher of the Year.' I'm
> going to run rings around them." So when I got there at 5:30
> AM, I parked right next to the principal's spot, because he was
> going to know, by God, I was in the building, and I busted my
> hump, and I got 'Teacher of the Year.' . . . You don't get that

[validation] when you're home with the kids. You really have
to trust yourself, and you have to be self-sustaining in terms of
feeling that you've accomplished something.

Alise Jansons experienced similar angst, but also recognizes a balancing benefit:

At home, you don't get a lot of praise. At a job you always have
some supervisor saying "Good job!" and "Great!" and "Here's
your performance review." Well, you don't get that at home. . . .
Nobody cheers you on like, "Wow! Great food, Mom!" But you
do get that at work. . . . That's sort of the thing you miss. But
on the other hand, I'm so much more relaxed . . . and a better
mom, and I think, a better member of society, because, like I
said, I can think about doing the right thing instead of just
rushing, rushing, rushing all the time.

When we opt out of a formal profession, we surrender more than
just the rewards of work; we also accept the risk of a certain degree
of professional shunning. Psychologist Bruce Levine reminds us that
our culture shames anyone who appears to be nonproductive or inefficient. Studies have repeatedly shown that women who leave the
workforce have an extremely difficult time returning.[37] David Peterson feels that women aren't the only ones who are unable to jump
into the workforce after a period at home:

I've never had to do a resume before, because I've always been
self-employed or worked for a friend. And, as it turns out, I
think that's the way most people get their jobs, but they have
to know somebody to do that. . . . If you're house-bound or a
house husband or house-oriented, then you don't make those
[professional] connections.

For most Radical Homemakers, the life choice to "quit" (a telling, value-laden word) is often irreversible. The professional world

will probably not want us back. Then again, most of us never want to return. "The common practice of being miserable in a job," warns William Coperthwaite:

> . . . creates a dangerous atmosphere which can affect grow-
> ing children who see the adults they love relating negatively
> to their work, coming home frustrated and unhappy. Imagine
> being able to face your kids honestly, having them know you
> cannot be bought — that you are among those who do not
> have a price. It is so much healthier for a child to see parents
> recognizing that their way of living is wrong and seeking a
> remedy rather than continuing to rationalize unhappiness,
> thereby encouraging the child to follow the same pattern.[38]

The irreversible nature of Radical Homemaking did not trouble Julie Hewitt in the least. Even though she was making substantial money at a fast-paced career, she was willing to surrender it. Nine years later, she hasn't looked back. "I just don't value that lifestyle the way I used to," she explains. "The whole idea of success is out the window in my opinion. It's not valid anymore. It's so myopic. [This idea that] 'It's all about me and success' — it's not going to get us anywhere [as a society]." Julie felt she had nothing to lose except extra dollars when she left her job, and everything to gain — a calmer life, better care for her family, better food, intellectual growth, and a more sustainable existence. Bettina Winston doesn't worry about missing out on a professional career, either. "I think [this lifestyle] is just choosing not to do what the media or whatever says you should be doing, which is working for some company and earn-ing a paycheck."

Once the parturition from the professional workplace has been cauterized, Radical Homemakers often confront pressure and judg-ment in the broader world — in their community, from their spouse's coworkers, even from their dubious extended family. "We were put-ting in a garden," said Penelope Sloan, recounting a story from her and John's days in New Jersey when she had to explain to her neighbor their apparently strange behavior of turning over sod for their first garden:

> We have our shovels out, and we're flipping the soil, the sod and the whole thing . . . and he's like, "What are you going to grow?" . . . "Tomatoes, zucchini, you know, the usual things you grow in a garden." So they called us "the weird people." . . . We were going out to dinner one night and we walked out of the house, and their kids were in their upstairs bedroom, which was right next to our driveway, and the kids were going, "Hey people! Weird People! Hi!"

Having argued that increasing domestic self-reliance is the Radical Homemakers' first step toward building self-sufficient communities, we find that the communities tend to lag behind the progress of the homemakers. Penelope's and John's former New Jersey neighborhood is a case in point. Educator Parker Palmer[39] has described a process whereby individuals grow out of a homogeneous "socialized consciousness" to experience an awakening "cultural consciousness" that ultimately leads to deep personal transformation. When an individual is functioning with only a "socialized consciousness," he or she is essentially subject to a trance induced by the prevailing cultural norms. Bettina and Justin Winston have often observed this socialized consciousness around them. "We have a little pet language that has to do with robots," explains Justin:

> . . . and it has to do with what is on the television, and how you watch TV, and how you watch commercials . . . and then we go and see people in town, and we see them doing the things in the commercials, and we consider that "robot behavior." They've been programmed to do something that doesn't really seem natural.

The process of maturing out of this conformity and into a state of "cultural consciousness" commonly leads to a disconnection between some members of the family and community. This schism happens as individuals struggle to choose between normative behaviors and expectations, and finding a way to be "true to themselves." And it can be painful. Those who choose to align their lives with their values typically experience a sense of isolation from anyone else whose outlook is defined by conventional cultural codes. David Korten explains that people undergoing this transition may even occasionally feel like creatures from outer space.[40] Rebecca James and her husband Steve had one of these "alienating" experiences. Even though Steve was continuing to work, he was penalized for Rebecca's decision to stay home. Rebecca tells the story:

> He had a really difficult boss. . . . She came to the job right after my daughter was born, literally the week she was born. So my daughter was a home birth, and Steve was trying to make himself available and help with two small children, and this boss was kind of taking her measure of him. And what she decided was that he had some wife at home [and] she placed herself in competition with me. She was this career person who didn't have a family, and "a career was important." And she would ask him questions about what his wife was like, as soon as she realized I was home with the kids. And [she] clearly disliked that any woman would choose to be home with the kids, and so she'd push him to work harder and more hours. . . . I could have two kids that had 102-degree fevers and were throwing up, and she'd say, "I don't understand why you need to go home. All she does is watch the kids. Why does she need you to go home? She doesn't have anything else to be responsible for."

Rebecca says there were many times, outside her husband's work, where she perpetually endured "little verbal pokes" about her "hippie mama" ways. "I was a person who got put in that box, not really because I was this fantastic hippie mama, but because I was the closest equivalent that there was in the room," she says. "People worked out their demons on my person."

The Winstons experience deep support from Bettina's family, but they endure the sense of alienation from Justin's side of the family, who suggest that their lifestyle is indulgent. "His dad makes us feel so guilty about it," Bettina explains. "It's a slave mentality," adds Justin. "I think he's a slave, and he has no consciousness of it." "It's so hard to talk to him," says Bettina, adding that her father-in-law believes "we are a danger to the fabric of this country." Since Justin handles most of the cleaning and cooking (and finds it really satisfying), he also puts up with occasional peer pressure from other men his age.

"When I'm around other men who want to brag about how much [money] they make or what they drive or something like that, it can get on my nerves," he says. All in all, however, since he finds his way of life satisfying, he doesn't let the social pressure bother him. "I was a poor artist for fifteen years in New York. So I got used to not having money and not having things and not feeling bad about it. Because it was my choice to do that, and it's the same thing here."

Carrie Lockwell feels that, because she keeps her son home from school, her community is of the opinion that "he's missing something." The pressure occasionally forces her to question her decision to home-school; but when she reexamines the assumptions, she concludes:

> What's he missing? Getting beat up on the bus? Getting the flu at school? Washing his hands with the antibacterial crap? . . . Eating the *E.coli* burger in the lunch line? What's he missing? . . . He's not missing much.

Nance Klehm suggests that there was a time when she worried more about impressions she made with her lifestyle choices. When she was the random victim of a brutal beating one night by members of a gang, those worries came to a grinding halt. Nance soon found herself surrounded by people who cared for her, and she discovered that, despite her injuries, "my core self, whatever that is, is okay, no matter what." Nance describes her next discovery:

> And then I realized that I needed to step into my power and be . . . *fearless*. . . . Really step into it, and not worry about it anymore. So I don't worry about it anymore. I don't try to impress people anymore.

Rejecting worries about people's opinions of how they choose to live clears a first big hurdle for many Radical Homemakers. Nonetheless, the choice of life over money is subjected to derision in simple, yet obvious ways. Penelope Sloan remembers how her beloved, care-worn, yet faithful little car never measured up to the expensive new ones in the parking lot where she used to work, and how it started to become a source of ridicule and embarrassment. Rebecca James talks about how her husband and children no longer buy Christmas presents. That works fine in their household, but giving their home-made crafts to other relatives often feels meager. "We both come from these suburban families that go and buy stuff from the mall," she explains. "Unless you can spend $80 on really beautiful angora yarn [for a knitted Christmas gift], your gift is just not going to stack up. It's going to sort of look like something a kindergartner made for you in art class." But to resist this sense of indignity is to reiterate and reaffirm the values that inform the choices the Radical Homemaker has made. "I tend to think most people learn what [things] they need from the culture. It's defined by the culture. They don't ask questions," argues Michael Mills, who refuses to succumb to the pressure for new and better. Alise Jansons says that, in order to break through the complicity, you need a little moment of epiphany:

> I just feel like you have to have this "ah hah!" moment and realize that this is a joke! This is a joke, and the system is making me do this because this is how we've decided our economy should be, and we [are expected] to buy into that. And I don't buy into that. I just worry, do we have an alternative economy?

But true to the Radical Homemakers' great work, Alise's energy flows toward building that alternative — the life-serving economy — *not* toward cowering in deference to the corrosive harrying of the extractive economy. The fearlessness we must cultivate to cope with social pressure helps us out as we pursue the simple daily actions to build our lives. Radical Homemaking is filled with tiny adventures where risks are taken.

"I'm the person who stands up for the chickens," declares Nance Klehm. "They were going to outlaw chickens in Chicago, and I'm the person who stood up for all my neighbors." Like many of her Hispanic city neighbors, Nance Klehm relies on her small flock of hens for her daily nutrition. Unlike many of them, however, she is a legal citizen of the country. When Chicago planned to outlaw chickens within the city limits, the majority of people who would suffer were also without a legal voice. Nance had the courage to step forward to defend everyone's traditions and needs.

Sometimes the courage comes from doing little things, like taking advantage of resources that will otherwise go to waste. Erik Knutzen and Kelly Coyne have planted a guerilla vegetable garden on city property in front of their house. They scout their neighborhood for empty houses and harvest the fruit that drops off the trees behind them. When a harsh winter storm blows down limbs in Chicago's city parks, Nance Klehm grabs her chainsaw and heads out to clean them up as though she owns the place, and in the process gleans some firewood. "You know, a chainsaw is better than a big dog!" she says. "You're, like, the white lady out there with a chainsaw. [People assume] you've got to be crazy," she says, and she is left alone to take care of things.

For other people, the envelope-pushing chance-taking may seem less obvious. For Carrie Lockwell, the homemaking adventure started with simply opening a cookbook and making her first batch of brownies from scratch, a simple step that snowballed into her and Chad growing, cooking and preserving nearly all of her family's food. Kelly Coyne has observed that, for some people, courage must be mustered for the simple act of picking and eating a piece of fruit, rather than buying it in the grocery store:

> People are afraid of a lot of things. I just talked in San Fran-
> cisco in a bookstore, and this woman said, "I have a pear tree
> in my yard, but I'm afraid to eat the pears." And I was like,
> "Well, why?" [To myself] I was thinking, "My God! A pear
> tree! I would die for a pear tree!" [She says] "Well, there's smog
> on them, and I don't think it'll ever come off." . . . [I thought]
> "You think the fruit you get from the store comes from the
> magic clean nirvana land? . . . Where do you think your fruit
> comes from? What clean, magic place? . . . [I said] I would eat
> the pear. I wouldn't even wash the pear. I would eat it off the
> tree, because I want the bacteria on the pear." [And she says]
> "What about the smog?" [I say] "I'm living in Los Angeles. . . .
> I'm breathing [the equivalent] of two packs of cigarettes a day,
> so if I'm eating a pear with some smog on it, I think my stom-
> ach can deal with that better than my lungs do."

"I think that there's a situation where we look at our lives and we read these stories about people who went off and started an organic farm, and it reads very hippie dippy," observes Rebecca James. "And you think, well, I'm not named after a flower . . . and I don't think I could do that":

> We tend to look at it as an all-or-nothing proposition. I have
> to go completely back to the earth in the sixties hippie way . . .
> or I have to do this thing that I'm qualified to do or trained
> to do. . . . The bottom line is that necessity is the mother of
> invention. . . . The more of our own needs that we can provide,
> the better it is for our family.

Holly Simmons believes that gaining confidence to make deci-sions that honor the tenets of the Radical Homemaker choice is the first step to bringing about cultural change. She suggests that if each of us could learn "to not let fear change [our] good clear thinking," the world would benefit. Dierdre Ianelli sees conquering these fears as part of her contribution to cultural change. "We need to come together, we need to build community and we need to stop with the video games. We need to shut off the TV, we need to start reading and thinking and talking to each other. . . . I want to change my culture," she says. "I'm a participant in culture change right now." It all starts with setting aside our fears and mustering our courage to live a life we truly believe in that will help to create a world we can all live in.

CHAPTER SEVEN

TOWARD A HOMEGROWN CULTURE

> "A minority is powerless
> while it conforms to the majority;
> it is not even a minority then;
> but is irresistible when it clogs
> by its whole weight."
>
> — *Thoreau*, Civil Disobedience [1]

Healing our planet, our hearts and our bodies, bringing peace to our society, finding happiness, social justice and creative fulfillment, all begin by turning our attention first to our homes. But it does not end there. Reclaiming our domestic skills is the starting point; our continued happiness, creative fulfillment, and further healing of our society and planet requires that we look beyond the back door and push ourselves to achieve more. It is not enough to just go home and put down roots; we must also cultivate tendrils that reach out and bring society along with us.

When Betty Friedan wrote her critique of postwar housewives, she argued that theirs was a stultifying vocation that provided no adequate opportunities for women to achieve a higher level of self-realization. Predictably, the same cautions may be urged upon today's Radical Homemakers, and perhaps rightly so. After an exuberant rush of finding new challenges and personal growth as we seek to reclaim lost domestic skills, a new yearning may emerge. Friedan argued that our human drive is deeper than seeking pleasures or the mere satisfaction of fundamental needs; it is a desire to grow, to realize our full potential. Rather than dwelling in malaise, we can see it as an inspired motivation that compels us to seek the next wellspring of fulfillment.

In chapter one I mentioned that the Radical Homemakers seemed to be on a three-stage path. In the first stage, *Renouncing*, most of them were still leading conventional lives, but were becoming increasingly aware of the illusory happiness of a consumer society. As a result of deep introspection, they would ultimately make the choice to step off their current path and become a homemaker. In the second stage, *Reclaiming*, the homemakers entered a period where they worked to recover many of the lost domestic skills that would enable their family to live without outside income. I observed that, depending on the individual, this phase could take years (especially if small children were at home) or a lifetime. As we saw in chapter six, it is an exciting and deeply fulfilling period. However, if homemakers dwelled in this phase for too long, a few of them admitted to manifesting symptoms of Friedan's "Housewife's Syndrome," including a sense of aimlessness, despair about the rest of the world, cynicism, or sporadic bouts with depression. Those homemakers who were truly fulfilled had moved into a third phase, what I've dubbed *Rebuilding*, in which they worked to expand their creative energies outward. Their homes had become more sustainable and meaningful places, and now they were applying their talents and skills to bring their communities and society along with them.

For certain, when we are first reclaiming our domestic skills and taking on new challenges on the home front, our creative spark will be well-kindled. This is a distinctive value of the Radical Homemaker life — because it is oriented around a philosophical base (the four tenets of family, community, social justice and ecological sustainability), its practical constructions, however mundane they may seem, are always laying the foundation for satisfying deeper social accomplishments. Homemaking is not something that stands in the way of our deeper fulfillment; it becomes the fertile ground that feeds it. Once the patterns for homemaking are set, there will appear opportunities to make the changes reach farther.

As the acquisition of new skills continues on the Radical Home-making path, creative momentum builds until all of our other talents and abilities begin to bubble to the surface and demand to be put to service toward deeper ambitions. As psychologist A.H. Maslow writes, "Capacities clamor to be used, and cease their clamor only when they are well used. That is, capacities are also needs. . . . The unused capacity or organ can become a disease center or else atrophy, thus diminishing the person."[2]

"When you take charge of your household through home economics, through being a citizen, through being able to do things yourself in your house," Erik Knutzen explains, "the next step beyond that is to work in your neighborhood, to make your neighborhood a better place." He approaches his civic involvement with a certain pragmatism:

> I know people get all worked up about national politics. My attitude with it is, certainly you should vote, but I cannot influence national politics as an individual. I can have a profound influence on my neighborhood and my community, and so I urge people to get involved in the community as the step beyond this. . . . So I'm involved in a local neighborhood council, I'm on the board of the bicycle coalition here to try to make L.A. a more bikeable, walkable place. So I think that's important with this lifestyle as well, and it is all part of local-izing . . . of getting in touch with the place you're in.

Eric's community participation exemplifies what sociologist Robert Putnam described as the rebuilding of social capital, or social networks, and "norms of reciprocity and trustworthiness" that result from them. Putnam points out that a society rich in virtuous people is still poor in social capital if those individuals are isolated. The presence of this social cohesion helps the community to solve problems more easily, to reduce the costs of business and social transactions, and to simply take better care of one another. This communal vitality also helps individual citizens to be happier and healthier.

"Mounting evidence suggests that people whose lives are rich in social capital cope better with traumas and fight illness more effectively," says Putnam.[3] Psychologist Bruce Levine notes that it is also an antidote to depression.[4] As we endeavor to put our homes in order, reaching out and building this capital not only helps to sustain our way of life and build a more self-reliant community, it keeps us happier in the long run and increases our collective power to bring about national change.

On that note, Frances Moore Lappé recently observed that we must define happiness as deeper than having nice relationships and satisfied needs:

> If happiness lies in covering basic needs plus satisfying personal ties and finding meaning, society's role is limited. It need only ensure that essential needs are met and provide opportunities to pursue personal relationships and meaning. Even a largely totalitarian government could do that. But, if we add power to that happiness equation, our agenda shifts. Maximizing happiness then requires engaging citizens in changing the rules and norms so that more and more of us are empowered participants. And, of course, joining with others in this exhilarating pursuit we achieve a double whammy: Such activity furthers the widely appreciated relational and meaning aspects of the happiness puzzle.[5]

It seems a natural consequence, then, that many of the Radical Homemakers in this study were conscientious about building social capital and increasing democratic power in their communities and even beyond. Erik Knutzen was working to make L.A. bike- and pedestrian-friendly. Kelly Coyne was planning a project to help fellow Urban Homesteaders identify one another and network together. Sylvia Tanner had created a community coalition for energy sustainability, and the Hewitts were part of a community group studying peak oil issues. Deirdre Ianelli was helping to start a new community food co-op. Michael Mills was organizing to battle gas drilling in his town. David Peterson established a local chapter of Neighbors-Helping-Neighbors. Carol Rydell and Amanda Shaw organize a farm-direct buying club that links local consumers with local farmers. A number of the homemakers I interviewed and many of those who wrote letters to me were nationally active on myriad issues, including health-care reform, fighting the National Animal Identification System, political campaigning, right-to-farm laws, food and energy policy and home-schooling activism. The mission to live well and sustainably does not keep Radical Homemakers confined to a small domestic sphere. While there will inevitably be periods of time when they might withdraw from the broader community to tend more intensely to family needs, their mission is something they take to the broader world, an issue that they see as greater than themselves.

As gratifying as participation in community work may be for some, many homemakers were driven to pursue personal creative achievements, which also nourish our culture and create a more vibrant society. Sylvia Tanner plays fiddle and is learning the bagpipes in addition to farming. David Hewitt meets a group every Tuesday night on an old schooner to play Irish music. Julie Hewitt is researching ways to innovatively integrate special education and home-schooling. Justin Winston is a painter. Sylvia Tanner, Alise Jansons, Erik Knutzen, Kelly Coyne and Maryann Heslier are all writers. Penelope Sloan is a photographer. Bettina Winston has a craft business. Eve Honeywell, Deirdre Ianelli, the Hewitts, the Simmons, the Lockwells, Anna Reynolds and Rebecca James are all farmers as well as home-schoolers. When we last spoke, David Peterson had also begun growing food to provide for his local community, and had resumed fine chair-making. Amanda Shaw, Kelly Robideau, Carol Rydell and Nance Klehm all teach classes to help community members reclaim domestic skills. "The greatest happiness comes from absorbing yourself in some goal outside yourself," explains Richard Layard. "Prod any happy person and you will find a project."[6]

According to the rules of the old extractive economy, once a person chooses to leave the workforce, they are seldom allowed to return. Their future role in the extractive economy will be forever marginal, except as consumers. By contrast, as Radical Homemakers work to build the new life-serving economy, that new paradigm will in turn find places for them: farmers find local customers for their food without supplicating to a commodity system; writers find more outlets for their work without contriving to conglomerate editorial boards; musicians are able to find viable local venues without striving to become corporate-fabricated rock stars; and painters and crafters find a cultural community that honors and values their work. There is room and a need for everyone.

AFTERWORD

It has been a year since my conversation with Susan Colter in her tomato-filled apartment, two years since I first posted a notice on my Web site:

> If you have learned to live on less in order to take the time to
> nourish your family and the planet through home cooking,
> engaged citizenship, responsible consumption and creative
> living, whether you are male, female, or two people sharing the
> role, with or without children, full or part-time, please drop me
> a line and tell me your story.

In that time, one of my daughters has gotten her first loose tooth, the other has learned to use the toilet. Every morning their father cooked them breakfast so that I could hide away in my office and pour over data, seeking answers to Susan's questions. Now, as I prepare to stand up from my desk, to return to that stack of firewood that needs piling, the garden that needs weeding, and the bushel of cucumbers in need of pickling, I wonder how this one manuscript has driven me to lay all my domestic work aside and consume so much of my attention. As I write this, the outside door to my office rattles as my five-year-old presses her nose to the glass and begs me to come play. My two-year-old longs for a morning snuggle and joins her sister in what has now become a sit-in.

Susan's questions haunted me for the past year, I thought, because I needed to come up with a volume that satisfied her critical dilemmas. In truth, her conversations were a stand-in for a future conversation with my own daughters. How will Bob and I answer for our own life paths? Did we sequester our children from a domineering extractive economy only to leave them unprepared to fight for a place in it, or did we help to create a world where they, as young women, will find a life of hope, magic, creativity, joy and peace? It is this second vision that has driven us and so many of our contemporaries to choose our path. But if that path is to be valid, then we cannot create it with a few hundred isolated believers scattered across the country. Our numbers must grow. We must join together, focusing our energies on creating a world that is not only pleasurable, socially just, healthy and beautiful, but very, very possible.

"Let ours be a time remembered for the awakening of a new reverence for life," states the Earth Charter, "the firm resolve to achieve sustainability, the quickening of the struggle for justice and peace, and the joyful celebration of life."[7] Each of us has the power to make this vision a reality. And it all begins at home.

STUDY PARTICIPANTS

AUTHOR'S NOTE: *In order to honor the privacy of the study participants, most of their names have been changed, as well as a few minor details about their lives. The exceptions are Kelly Coyne, Erik Knutzen and Nance Klehm, all who write and speak actively on subjects that tie in very closely with Radical Homemaking.*

SUSAN COLTER

Susan Colter describes the Boston suburb where she grew up as "a rich, white town." Both of Susan's parents had demanding professional careers, and both "poured their time and energy into work." As a result, she describes her mother and father as "not *uninvolved* parents, but it was like, we [she and her brother] came after everything else had been done." Following her parents' divorce, Susan felt left to her own devices as a high-schooler, so she taught herself to cook (no one was cooking at home). A good student, she went on to a prestigious private school, where she spent a semester in South Africa. There she witnessed both widespread hunger and a slower pace of life that led her to seriously question her current trajectory. Susan graduated from college in 2007, then returned home to take care of her mother, who was dying. In spite of the impending loss, Susan explains, "It felt so good to have my family . . . to all eat together and to talk together and to spend time together." At the time of our interview, Susan was at a crossroads. She was living in a rundown rental unit on the edge of Durham, New Hampshire, with her boyfriend and two other roommates. She and her boyfriend had spent their summer working on nearby CSAs and, as the growing season was winding down, she was trying to figure out what to do next. Her peers were launching their careers, and she was feeling estranged from the idea of putting that above all else; yet she feared that an alternative lifestyle was something that she couldn't survive economically or physically.

KELLY COYNE AND ERIK KNUTZEN

Kelly Coyne grew up moving around the West Coast and Southwest while her father was "chasing better jobs." In her words, her parents "liked living well" and aspired to better their position from their middle-class roots. Thus, she lived in beautiful homes with "swimming pools in San Jose and a beautiful ocean view in Eureka and a beautiful mountain view in Evergreen . . . but we were always living outside our means." Her dad was in human resources and sales; her mom worked in real estate. Erik grew up in West L.A. His dad was a real-estate appraiser; his mom was a schoolteacher. They never moved once. And, Kelly adds, he came from "generations of penny-pinchers." Kelly and Erik met in graduate school at the University of California at San Diego. Upon finishing their degrees, they lived in L.A. and worked for various arts organizations. They recently left their jobs and are now, Kelly says, working to "cobble together an income with a blend of part-time work, writing, teaching, speaking" and, of course, keeping their expenses extremely low by farming their tiny backyard in the heart of Los Angeles. Kelly and Erik described themselves as not being "particularly aspirational" as far as careers are concerned. Kelly confesses, "I never had any particular vision of myself as a successful business person, even though my family was all about business." Erik says that, as a kid, he'd wanted to be a scientist, "unfortunately, math did me in . . . and then I made this weird decision to study music." While both completed degrees preparing them for lives in academia, they admitted to themselves that, upon graduation, neither "wanted anything to do with it." Instead, explains Erik, "we found our way to be academics without being academics." As urban farmers, Erik and Kelly have spent the last ten years exploring how to make a sustainable, self-reliant life from their little "mini-farm," where they've studied, practiced, failed, retried and "just sort of moved from one kind of fascination to the next," says Kelly. Today their postage-stamp yard houses four chickens, raised vegetable beds, and a homemade solar dehydrator for tomatoes and figs. They teach and write about (and personally practice) urban foraging, canning, food preservation, home brewing, gardening, water harvesting, and just about anything that can help city dwellers enjoy a more sustainable and — most importantly in their opinions — *flavorful* lifestyle. Erik and Kelly are proprietors of homegrownevolution.com, a popular urban homesteading blog, and they are also authors of the recent book, *The Urban Homestead: Your guide to self-sufficient living in the heart of the city.* When we spoke in November of 2008, they had an annual combined income goal of $36,000, which they felt would provide for all their needs living in downtown Los Angeles, including $800 per month for health insurance premiums. While they had not attained that goal yet, they had just completed their first year of gainful unemployment and were happy to report that, to date, their bills had all been paid.

MARYANN AND THOMAS HESLIER

Maryann grew up in a poor suburb of Washington, D.C., where the back lot of her family home butted up against a four-lane highway. Her mother hated cooking and cleaning, yet dutifully performed her job and fed their family as thriftily as possible on foods such as margarine and powdered milk. Maryann went away to a small, part-"hippie" and part-"redneck" college in Appalachia, where she worked for her room and board. When she was in her twenties, she lived in her truck, traveled, backpacked, completed a masters degree in poetry and worked as a rafting guide. During that time, she befriended a number of slightly older women who shared her interest in outdoor pursuits, and she credits them with teaching her the foundations of her domestic skills. Under the mentorship of these women, she grew to love cooking, especially with whole foods. Toward the end of her twenties, she took a job as a teacher at an experiential outdoor school where the politics of food, the power of community and the beauty of handmade objects made a lasting impression on her. She married Thomas, and they moved partway across the country, where he completed his dissertation, she began working toward a second masters degree in literature and the environment, and they became pregnant. Upon Thomas' graduation, they moved to a rural college town in the Mid-Atlantic region, where he now works as a professor and she has, in her words, "made our life my art as well as my career." At the time of our interview, Maryann had a four-year-old and nine-month-old baby, and she was continuing to write and publish poetry and academic journal articles, as well as present research in the field of literature and the environment. The family is living on Thomas' annual income of about $55,000 per year.

JULIE AND DAVID HEWITT

Julie Hewitt grew up in a West Coast suburb. Her father was an executive for a health-care company, and her mother worked as a teacher until she had children. In Julie's words, her life was "as suburban as you could get." She never imagined having kids, she never thought about homemaking, never thought about growing her own food. After completing a degree in journalism, she worked as a travel editor for a small West Coast publisher. She met and married David, who was in the same line of work, and they wrote and edited travel books until they felt they could no longer make ends meet on $12-an-hour incomes. At that point, they "went corporate" and took jobs with a very large computer software company. After three years on the job, Julie became pregnant. Following complications in her third trimester, she had an emergency cesarean and gave birth to a three-and-a-half-pound baby girl with Down syndrome. Julie took her six-month pregnancy leave, and following that, David took his three-month paternity leave. Julie explains, "I was just kind of not fully in my body for those nine months. I was working . . . I couldn't get any more time off; my boss said 'no.'" Thus, "I went back to work kind of numb." The final straw was when, at the age of six months, their daughter required open heart surgery, and Julie found herself driving from work to the hospital every day of the week. In spite of what Julie and her fellow coworkers called "the golden handcuffs," where employees are not fully vested until they have put in four and a half years of service, Julie couldn't continue. She and David studied their financial statements and discovered they had acquired enough stock options for a nest egg. Julie quit work and stayed with their daughter while David continued to work. During that time, they lost a considerable amount of their money in some bad investments, which resulted in the couple becoming deeply conservative with their finances. They went through a period where they were constantly asking themselves, "What's really important?" Finally, they decided that they didn't need as much money. David then quit his job, they bought a fixer-upper, renovated it, gave birth to their son, then sold their home for a good profit. With the proceeds they moved to an isolated rural coastal community in the Pacific Northwest. Once more they bought a rundown home that David was able to repair with minimal outside help. David started a garden. Julie learned how to preserve their food. They got chickens and realized that if they just had a source of milk, they could greatly reduce their trips to the grocery store. Today, David works part-time from home, raises the vegetables, fixes old boats, and plays music each week with a group of friends. Julie tends the goats, home-schools the children, and puts up the harvest. The family of four lives on $48,000 per year.

EVE HONEYWELL

Eve and her husband Paul met in the fifth grade in their rural New Hampshire community. Eve lived in town until her parents divorced and her mother remarried when she was twelve. Her mother stayed home until her four children were in school, and then she worked in retail. Raising a large family, Eve's mother kept to a strict food budget by avoiding processed foods and cooking most of their meals. She also sewed clothes for her children, making sure they each received a new pair of pajamas every Christmas. As a teenager Eve had no plans to become a farmer. She went to a private liberal arts college, where she earned her teacher certification, then found herself back in her home community for her first teaching job, where she reconnected with Paul, who had completed a two-year degree in automotive mechanics at the state technical college. After two years working in the public education system, Eve was burned out, and she and Paul moved to the Midwest, where he had an opportunity to further his credentials while she worked three part-time jobs. During that period they decided they wanted to return to the family farm where Paul grew up. His dad had retired and was leasing the land to another farmer in the area. The couple paired up with Paul's sister, and together they formulated a business plan to take over the family farm. After a series of family negotiations, Eve and Paul moved back at the end of 2003. They settled into the tenant side of the farmhouse, where Paul's parents still live next door. They gave birth to their first child at home in early 2004. Paul opened a repair shop in one of the barns; Eve starting gardening and selling produce at the farmers' market and took a job as the community librarian. Three years later, she says, "I got to the point where I was juggling way too much. I had too many things going on and felt like the farm wasn't getting the attention it needed, the kids weren't getting the attention they needed and the library wasn't getting the attention it needed, and I had to cut something out . . . and it wasn't going to be my home, my kids or my farm." At that point Eve resigned from her position, although she continues to volunteer at the library during the winter months. Eve and Paul now have two children and they live on $30,000–35,000 per year, a large portion of which goes to pay for leasing the family farm from Paul's parents.

DEIRDRE AND RICK IANELLI

Deirdre and Rick grew up in the same town in rural Vermont where they live today. Deirdre described herself as very "career-oriented" prior to getting pregnant, having worked as a school teacher for three years and in radio prior to that. She quit her job once she and Rick decided to start a family, and he continued to work at his family's financial planning business, which his mother started in the community in the late 70s by going door to door while his father worked as a deliveryman. They live in one half of a duplex house that sits on a farmstead owned by Rick's parents. The organic farmstead has become an enterprise that involves much of their extended family. Rick manages the livestock, his sister and her partner manage an on-farm bed and breakfast for guests seeking agricultural tourism opportunities, and Deirdre assists with the livestock and helps out with the B&B. At the time of our interview, Deirdre and Rick had one son, Jeff, and a second child was due any day. Their annual income is between $30,000 and $35,000.

REBECCA AND STEVE JAMES

Growing up, Rebecca moved all around the country as a result of her father's employment with a multinational corporation. She never lived anywhere more than four years. She always lived in suburban neighborhoods, and describes her mother as "Suzy Homemaker. And she did it very well . . . but she is an extremely intelligent woman and she felt she wasn't using her gifts." When Rebecca was in high school, her mother returned to law school and became a corporate attorney. Rebecca describes her family's dining culture as "metal lunchbox cuisine," cream of mushroom soup, canned vegetables and iceberg lettuce. She never ate a winter squash or herbs until she became an adult. Rebecca was very strongly encouraged to "go away to college and get a career" and, she adds, "in my mom's head it would be something really spectacular, like a doctor or an astronaut . . . a career with panache. . . . And I found that difficult, because I liked a lot of home things. . . . I liked to be outdoors." Rebecca eventually became a teacher for children who suffered severe behavior handicaps. She met her husband in college, and while she had always wanted to home-school her future children, she continued to work because they required two salaries in order to make ends meet. Following stress-related birth complications with her third child, she and her husband Steve "had enough." He found a new, better paying job that would enable them to live in a rural setting. She quit her job, they moved to a rural area in the Northeast and purchased a small three-acre homestead. Rebecca home-schools their three children and has begun operating a small backyard farm, where she raises food for her family and sells or barters the surplus organic vegetables and eggs. Steve commutes to a nearby city to work. The family's annual income is $39,000.

ALISE AND EDUARDS JANSONS

Alise Jansons' mother and father immigrated to the United States from Latvia and settled in northern New Jersey prior to starting their family. Although her mother held a college degree in biology, she opted to stay home with her children. "She loved it," says Alise, "and I saw that." While she wasn't much of a cook, her mother had a passion for her garden in their little yard, just fifteen miles outside of Manhattan. Growing up, Alise felt like the "New Jersey Rat Race" didn't suit her. She dreamed about living in Alaska and, she adds, "I really loved being in the woods. I didn't really belong in New Jersey." As a teenager she traveled to Canada for a Latvian song festival, and there she met her future husband, Eduards, who lived in Minnesota. In order to be closer together, she went to college in Michigan so that they could travel to see each other by train. Then, she moved out to Minnesota to complete her masters degree in Community Health Education. She finished her degree, married Eduards, and two months later her mother suffered a brain hemorrhage. Alise and Eduards moved back East and settled into her parents' home. Her father had gone back to Latvia, and so Alise took on the job of caring for her mother, and Eduards worked a part-time job and enrolled in Rutgers to complete his bachelor degree. When Alise's mom passed on a year later, she and Eduards took on the task of settling the estate and selling the family home. With no ties left in New Jersey, they considered their next steps. Alise mentioned her childhood dream of living in Alaska. Eduards was keen on living anywhere that wasn't New Jersey. So they rented a small U-Haul trailer, bought a pickup truck, towed their little car behind it, and drove up the Alaskan Highway with their few belongings and Alise's $10,000 inheritance. Within three days of arriving, they rented a house. Within a month, Alise had a job as a manager in a brain injury program. Eduards worked as a temp, which eventually led him to his "dream job" of working for the Fish and Wildlife Service. With some help from Eduard's family, they got a downpayment together to purchase an old sawmill that had been converted to a house, and Alise gave birth to their son. Since she was the primary wage-earner, she continued with her job, bringing her son to work with her. When he was fourteen months old, "he was starting to get into things, and the Human Resources guy saw that, and didn't like it." When she was told she could no longer bring her son to work, Alise decided she would leave her job, give up her $44,000 income, and try to live on Eduards' $25,000 salary while she patched together odd jobs to make ends meet. Alise did everything from selling things on eBay to working as a "secret shopper" to help grocery store chains evaluate their customer service initiatives. Eduards' salary eventually increased, secret shopping work was no longer necessary, and the family of three (with hopes of adding an additional member at some point) lives on about $50,000. In the summer they forage berries and eat from their yard, and they dip-net fish as a family. This garners them about forty pounds of red salmon and thirty pounds of halibut per year. Eduards trades their surplus fish for caribou from coworkers who hunt, and Alise is a member of the local Mom's Club International, which participates in the state's Moose Kill List. Whenever a moose is killed by a car, whoever is at the top of the list is called immediately and then has a chance to drive to the site, process the road kill and bring the meat home for their family (moose, I've learned, is something of a coveted delicacy in Alaska).

NANCE KLEHM

Nance Klehm grew up on her parents' farm in northwest Illinois. Upon graduating from high school, she traveled, then eventually went to college and earned a bachelor degree in archeology. From there, she traveled to South America, where she worked for a spell until she got blood poisoning and returned to the Midwest. Today, she lives in a little Mexican neighborhood on the southwest side of Chicago, which she describes as "a friendly ghetto." Nance raises or forages for most of her food while living in the heart of the city. She gardens in her backyard, in the lot next to her, on her rooftop and in her basement. She created a "neighborhood orchard" in her community, where she helps her neighbors design and plant backyard gardens to meet their food needs, then takes unused portions of their harvest as her compensation. Nance teaches myriad courses for urban living — foraging, wild plants, cooking, food preservation, lacto-fermentation, wine and cheese making and ecosystem design. "I call myself a bio-instigator," she explains. At the time of our interview, she was wrapping up a project at a nearby homeless shelter where she designed on-site greenhouses that would grow food in soil made from the shelter's own food waste and discarded newspapers with the help of one million worms. She works just enough to garner the cash she needs — less than $20,000 per year — and then chooses to operate in the non-cash economy through trades and shared resources to provide for the bulk of her needs. Nance owns her home in her urban neighborhood, but she shares it with two chickens, a rabbit, two cats and three dogs.

CARRIE AND CHAD LOCKWELL

Carrie Lockwell grew up seven miles away from where she and Chad live today. Chad grew up just down the country road. Uncomfortable with the idea of taking on college debt, when she finished high school Carrie opted for a career in the military, where she worked as a mechanic in the Air Force. She met Chad upon her return home, and married him a year later and continued to work a series of jobs as a grocery store manager, typist, and house-cleaner. While in his twenties and before marrying Carrie, Chad opted to pay rent to his family and live at home, which enabled him to build up his savings, which he then used to buy a barn and twenty-six acres of neighboring land. When Carrie and Chad were ready to set up housekeeping, they were short on capital to buy or build a home. Instead, they borrowed $10,000 and built a 30-by-30-foot apartment in Chad's barn, which has expanded to accommodate the family's growing needs over the past fourteen years. Seeking an inexpensive way to manage the twenty-six acres behind their barn, the couple used their tax return one year to purchase two Herefords. They put up a single strand of wire to contain the beef cows, and officially started farming. Today, Chad works as a mechanic and Carrie home-schools their eleven-year-old son, Shawn, and manages their grass-fed meat business, where they now raise beef, pork and chicken, and keep one dairy cow. The family lives on about $40,000 per year in a rural community in the Northeast.

STORMY MCGOVERN

Stormy McGovern, now in her mid-twenties, grew up in the Pacific Northwest in "a little town with one bar, one gas station, a gun shop and a church that doesn't run anymore . . . just a bunch of back-to-the-landers and other folks scattered out in the woods." Her parents met in Seattle and acquired for very little money the land where she grew up. At first they lived in a platform tent. By the time Stormy was born, they had upgraded to a homemade two-room cabin with an outhouse. When her sister was born, they added a bedroom, and then, years later, they eventually added a bathroom. "They just kept kind of tacking on" as the family grew. They raised pigs, composted, used no chemicals and kept a garden. "It wasn't like we were trying to be back-to-the-land," she explains, "this was where [and how] we could afford to make it happen." Her dad owned a small paint shop, and she learned the basics about cooking and canning from her mom. While Stormy was able to get good grades in high school, she had a hard time feeling comfortable in the system and she became "a very troubled teen." "My rage came out, and eventually I left in a big explosion and I ran away." She dropped out of high school, went to Rainbow Gatherings, then eventually finished both high school and an associate degree through a series of sporadic enrollments in community colleges while she hitchhiked around the country and lived out of a backpack. During that time, "I realized I needed to eat," she explains, "so I started doing a lot of grassroots cooking." She joined the "Food Not Bombs" movement, where she would glean through cities for discarded and surplus food and would then use it to create meals "for the homeless, or for whoever wants to eat." In between she'd work on farms or find her way to Rainbow Gatherings, where, she says, "a lot of nomads mostly just live in the woods" and pray for peace and healing. Wherever she drifted, whether to a city street or Rainbow Gatherings, a farm, or toward a guerilla food-relief site following hurricane Katrina, Stormy would find her way to a makeshift kitchen to cook. "Food is my religion," she explains. "If you surround yourself with food, you're not going to starve, even if you don't have money." The trick, she explains, is to "use your energy to feed people." In recent years Stormy describes her life as more "grounded." At the time of our interview, she was living in a trailer on a small farmstead where, in exchange for rent, she helped manage the garden, tend livestock and preserve the harvest. She was working a series of odd jobs as members of her community needed her, doing everything from welding and rehabbing boats to babysitting, and was bringing in the most money she'd ever earned, about $200 per week. "It's a lot easier to be self-sufficient," she observes, "when you're in one spot. You're not going to hitchhike all over the country with all of your canned goods and your freezer of venison and your dried herbs, you know?"

MICHAEL AND SARAH MILLS

Michael and Sarah Mills were high-school sweethearts in a middle-class suburban community outside New York City. Upon graduating from high school, both began college but left early, feeling that higher education wasn't suiting their needs at that point in their life. Aces in frugality, Michael worked first in a hardware store, and then in a glass shop. Sarah taught, then worked a few other jobs. Michael lived at home, borrowed a car if he needed it, and he and Sarah found they preferred dates that required very little money, such as going canoeing. As a result, when they were twenty and twenty-one respectively, they were able to put 40 percent down on their first home. "I really wanted to own property and own a house," Michael explains. "I didn't want to be in debt and I didn't want to ever be concerned thinking somebody could take away where I live, that I could lose it." Thus, by the time he was twenty-seven and Sarah was twenty-eight, the mortgage was paid off. Seeking a more suitable community to meet their needs, the couple eventually decided to purchase eighty acres in the northern Catskills. Michael had been working in a factory at the time, where he eventually worked his way into the tool room, then became a metal pattern-maker. However, once they owned property, he left his job in order to build their passive solar home, while Sarah

took work as a teachers' aide in order to procure health insurance. For
a short period, they lived next door while Michael built, then they
moved into a camper on the property along with their son, who was
four, their daughter, who was two, and, Sarah adds, "a big dog." Once
they had moved into the home, Michael temporarily resumed work
as a machinist, and Sarah took care of the children and went back to
school, eventually earning her masters degree, enabling her to take a
job teaching while Michael once more returned home. While raising
their family, they kept and processed chickens, ducks, pigs, sheep and
geese; Michael planted and sold Christmas trees; and they grew all
their own fruit and vegetables. Now, with the children grown and
on their own (their college educations all paid for, debt-free), they
have stopped producing meat. "I was killing all of it, and I just got
this hard shell," Michael explains, "and I lost it. . . . I'd much rather
kill something that doesn't trust me." Thus, these days Michael hunts
deer for their meat, and they've begun raising trout in addition to
keeping their garden, apples trees and an enormous blueberry patch.
Michael and Sarah have an adjusted annual gross income of less than
$30,000, and they continue to put about 20 percent of it into savings
each year.

DAVID PETERSON

David Peterson met his future wife, Janice, when they were both
thirty-two years old. He was a woodworker, sleeping at night on his
shop bench in Boston; she was completing her residency for her MD.
They married when they were thirty-five. A New Englander from
many generations back, David wanted to return to his roots in rural
Vermont, and so they moved back north. David and Janice wanted
to have children but, he says, "we hadn't figured out beyond that at
all, and when he was born, we didn't know what to do. We had both
been planning on working, and we couldn't. We didn't want to put
him off in day care and just see him for two or three hours a day.
[After completing a one-year mediation program] I wasn't finding a
job, and I had a better temperament for staying home with him." He
adds, "I could never make as much money as she did . . . and it was

great." Once their son was enrolled in kindergarten, David and Janice acquired some land, and he hired himself on as his own contractor. First, he built himself a shop, then a garage, and finally, once he felt his carpentry skills were up to the challenge, he built the family a house. While Janice's income was adequate to support the family, they recently lost much of their savings, which had previously been ample, because "we'd done it in a very traditional way . . . the IRA-type thing, and you know, we've watched our money go. . . . We were told this was the way to do it, and I've learned not to believe that any-more!" David, who has no regrets about his time as a stay-at-home dad, is facing the challenge of his empty nest now that his son, one of his dearest friends, has gone away to college. Knowing that Janice would like to reduce her work hours, yet keenly aware that, at age sixty-one, their retirement plans have suffered a considerable setback, David was looking for meaningful work to supplement their savings when we spoke in July of 2008. In addition to serving as a substitute teacher (and riding the school bus to work), he had enlisted with a temp service, eager to try something different from carpentry and woodworking. David and Janice had also recently begun keeping livestock in addition to their home garden. In later months, follow-ing our interview, he abandoned the temp work and career search and ultimately decided to expand his farm production to sell food to his neighbors, and to resume his craft work.

ANNA REYNOLDS

Anna Reynolds grew up in Brooklyn in the 1950s, one of six children. One of her brothers developed a terminal illness, and so her parents worked three and a half jobs between them in order to pay for his medical expenses and support the family. Anna's mother, in addition to being a dietician, could knit, crochet, tat, garden and preserve food. Torn between work, a sick child and raising a family, Anna's mother abandoned the notion of keeping a tidy home. As a child, her family would visit the Hunts Point Market each year to buy bulk quanti-ties of whatever vegetables and fruits they couldn't raise in their own backyard; then they would can and freeze them for the winter. Anna attended NYU, then worked as a chemical engineer for a corporation in the Midwest. Upon getting pregnant for her second child, she was fired and became a stay-at-home-mom and farmed while her husband worked. Feeling that the public school system could not meet her family's needs, she opted to home school all four of her children through high school. At age fifty-two, with three children still at home, Anna and her husband divorced. She used her portion of her small settlement to relocate to a rundown farm in rural Pennsylvania, within commuting distance of the state's land grant college. One of the children opted to forego college, and the other two sons, now in their twenties, continue to live at home. They are taking turns attending college and living at home to help their mother operate the small dairy farm. Anna has also enrolled at the land grant, intent on updating her credentials (and manages to procure her health insurance as well). The family is living on about $30,000 per year.

KELLY ROBIDEAU

Kelly Robideau grew up in an affluent San Francisco suburb, where her father worked as an architect and her mother stayed home until she was eight years old. "I always felt like she was home," Kelly remarks, "even when she was working, because I'd just go to the fabric store and hang out with her there. . . . Friends of mine that I grew up with always say that, going over to our house, there was always something baking." Most of her friends had two parents who worked full-time, so Kelly's family was an exception in her neighborhood. Kelly was strongly encouraged to find a career for herself but, she confesses, "I was always much more interested in home kinds of things. . . . [In college] I was in the 'consumer and family studies' department, which was what they used to call 'home economics,' and people razzed me for that . . . it was really kind of frowned upon to be interested in domestic things." Kelly married after college, started working on her masters degree, got pregnant, then split up with her husband prior to the birth of her daughter. To give herself the flexibility to be able to spend more time with her baby, she moved back home with her family, finished her masters degree, then began working at a hospital as a dietician. Wanting to find a way to support herself and her daughter from home, she began publishing a newsletter on children's nutrition and periodically taught nutrition classes at parenting centers. Kelly eventually remarried, and she and her husband and teenage daughter now live in a tiny house about an hour north of San Francisco, where he works as a psychologist. Kelly loves the subject of food and nutrition, so she continues to teach at a nearby college two days per week. The family's tiny backyard provides them with herbs, vegetables, peaches, apples and figs, which they enjoy fresh and preserve. They pick their olives from a nearby cemetery, cure them themselves, make their own wine and brandy, buy pork from a friend, and cure their own bacon and pancetta.

CAROL RYDELL AND AMANDA SHAW

Carol and Amanda do not share a home. Rather, they are members of the same community who have built a powerful friendship and serve as one another's support. Since their domestic pursuits and community involvement are so intertwined, I have chosen to blend their biographies together.

Carol Rydell, seventy-five, moved to her home in the suburbs of a Midwestern city over thirty years ago when her husband took a job as a pastor at a local church. There, she raised her family and, once her children were in junior high, she resumed her work as a registered dietician. Following her retirement, she learned about the nutritional principles advocated by the Weston Price Foundation and became an advocate for eating sustainably produced meat, animal fats, raw (unpasteurized) dairy products, and fruits and vegetables acquired directly from local farms or, in her case, from her suburban backyard, which she converted into a four-season fruit and vegetable garden, complete with Carol's own "humanure" composting system for added nutrients.

Amanda Shaw, now in her late forties, grew up twenty miles outside of the city and wound up moving back to the area with her children following her husband's career. Amanda was a stay-at-home mom and active gardener. In 2001 with their children out of the house, her husband left, seemingly, in Amanda's words, "overnight." At that point, says Amanda, she had no choice but to set out on "this healing journey. Just looking to get my health and my life back and find my own life — find *me*." On that journey she met and befriended Carol. The two women teamed up to lead the local chapter of the Weston Price Foundation in an effort to help more members of their community find sustainable, nutritious food. Meanwhile, Amanda, with greatly reduced financial resources and no land available through her rental property, took on a community garden plot to procure food for herself.

When Carol's husband passed suddenly in 2006, and Amanda's efforts to complete her certification in integrative nutrition made her garden work seem overwhelming, they joined forces once more, this time in Carol's backyard. Ever since, the two women have shared the labor and harvest in Carol's garden. Amanda comes over once per week to work, and then they share a meal. Together they also coordinate one of the many underground farm clubs that are sprouting up nationwide, where nearby farmers supply raw milk and other fresh, local products not sanctioned by the state department of agriculture (or the industrial agricultural complex). With over 200 members, they've set up a guerilla farm market twice per month in a back lot behind a local church that supports their efforts to provide ecologically and nutritionally beneficial foods for their community. The "club" has meetings twice per month where products are exchanged for three hours, and then everyone packs up and disappears. In addition, Carol and Amanda teach nutrition and cooking classes through several local venues, including nonprofit ecological centers, church groups and cancer support programs.

HOLLY AND BRIAN SIMMONS

When Holly Simmons' mom and dad finished college in the early sixties, they abandoned city life on the coast and bought a ranch out west. "My dad always wanted to be a cowboy," she explains. Her parents operated a marginal livestock venture while raising five children. Once the kids were grown and on their own, seeing no future in ranching, they made plans to throw in the towel and convert the 400 acres to a golf course. During the same period, Holly had gone to college and majored in art, then moved to New York City, where she worked a brief period in the fashion industry. She quickly discovered that the lifestyle held no appeal for her and moved back home to assist in the waning family business. Once home, she met Brian, who was working as a geologist. Soon after, they got married and started a family as Holly's dad finalized plans to "develop" the ranch. At the eleventh hour, a friend convinced Holly's dad to attend a workshop for ranchers on a process called Holistic Management, where (to simplify the teachings somewhat) attendees were taught techniques for integrating social and ecological analysis in their decision-making processes. Brian accompanied Holly's dad to the workshop. One of the first things they learned, explains Holly, was that in Holistic Management, "*Everybody* comes to the table, *not* just the papas — the kids, the moms, *everybody* is making decisions together, and it's huge." That lesson hit home. Today, Holly and two of her siblings, along with their spouses and children, have rejoined their parents on the family ranch, with a fourth sibling making plans to return as soon as possible, and the fifth living in the area. There are no golf courses on the horizons, as each nuclear family unit has their own business enterprise that operates using the shared land base. Some grow organic vegetables; others operate a grass-based dairy; someone else produces grass-fed meat. Holly and Brian started a landscaping business that keeps them busy during the growing season, but allows them freedom to home-school their three boys during the winter months, plus attend the boys' races with the local cross-country ski team. The family of five lives on $40,000 per year.

PENELOPE AND JOHN SLOAN

Penelope and John grew up in the same town in suburban New Jersey, but they didn't meet until after Penelope had graduated from college with a major in political science and was selling clothing in a chain store in a shopping mall. A few months later, they moved in together in the small city where John was working on his masters degree, and Penelope worked a series of temporary jobs. When he graduated and found work at an agricultural chemical company, they purchased a small home with the help of their family. Penelope began working on a second degree, this time in nutrition. In the course of her studies, she met a number of nutritionists who "were really down on the whole field." She decided she "didn't want to be a killjoy," telling heart attack victims to stop eating eggs, especially when she felt eggs were part of a wholesome diet. Penelope then took what she describes as yet another "soul-sucking job" in a computer lab, and eventually found a position as an assistant teacher in a Montessori school, which she enjoyed. In the interim she came across the book *Your Money or Your Life,* and she and John became interested in voluntary simplicity and living job-free. Thus, they converted a piece of their "postage stamp" suburban yard into a garden, lived as frugally as possible, and earned the title of "the weird people" from their New Jersey neighbors. "We started to kind of feel like we didn't belong in that suburban setting," Penelope explains. So they made a plan with the aim of eventually achieving financial independence and moving to the country. Five years before their anticipated "retirement date," they received an unexpected inheritance and decided they had enough money to relocate to their new lives. They sold their house and bought a cheaper fixer-upper farm in rural Vermont. They put their inheritance money into a series of five-year certificates of deposit, which now provide them a relatively stable and modest income of $20,000–22,000 per year. Now thirty-six and forty-one, respectively, Penelope and John grow most of their fruit and vegetables, brew their own wine and beer, raise chickens and a Thanksgiving turkey, are considering plans for acquiring a few goats, and travel to town no more than twice per week.

SYLVIA TANNER

Upon crossing the threshold to Sylvia Tanner's solar, off-grid cabin, you are greeted with a bumper sticker hung over her drain board: *I wanted to save the world, but I couldn't find a babysitter.* Sylvia was raised in New York City, where both of her parents worked full-time. Sylvia was married soon out of college, living in Delaware while she pursued a masters degree in agronomy. Her marriage was brief, however, and soon after she and her husband separated, she found out she was pregnant. Sylvia was funded to complete her Ph.D., but after her son was born, she was confronted with a different reality. "I had these images that you just sort of have this kid and you just went right back to everything, and they just slept or something," she recalls, laughing. "And then I found out that wasn't the case. . . . I had no clue that everything would turn into total upheaval . . . I finally realized I couldn't do it all." Needing to find some income to support her son and herself, Sylvia worked part-time as a solar scientist and fed her little family of two from a plot she maintained in a community garden. She and her son eventually returned to Boston, where she worked full-time as an environmental analyst once he was old enough to go to school. She had read the book *Your Money or Your Life* and chose to save every dime she could with a goal to have a form of financial independence that, rather than not having to work at all, would enable her to do only the type of work she wanted to do and have time for other things. She was soon able to buy a plot of land in Maine with a derelict cabin. While she continued to work, she and her son would drive up every weekend to plant an orchard and blueberry bushes. Her next step was to hire on a friend as a carpenter. Since she had no carpentry skills, she hired herself on as his assistant. Over the next few years, Sylvia did much of the rehab work on her cabin herself, with the help of friends. When she and her son were ready for a living room, she recruited a master carpenter and promoted a building workshop throughout New England. She managed to secure a core of eager students who paid her friend for the privilege to learn to build her addition, while she helped out and fed everyone. Once she and her son were ready to move into the cabin full-time, she switched her job to part-time and commuted, staying away from home one night each week while her neighbors took care of her son. When the stress became too much for the little family, she threw up her white flag on her career and said, "I'm going to wing it from here." Since 1997 she has supported herself and her son by raising much of their own food, operating a small CSA, selling organic blueberries, and through myriad part-time jobs that would enable her to make ends meet, including freelance writing, adjunct teaching, cooking, anything that, in Sylvia's words, is "interesting," "meaningful," and "*not* full-time." Now that her son is grown, she spends much of her time community organizing and playing music, in addition to running her farm and working as needed. Because of the fluctuating nature of her income, Sylvia was unable to pin down an actual annual income on which she raised her son, or on which she lives now, although she says it has always been near poverty level.

BETTINA AND JUSTIN WINSTON

Bettina Winston spent her earliest years living with her parents, siblings, a couple of her aunts and their boyfriends in a large rented farmhouse on the outskirts of Saratoga Springs, New York. There, her family heated only with firewood, kept a big garden, and ate no processed foods. When she was five, her nuclear family moved to a small house in the village, where her parents started a home-based business. By contrast, Justin grew up in a suburb in the Midwest where his father worked for a large corporation and his mother went to work after he and his brother started school. Bettina and Justin met in New York City, where Justin was employed by a small shop and worked as a self-described "poor artist," who was "really used to not having money, and not having things and not feeling bad about it." Bettina describes her former "career" as being plugged into a "network for odd jobs," where she did various things, including sewing, puppet-making, and painting. After the birth of their first child, they moved back to the Saratoga area to be near Bettina's family. They work as artists, operate a small craft business and live on less than $45,000 per year. They garden, make maple syrup, can and freeze their harvest, and harbor hopes of someday being able to have more land to grow more of their food. They now have two children, ages five and one (Camille and Devon).

ENDNOTES

INTRODUCTION / **RADICAL HOMEMAKING**

1. David Korten, "What's an Economy For?," in *Take Back Your Time*, ed. John De Graaf (San Francisco: Berrett-Koehler, 2003).

2. Ruth Schwartz Cowan, *More Work for Mother* (New York: Basic Books, Inc., 1983), p. 17.

3. Betty Friedan, *The Feminine Mystique*, 5 ed. (New York: W.W. Norton and Company, Inc., 2001).

4. United States Department of Health and Human Services, *2008 Poverty Level Guidelines*.

PART ONE: WHY

CHAPTER ONE / **A WOMAN'S PLACE**

1. William S. Coperthwaite, *A Handmade Life* (White River Junction, VT: Chelsea Green, 2002), p. 16.

2. David C. Korten, *The Great Turning: From Empire to Earth Community*, First ed. (San Francisco — Bloomfield: Berrett-Koehler Publishers, Inc., and Kumarian Press, Inc., 2006), p. 24.

3. Riane Eisler, *The Chalice and the Blade* (New York: Harper and Row, 1987).

4. Korten, *The Great Turning: From Empire to Earth Community*.

5. Eisler, *The Chalice and the Blade*.

6. Ibid., p. 45

7. Glenna Matthews, *"Just a Housewife" The Rise and Fall of Domesticity in America* (New York: Oxford University Press, 1987).

8. Ibid.

9. Korten, *The Great Turning: From Empire to Earth Community*, p. 107.

10. Betty Friedan, *The Feminine Mystique*, 5 ed. (New York: W.W. Norton and Company, Inc., 2001).

11. Ibid., p. 91.

12. Ibid., p. 57.

13. Ibid., p. 71.

14. Ibid., p. 126.

15. Ibid., p. 83.

16. Ibid., p. 299.

17. Ibid., p. 300.

18. Ibid., p. 301.

19. Ibid., p. 323.

20. Ibid., p. 305.

21. Ibid., p. 310.

22. Ibid., p. 310.

23. Ibid., p. 321.

24. Ibid., p. 320.

25. Ibid., p. 330.

26. Lee Drutman and Charlie Cray Drutman, *The People's Business* (San Francisco: Berett-Koehler, 2004), p. 3.

27. USDA/ERS, 2009, available from http://www.ers.usda.gov/Data/FoodConsumption/FoodAvailQueriable.aspx#midForm.

28. National Center for Health Statistics, "Health, United States, 2007," (Hyattesville, MD: 2007).

29. Pamela Stone, *Opting Out?* (Los Angeles: University of California Press, 2007).

30. Ibid., p. 82.

31. Ibid., p. 19.

32. National Women's Law Center, *Congress Must Act to Close the Wage Gap for Women*, 2008, available from http://www.nwlc.org/pdf/Pay_Equity_Fact_Sheet_Nov2008.pdf.

33. Stone, *Opting Out?*

34. Leslie Bennetts, *The Feminine Mistake: Are We Giving up Too Much?* (New York: Hyperion, 2007).

35. Ibid., p. 84–85.

36. David Korten, "What's an Economy For?" in *Take Back Your Time*, ed. John De Graaf (San Francisco: Berrett-Koehler, 2003).

37. Stone, *Opting Out?* P. 11.

38. Ibid., p. 15.

39. Wendell Berry, "Does Community Have a Value?" in *Home Economics* (San Francisco: North Point Press, 1987), p. 191–192.

40. John De Graaf, David Wann, and Thomas H. Naylor, *Affluenza* (San Francisco: Berrett-Koehler Publishers, 2005), p. 59.

41. Thomas Berry, *The Great Work* (New York: Bell Tower, 1999), p. 180.

42. Matthews, *"Just a Housewife" The Rise and Fall of Domesticity in America.*

43. Ibid., p. 139.

44. Dolores Hayden, *The Grand Domestic Revolution* (Cambridge: The MIT Press, 1981).

45. Ibid., p. 6.

46. Ibid., p. 6.

47. Matthews, *"Just a Housewife" The Rise and Fall of Domesticity in America.*

48. Hayden, *The Grand Domestic Revolution*, p. xiv.

49. Friedan, *The Feminine Mystique*, p. 341.

50. Ibid., p. 472.

51. Ibid., p. 472.

52. Hayden, *The Grand Domestic Revolution*, p. 5.

53. Matthews, *"Just a Housewife" The Rise and Fall of Domesticity in America*, p. xv.

CHAPTER TWO / **HOME ECONOMICS**

1. John De Graaf, David Wann, and Thomas H. Naylor, *Affluenza* (San Francisco: Berrett-Koehler Publishers, 2005), p. 131.

2. Betty Friedan, *The Feminine Mystique*, 5 ed. (New York: W.W. Norton and Company, Inc., 2001), p. 23.

3. Ibid., p. 23.

4. Henry David Thoreau, *Walden and Civil Disobedience* (New York: Penguin, 1983), p. 399.

5. John De Graaf, "What's the Economy for, Anyway?", *In Balance*, no. 37 (2008).

6. Ibid.

7. Lee Drutman and Charlie Cray Drutman, *The People's Business* (San Francisco: Berett-Koehler, 2004).

8. David C. Korten, *The Great Turning: From Empire to Earth Community*, First ed. (San Francisco — Bloomfield: Berrett-Koehler Publishers, Inc., and Kumarian Press, Inc., 2006).

9. Drutman, *The People's Business*.

10. Ibid., p. 4.

11. Ibid., p. 16.

12. Ibid., p. 14.

13. Korten, *The Great Turning: From Empire to Earth Community*, p. 138.

14. Drutman, *The People's Business*, p. 13.

15. Korten, *The Great Turning: From Empire to Earth Community*, p. 41.

16. Thoreau, *Walden and Civil Disobedience*, p. 69.

17. Taken from remarks by former President George W. Bush to airline employees at Chicago O'Hare International Airport on September 27, 2001.

18. Thomas Berry, *The Great Work* (New York: Bell Tower, 1999), p. 63.

19. Jonathan Rowe, "Wasted Work, Wasted Time," in *Take Back Your Time*, ed. John De Graaf (San Francisco: Berrett-Koehler, 2003).

20. Sean Cole, "The Fix Is in Decline," *Marketplace Radio*, November 9, 2007.

21. Wendell Berry, "Does Community Have a Value?", in *Home Economics* (San Francisco: North Point Press, 1987).

22. Jeffrey Goldbert, "How Big Is Wal-Mart?" (*The Atlantic*, 2009, cited March 5); available from http://jeffreygoldberg.theatlantic.com/ archives/2009/03/how_big_is_walmart.php.

23. Bill McKibben, *Deep Economy: The Wealth of Communities and the Durable Future* (New York: Times Books, 2007), p. 124.

24. John Talberth, Clifford Cobb, and Noah Slattery, "The Genuine Progress Indicator 2006," (Oakland, CA: Redefining Progress, 2006).

25. U.S. Dept of Commerce, "Gross Domestic Product, 1 Decimal," (U.S. Dept of Commerce, Bureau of Economic Analysis, 1947.01.01 to 2008.01.01).

26. Talberth, Cobb, and Slattery, "The Genuine Progress Indicator 2006."

27. G. William Domhoff, *Who Rules America?* (University of California Santa Cruz, 2006; available from http://sociology.ucsc.edu/ whorulesamerica/power/wealth.html.)

28. Drutman, *The People's Business.*

29. De Graaf, Wann, and Naylor, *Affluenza.*

30. Merriam Webster, *Webster's New Collegiate Dictionary* (Springfield, MA: G.&C. Merriam Company, 1979).

31. Earth Charter USA, Www.Earthcharterus.Org, 2009.

32. Berry, "Does Community Have a Value?"

33. Widmeyer Research and Polling, *New American Dream: Polls and Research* (Center for a New American Dream, 1998–2006; available from http://www.newdream.org/about/polls.php.)

34. Ibid.

35. Ibid.

36. Ibid.

CHAPTER THREE / **FROM SELF-RELIANCE TO COMMODIFICATION**

1. William S. Coperthwaite, *A Handmade Life* (White River Junction, VT: Chelsea Green, 2002), p. 7.

2. As quoted in John De Graaf, David Wann, and Thomas H. Naylor, *Affluenza* (San Francisco: Berrett-Koehler Publishers, 2005).

3. Ruth Schwartz Cowan, *More Work for Mother* (New York: Basic Books, Inc., 1983), p. 17.

4. Ibid.

5. Ibid., p. 26.

6. Ibid., p. 25.

7. Ibid.

8. Ibid.

9. Glenna Matthews, *"Just a Housewife" The Rise and Fall of Domesticity in America* (New York: Oxford University Press, 1987).

10. Cowan, *More Work for Mother.*

11. Matthews, *"Just a Housewife" The Rise and Fall of Domesticity in America*, p. 4.

12. Ibid., p. 6.

13. Mary Tolford Wilson *The First American Cookbook*, in Amelia Simmons, *American Cookery* (New York: Dover, 1796/1958).

14. Amelia Simmons, *American Cookery*, first printed in 1796 (facsimile of *American Cookery:* New York: Dover, 1958).

15. Matthews, *"Just a Housewife" The Rise and Fall of Domesticity in America.*

16. Ibid., p. 21.

17. Ibid.

18. Ibid., p. 61.

19. Ralph Waldo Emerson, "Domestic Life," in *Volume VII, Society and Solitude* (Boston: Houghton Mifflin, 1893).

20. Ibid.

21. Cowan, *More Work for Mother.*

22. Ibid.

23. Sherrie McMillan, "Evolution of Mealtimes," *History*, October/ November issue (2001).

24. Ibid.

25. Cowan, *More Work for Mother.*

26. As quoted in Matthews, *"Just a Housewife" The Rise and Fall of Domesticity in America.* p. 99.

27. Ibid.

28. Ibid.

29. Ibid.

30. Cowan, *More Work for Mother*.

31. Ibid.

32. Matthews, *"Just a Housewife" The Rise and Fall of Domesticity in America*, p. 180.

33. Ibid.

34. Ibid.

35. Cowan, *More Work for Mother*.

36. Pamela Stone, *Opting Out?* (Los Angeles: University of California Press, 2007), p. 182.

37. Bruce E. Levine, *Surviving America's Depression Epidemic* (White River Junction, VT: Chelsea Green, 2007).

38. Dolores Hayden, *The Grand Domestic Revolution* (Cambridge: The MIT Press, 1981).

39. Ibid.

40. Matthews, *"Just a Housewife" The Rise and Fall of Domesticity in America*.

41. Ibid., p. 145–146

42. Ibid., p. 171.

43. Ibid., p. 162.

44. Christine Frederick, *Selling Mrs. Consumer* (New York: The Business bourse, 1929), p. 5.

45. Ibid., p. 12.

46. Ibid., p. 21.

47. Ibid., p. 23–24.

48. As quoted in Matthews, *"Just a Housewife" The Rise and Fall of Domesticity in America*, p. 157.

49. Ibid.

50. Ibid.

51. Ibid., p. 151.

52. Ibid.

53. Ibid.

54. Frederick, *Selling Mrs. Consumer*, p. 129–130.

55. John L. Hess, and Karen Hess, *The Taste of America* (Champaign, IL: University of Illinois Press, 2000), p. 8.

56. Greg Horn, *Living Green* (Toanga, CA: Freedom Press, 2006).

57. Hess, *The Taste of America*, p. 45.

58. Bill McKibben, *Deep Economy: The Wealth of Communities and the Durable Future* (New York: Times Books, 2007).

59. Hess, *The Taste of America*.

60. From Food and Agriculture Organization, Agricultural Biodiversity in FAO Factsheets: http://www.fao.org/docrep/010/i0112e/i0112e00.htm.

61. Ibid.

62. Barbara Kingsolver, *Animal, Vegetable, Miracle: A Year of Food Life* (New York: HarperCollins, 2007).

63. McKibben, *Deep Economy: The Wealth of Communities and the Durable Future*.

64. Ibid.

65. Lance Gay, "Americans Are Tossing $100 Billion of Food a Year," *Organic Consumers Association*, August 10, 2005.

66. Andrew Martin, "One Country's Table Scraps, Another Country's Meal," *The New York Times*, May 18, 2008.

67. Oberlin College, *Oberlin College Recycling Program* (Oberlin College, 2001); available from http://www.oberlin.edu/recycle/facts.html.

68. USDA/ERS, (2009); available from http://www.ers.usda.gov/Data/FoodConsumption/FoodAvailQueriable.aspx#midForm.

69. National Center for Health Statistics, "Health, United States, 2007" (Hyattesville, MD: 2007).

70. De Graaf, Wann, and Naylor, *Affluenza*.

71. Kingsolver, *Animal, Vegetable, Miracle: A Year of Food Life*.

72. Richard Layard, *Happiness: Lessons from a New Science* (New York: Penguin, 2005).

73. Hara Estroff Marano, *Suburban Blues* (March 22, 2005); available from http://www.psychologytoday.com/articles/pto-20050322-000002. html.

CHAPTER FOUR / **HOME WRECKERS**

1. Bruce E. Levine, *Surviving America's Depression Epidemic* (White River Junction, VT: Chelsea Green, 2007), p. 3.

2. Juliet Schor, "We Must Reduce Our Super-Sized Appetites," *Marketplace Radio*, November 13, 2007.

3. Ibid.

4. Greg Horn, *Living Green* (Toanga, CA: Freedom Press, 2006).

5. Tess Vigeland, "Tess' Trash Tour," *Marketplace Radio*, November 9, 2007.

6. Martin E.P. Seligman and Ed Diener, "Beyond Money," *Psychological Science in the Public Interest* 5, no. 1 (2004).

7. Levine, *Surviving America's Depression Epidemic*. p. 7.

8. Ibid., p. 3.

9. Ibid., p. 172.

10. John De Graaf, David Wann, and Thomas H. Naylor, *Affluenza* (San Francisco: Berrett-Koehler Publishers, 2005).

11. Jonathan Rowe, "Wasted Work, Wasted Time," in *Take Back Your Time*, ed. John De Graaf (San Francisco: Berrett-Koehler, 2003).

12. Richard Layard, *Happiness: Lessons from a New Science* (New York: Penguin, 2005), p. 183

13. Stephen Bezruchka, "The (Bigger) Picture of Health," in *Take Back Your Time*, ed. John De Graaf (San Francisco: Berrett-Koehler, 2003), p. 85.

14. Bill McKibben, *Deep Economy: The Wealth of Communities and the Durable Future* (New York: Times Books, 2007).

15. Levine, *Surviving America's Depression Epidemic*, p. 29.

16. De Graaf, Wann, and Naylor, *Affluenza*, p. 115.

17. Ed Diener, "Beyond Money."

18. Henry David Thoreau, *Walden and Civil Disobedience* (New York: Penguin, 1983).

19. Taken from William Morris' 1884 lecture, "Art and Socialism," available online at http://www.marxists.org/archive/morris/works/1884/as/as.htm.

20. John De Graaf, "Preface," in *Take Back Your Time*, ed. John De Graaf (San Francisco: Berrett-Koehler, 2003).

21. Juliet Schor, "The (Even More) Overworked American," in *Take Back Your Time*, ed. John De Graaf (San Francisco: Berrett-Koehler, 2003).

22. John De Graaf, "What's the Economy for, Anyway?", *In Balance*, no. 37 (2008).

23. McKibben, *Deep Economy: The Wealth of Communities and the Durable Future*.

24. Schor, "The (Even More) Overworked American," p. 9–10.

25. Barbara Brandt, "An Issue for Everybody," in *Take Back Your Time*, ed. John De Graaf (San Francisco: Berrett-Koehler, 2003).

26. Joe Robinson, "The Incredible Shrinking Vacation," in *Take Back Your Time*, ed. John De Graaf (San Francisco: Berrett-Koehler, 2003).

27. Steven Greenhouse, "Forced to Work off the Clock, Some Fight Back," *The New York Times*, November 19, 2004.

28. Jonathan Rowe, "Out of Time," *Yes!*, Winter (2006).

29. De Graaf, Wann, and Naylor, *Affluenza*.

30. Brandt, "An Issue for Everybody," p. 13.

31. Camilla H. Fox, "What About Fluffy and Fido?", in *Take Back Your Time*, ed. John De Graaf (San Francisco: Berrett-Koehler, 2003), p. 54.

32. Taken from Joaquin Almunia's June 1, 2007, report, "More and Better Statistics for an Improved Economic Governance," press conference to present new economic quarterly statistics, Brussels.

33. Thoreau, *Walden and Civil Disobedience*, p. 47–48.

34. De Graaf, "Preface," *Take Back Your Time*.

35. Schor, "The (Even More) Overworked American."

36. McKibben, *Deep Economy: The Wealth of Communities and the Durable Future*, p. 115.

37. Tim and Kirk Warren Brown Kasser, "On Time, Happiness, and Ecological Footprints," in *Take Back Your Time*, ed. John De Graaf (San Francisco: Berrett-Koehler, 2000).

38. Ibid., p. 110.

39. De Graaf, Wann, and Naylor, *Affluenza*, p. 137.

40. Rowe, "Out of Time."

41. De Graaf, Wann, and Naylor, *Affluenza*, p. 2.

42. David C. Korten, *The Great Turning: From Empire to Earth Community*, First ed. (San Francisco — Bloomfield: Berrett-Koehler Publishers, Inc., and Kumarian Press, Inc., 2006), p. 59.

43. Justin Fox/Davos, "Can the World Stop the Slide?", *Time Magazine*, January 24, 2008.

44. De Graaf, Wann, and Naylor, *Affluenza*, p. 143.

45. Associated Press, "Average Home Has More TVs Than People," *USA Today*, September 21, 2006.

46. As quoted in McKibben, *Deep Economy: The Wealth of Communities and the Durable Future*.

47. Layard, *Happiness: Lessons from a New Science*.

48. McKibben, *Deep Economy: The Wealth of Communities and the Durable Future*, p. 132.

49. MPA, *Under the Influence of Magazines* (Magazine Publishers of America, 2008).

50. Juliet Schor, "The New Politics of Consumption: Why Americans Want So Much More Than They Need," *Boston Review*, Summer 1999.

51. Levine, *Surviving America's Depression Epidemic*, p. 28.

52. Layard, *Happiness: Lessons from a New Science*.

53. Levine, *Surviving America's Depression Epidemic*, p. 82.

54. Ed Diener and Shigehiro Oishi, "The Nonobvious Social Psychology of Happiness," draft of invited paper for journal (University of Illinois at Urbana — Champaign 2004; available from www.psych.uiuc.edu/~ediener/hottopic/nonovious.htm), p. 4.

55. Scott Jagow, "Greed as a Disease," *Marketplace Radio*, November 12, 2007.

56. De Graaf, Wann, and Naylor, *Affluenza*.

57. Kasser, "On Time, Happiness, and Ecological Footprints," p. 111.

58. Korten, *The Great Turning: From Empire to Earth Community*.

59. K. Harrison, and K and A. Marske, "Nutritional content of foods advertised during the television programs children watch most," *American Journal of Public Health*, 2005; 95:1568-1574.

60. Associated Press, "Average Home Has More TVs Than People," *USA today*, September 21, 2006.

61. Trans-Atlantic Consumer Dialogue, Doc # Food 26-06, May 2006.

62. Hara Estroff Marano, "Suburban Blues," March 22, 2005; available from http://www.psychologytoday.com/articles/pto-20050322-000002.html.

63. McKibben, *Deep Economy: The Wealth of Communities and the Durable Future*, p. 98.

64. June Fletcher, "New Floor Plans Provide Peace, Quiet and Privacy," *Wall Street Journal Online*, 2004.

65. Ibid.

66. Clemson Extension, "Making Mealtimes Pleasant," *Home and Garden Information Center*, 2008.

67. McKibben, *Deep Economy: The Wealth of Communities and the Durable Future*, p. 117.

68. Robert Putnam, *Bowling Alone: The Collapse and Revival of American Community* (New York: Simon and Schuster, 2000), p. 288–289.

69. Layard, *Happiness: Lessons from a New Science*.

70. McKibben, *Deep Economy: The Wealth of Communities and the Durable Future*, p. 101.

71. Institute for Local Self Reliance, "The Impact of Locally Owned Businesses Vs Chains: A Case Study in Midcoast Maine," 2003.

72. Thoreau, *Walden and Civil Disobedience*, p. 56.

PART TWO: HOW

CHAPTER FIVE / HOUSEKEEPING

1. Barbara Kiviat, "10 Ideas That Are Changing the World: obs Are the New Assets," *Time*, March 23, 2009.

2. Martin E.P. Seligman and Ed Diener, "Beyond Money," *Psychological Science in the Public Interest* 5, no. 1 (2004).

3. Juliet Schor, "The New Politics of Consumption: Why Americans Want So Much More Than They Need," *Boston Review*, Summer 1999.

4. David C. Korten, *The Great Turning: From Empire to Earth Community*, First ed. (San Francisco - Bloomfield: Berrett-Koehler Publishers, Inc., and Kumarian Press, Inc., 2006), p. 77.

5. United States Department of Health and Human Services, *2008 Poverty Level Guidelines*; available from http://aspe.hhs.gov/poverty/09poverty.shtml.

6. Ralph Waldo Emerson, "Domestic Life," in *Volume VII, Society and Solitude* (Boston: Houghton Mifflin, 1893).

7. John De Graaf, David Wann, and Thomas H. Naylor, *Affluenza* (San Francisco: Berrett-Koehler Publishers, 2005), p. 142–143.

8. Korten, *The Great Turning: From Empire to Earth Community*, p. 138.

9. Ed Diener, "Beyond Money."

10. Bradford Plumer, "The Two-Income Trap," *MotherJones.com*, November 8, 2004.

11. Doug Krizner, "Priced out of The American Dream," *Marketplace Radio*, November 13, 2007.

12. Chris Balish, *How to Live Well without Owning a Car* (Berkeley: Ten Speed Press, 2006).

13. De Graaf, Wann, and Naylor, *Affluenza*.

14. David Wann, "Haste Makes Waste," in *Take Back Your Time*, ed. John De Graaf (San Francisco: Berrett-Koehler, 2003).

15. Richard Layard, *Happiness: Lessons from a New Science* (New York: Penguin, 2005).

16. Kelly Coyne and Erik Knutzen, *The Urban Homestead* (Los Angeles: Process Self-Reliance Series, 2008), p. 288.

17. De Graaf, Wann, and Naylor, *Affluenza*.

18. Ibid., p. 78.

19. Henry David Thoreau, *Walden and Civil Disobedience* (New York: Penguin, 1983).

20 Ed Diener and Shigehiro Oishi, *The Nonobvious Social Psychology of Happiness*, draft of invited paper for journal (University of Illinois at Urbana — Champaign 2004; available from www.psych.uiuc.edu/~ediener/hottopic/nonovious.htm).

21. Ibid.

22. Ibid.

23. Ibid.

24. Suzanne Schweikert, "An Hour a Day (Could Keep the Doctor Away)," in *Take Back Your Time*, ed. John De Graaf (San Francisco: Berrett-Koehler, 2003).

25. Bruce E. Levine, *Surviving America's Depression Epidemic* (White River Junction, VT: Chelsea Green, 2007).

26. United Health Foundation, *America's Health Rankings 2008*; available from http://www.americashealthrankings.org/2008/othernations.html.

27. Dave Lemmon, Geraldin Henrich-Koenis, and Robert Meissner, "Families USA Report" (Washington, DC: Families USA, 2007).

28. Ruth Schwartz Cowan, *More Work for Mother* (New York: Basic Books, Inc., 1983), p. 76.

29. Thomas Berry, *The Great Work* (New York: Bell Tower, 1999), p. 113.

30. De Graaf, Wann, and Naylor, *Affluenza*.

31. Ibid.

32. Clemson Extension, "Making Mealtimes Pleasant," *Home and Garden Information Center*, 2008.

33. Ibid.

34. Ibid.

35. Oishi, *The Nonobvious Social Psychology of Happiness*.

36. Levine, *Surviving America's Depression Epidemic*, p. 80.

37. Korten, *The Great Turning: From Empire to Earth Community*, p. 307.

38. Oishi, *The Nonobvious Social Psychology of Happiness*.

39. Ed Diener, "Beyond Money."

40. As quoted in Leslie Bennetts, *The Feminine Mistake: Are We Giving up Too Much?* (New York: Hyperion, 2007), p. 269.

41. Korten, *The Great Turning: From Empire to Earth Community*, p. 283–284.

42. Betsy Taylor, "Recapturing Childhood," in *Take Back Your Time*, ed. John De Graaf (San Francisco: Berrett-Koehler, 2003).

43. Ibid., p. 47.

44. Ibid., p. 47.

45. Alex Spiegel, *Creative Play Makes for Kids in Control,* Morning Edition, National Public Radio, February 28, 2008.

46. Korten, *The Great Turning: From Empire to Earth Community*, p. 68.

47. Schor, "The New Politics of Consumption: Why Americans Want So Much More Than They Need."

48. Bill McKibben, *Deep Economy: The Wealth of Communities and the Durable Future* (New York: Times Books, 2007).

49. Bob Herbert, "Clueless in America," *New York Times*, April 22, 2008.

50. Korten, *The Great Turning: From Empire to Earth Community*, p. 289.

51. Jonathan Rowe, "Out of Time," *Yes!*, Winter 2006.

52. William Doherty and Barbara Carlson, "Overscheduled Kids, Underconnected Families," in *Take Back Your Time*, ed. John De Graaf (San Francisco: Berett-Koehler, 2003).

53. Layard, *Happiness: Lessons from a New Science.*

54. Hara Estroff Marano, *Suburban Blues*, March 22, 2005; available from http://www.psychologytoday.com/articles/pto-20050322-000002.html.

55. Taylor, "Recapturing Childhood."

56. Levine, *Surviving America's Depression Epidemic*, p. 30.

57. Ibid., p. 30.

58. Wendell Berry, "Higher Education and Home Defense," in *Home Economics* (San Francisco: North Point Press, 1987).

59. Levine, *Surviving America's Depression Epidemic*, p. 83.

60. Cowan, *More Work for Mother.*

61. Berry, *The Great Work*, p. 73.

62. Plumer, "The Two-Income Trap."

63. Sarah van Gelder and Doug Pibel, "Be Happy Anyway," *Yes!*, Winter 2009.

64. Ibid.

65. De Graaf, Wann, and Naylor, *Affluenza.*

66. Ibid.

67. Layard, *Happiness: Lessons from a New Science*, p. 42.

68. McKibben, *Deep Economy: The Wealth of Communities and the Durable Future*, p. 120.

CHAPTER SIX / **RECLAIMING DOMESTIC SKILLS**

1. Henry David Thoreau, *Walden and Civil Disobedience* (New York: Penguin, 1983).

2. Martin E.P. Seligman and Ed Diener, "Beyond Money," *Psychological Science in the Public Interest*, 5, no. 1 (2004).

3. Ibid.

4. David C. Korten, *The Great Turning: From Empire to Earth Community*, First ed. (San Francisco - Bloomfield: Berrett-Koehler Publishers, Inc., and Kumarian Press, Inc., 2006).

5. Richard Layard, *Happiness: Lessons from a New Science* (New York: Penguin, 2005), p. 63.

6. Ibid., p. 72.

7. Ed Diener and Shigehiro Oishi, *The Nonobvious Social Psychology of Happiness*, draft of invited paper for Journal (University of Illinois at Urbana - Champaign, 2004; available from www.psych.uiuc.edu/~ediener/hottopic/nonovious.htm).

8. Ed Diener, "Beyond Money."

9. Ibid.

10. Ibid.

11. Oishi, *The Nonobvious Social Psychology of Happiness*.

12. Ibid.

13. Layard, *Happiness: Lessons from a New Science*, p. 180.

14. As quoted in Glenna Matthews, *"Just a Housewife" The Rise and Fall of Domesticity in America* (New York: Oxford University Press, 1987), p. 163.

15. As quoted in Leslie Bennetts, *The Feminine Mistake: Are We Giving up Too Much?* (New York: Hyperion, 2007), p. 247.

16. Lisa Napoli, "Who Does More Housework?" *Marketplace Radio*, April 25, 2008.

17. Bill McKibben, *Deep Economy: The Wealth of Communities and the Durable Future* (New York: Times Books, 2007), p. 112.

18. Wendell Berry, "Does Community Have a Value?" in *Home Economics* (San Francisco: North Point Press, 1987).

19. Betty Friedan, *The Feminine Mystique*, 5 ed. (New York: W.W. Norton and Company, Inc., 2001).

20. William S. Coperthwaite, *A Handmade Life* (White River Junction, VT: Chelsea Green, 2002), p. 14.

21. Ralph Waldo Emerson, "Domestic Life," in *Volume VII, Society and Solitude* (Boston: Houghton Mifflin, 1893).

22. Thoreau, *Walden and Civil Disobedience*, p. 113.

23. John De Graaf, David Wann, and Thomas H. Naylor, *Affluenza* (San Francisco: Berrett-Koehler Publishers, 2005), p. 41.

24. Oishi, *The Nonobvious Social Psychology of Happiness*.

25. Berry, "Does Community Have a Value?" p. 182.

26. Emerson, "Domestic Life."

27. Amy Alkon, "The Advice Goddess," *Metroland*, 2007.

28. De Graaf, Wann, and Naylor, *Affluenza*, p. 202.

29. Greg Horn, *Living Green* (Toanga, CA: Freedom Press, 2006).

30. Ibid.

31. Bruce E. Levine, *Surviving America's Depression Epidemic* (White River Junction, VT: Chelsea Green, 2007), p. 80.

32. Emerson, "Domestic Life."

33. Jerome Segal, "A Policy Agenda for Taking Back Time," in *Take Back Your Time*, ed. John De Graaf (San Francisco: Berrett-Koehler, 2003).

34. John L. Hess, and Karen Hess, *The Taste of America* (Champaign, IL: University of Illinois Press, 2000), p. 8.

35. Barbara Kingsolver, *Animal, Vegetable, Miracle: A Year of Food Life* (New York: HarperCollins, 2007), p. 17.

36. Pamela Stone, *Opting Out?* (Los Angeles: University of California Press, 2007), p. 147.

37. Bennetts, *The Feminine Mistake: Are We Giving up Too Much?*

38. Coperthwaite, *A Handmade Life*, p. 38.

39. Cited in Korten, *The Great Turning: From Empire to Earth Community*, p. 84.

40. Ibid.

CHAPTER SEVEN / **TOWARD A HOMEGROWN CULTURE**

1. Henry David Thoreau, *Walden and Civil Disobedience* (New York: Penguin, 1983), p. 399.

2. As quoted in Betty Friedan, *The Feminine Mystique*, 5 ed. (New York: W.W. Norton and Company, Inc., 2001), p. 437.

3. Robert Putnam, *Bowling Alone: The Collapse and Revival of American Community* (New York: Simon and Schuster, 2000), p. 288–289.

4. Bruce E. Levine, *Surviving America's Depression Epidemic* (White River Junction, VT: Chelsea Green, 2007), p. 149.

5. Frances Moore Lappe, "Voices Carry," *Yes!*, no. 48 (2009).

6. Richard Layard, *Happiness: Lessons from a New Science* (New York: Penguin, 2005), p. 73–74.

7. Earth Charter USA, "Www.Earthcharterus.Org," 2009.

INDEX

Learn more.

Ask questions.

Find resources.

Discuss ideas.

Meet others.

RadicalHomemakers.com